The Centrelink Experiment

Innovation in service delivery

The Centrelink Experiment

Innovation in service delivery

John Halligan

(with Jules Wills)

ANU

THE AUSTRALIAN NATIONAL UNIVERSITY

E PRESS

ANU
E PRESS

the Australia and New Zealand
School of Government

Published by ANU E Press
The Australian National University
Canberra ACT 0200, Australia
Email: anuepress@anu.edu.au
This title is also available online at: http://epress.anu.edu.au/centrelink_citation.html

National Library of Australia
Cataloguing-in-Publication entry

Author:	Halligan, J. (John)
Title:	The Centrelink experiment [electronic resource] : innovation in service delivery / John Halligan, Jules Wills.
ISBN:	9781921536427 (pbk.)
	9781921536434 (pdf)
Series:	ANZSOG series.
Notes:	Bibliography.
Subjects:	Australia. Centrelink.
	Administrative agencies--Australia.
	Public welfare administration--Australia.

Other Authors/Contributors:
Wills, Jules.

Dewey Number: 353.50994

Cover design by John Butcher

Funding for this monograph series has been provided by the Australia and New Zealand School of Government Research Program.

John Wanna, *Series Editor*

Professor John Wanna is the Sir John Bunting Chair of Public Administration at the Research School of Social Sciences at The Australian National University. He is the director of research for the Australian and New Zealand School of Government (ANZSOG). He is also a joint appointment with the Department of Politics and Public Policy at Griffith University and a principal researcher with two research centres: the Governance and Public Policy Research Centre and the nationally-funded Key Centre in Ethics, Law, Justice and Governance at Griffith University. Professor Wanna has produced around 20 books including two national text books on policy and public management. He has produced a number of research-based studies on budgeting and financial management including: *Budgetary Management and Control* (1990); *Managing Public Expenditure* (2000), *From Accounting to Accountability* (2001); *Controlling Public Expenditure* (2003); *Yes Premier* (2005); *Westminster Legacies:Democracy and Responsible Government in Asia and the Pacific* (2005); *Westminster Compared* (forthcoming) and most recently *The Reality of Budget Reform in the OECD* (forthcoming). He is completing, with John Butcher and Ben Freyens, a study of service delivery in the Australian government, entitled *Policy in Action* (with UNSW Press). He was a chief investigator in a major Australian Research Council funded study of the Future of Governance in Australia (1999-2001) involving Griffith and the ANU. His research interests include Australian and comparative politics, public expenditure and budgeting, and government-business relations. He also writes on Australian politics in newspapers such as *The Australian*, the *Courier-Mail* and *The Canberra Times* and has been a regular state political commentator on ABC radio and TV.

Table of Contents

8. Entrepreneurship and challenging boundaries

9. Lessons from Centrelink's formative years

Epilogue: Back to the future

Appendices

Professor John Halligan

John Halligan is Research Professor of Government and Public Administration, Faculty of Business and Government, University of Canberra, Australia.

Recent books with colleagues are *Managing Performance: International Comparisons*, Routledge, London, 2008; *Parliament in the 21st Century*, Melbourne University Press, 2007; *Civil Service Systems in Anglo-American Countries*, Edward Elgar, London, 2003.

His research interests are comparative public management and governance, specifically public sector reform, performance management, political-bureaucratic relationships, and government institutions. He is currently drafting studies of public sector governance, performance management and a comparative analysis of public management in Anglophone countries.

Professional activities include Deputy President, Institute of Public Administration Australia (ACT Division).

Preface

Two images of Centrelink capture the essence of its foundation years of innovation and change. The first is the spirit of Centrelink—in its creation and in its operation in these formative years. This spirit is captured in the observation about

> organisations that want to shape the future...The leaders of these companies encourage their people to challenge conventional thinking, to change the business dramatically, and to create continuous renewal and progress. These companies don't just want to survive—they want to lead. They want to write the rules that others will follow. (Pfeiffer 1998 quoted in Hamilton 2007:94)

The atmosphere in Cosmo,[1] the headquarters of Centrelink in the ACT suburb of Woden, was often charged with excitement and energy unlike anything encountered in conventional departments of state. Here one was struck by a concern with ideas and experiments, with seeking to push the frontiers of public management in the public interest and with doing the best for customers.

A second image was that of the guiding coalition, a regular two-day meeting of senior executives who would consider an issue and how to respond to it. Originally 55, later 80 or more, staff would wrestle with the dimensions of the problem, reach a consensual position and develop a means of proceeding.

This study concentrates on the first decade of Centrelink—the years in which Sue Vardon was chief executive officer (CEO)—which extended from 1996 to the end of 2004. Consideration is also given to the transition to the new governance arrangements in 2005–06 and a comparison is offered between the formative and restructured Centrelink by Margaret Hamilton, a former senior executive of the agency.

Centrelink was established in 1997 as the main service delivery agency for the Australian Government in the field of social policy and administration. It was to be a one-stop, multipurpose delivery agency providing services on behalf of several purchasing departments. The new agency took on the responsibility of delivering government services to some 7.8 million recipients of social welfare benefits and services, accounting for almost one-third of Commonwealth expenditure and employing well more than 20 000 staff spread across service delivery sites across Australia.

The Centrelink experiment has arguably generated more research attention than any other agency during this time, with doctoral dissertations (Hamilton 2007; Rowlands 2003; Wills 1999) and numerous publications (for example, Halligan 2004; Husock and Scott 1999a). Centrelink continues in 2008 to be an exemplar that engages international attention.

ENDNOTES

[1] The executive area of the Cosmopolitan Building in Canberra.

Acknowledgments

This book originated from a conversation with Sue Vardon, chief executive of Centrelink, in which she expressed interest in seeing a good Australian study of the agency. The study results from a partnership between Centrelink and staff of the Centre for Research in Public Sector Management at the University of Canberra. The CEO of Centrelink provided full support for the study, which covered funding for a research officer, access to staff and records and included opportunities for the researchers to attend senior management meetings. She also read the draft manuscript.

Numerous interviews were conducted with national and area office staff of Centrelink and with other stakeholders including portfolio ministers, members of the board, client departments and central agencies. We appreciate the time given and the willingness to assist with our study.

A major study of a complex organisation requires a team. A major debt is owed to three academically oriented public servants. Jules Wills was an original participant in the project and his doctoral thesis on strategic planning featuring Centrelink influenced several chapters. David Rowlands, now with the Australian National Audit Office, made a significant contribution by encouraging us to draw on his thesis on 'agencification' and Centrelink and by commenting on the manuscript. Jill Adams, formerly of the Australia Public Service Commission, undertook major drafting and strengthening of several chapters while on the staff of the Centre for Research in Public Sector Management, and subsequently reviewed the manuscript.

Margaret Hamilton, formerly with Centrelink, provided a post-Vardon consideration of Centrelink in the chapter under her name. Thanks are due also to Michael O'Donnell (now at The Australian National University) for letting us draw on a paper that presented a preliminary examination of human resource management in Centrelink.

The Centre for Research into Public Sector Management at the University of Canberra was the project's 'home', and research staff associated with the centre provided much help with research tasks, notably Zoe Gardner, Lisa Skelly and Suzanne Vaisutis-White. Paddy Onton, Kate Ransley and Lisa Strickland provided support during the project and with the preparation of the manuscript. Centre colleagues Chris Aulich and Roger Wettenhall commented on chapters and asked questions about Centrelink as an agency.

John Wanna, Australia New Zealand School of Government (ANZSOG) Professor at The Australian National University (ANU), provided consistent encouragement to produce the book for the ANU series that he edits, and financial support for Margaret Hamilton's contribution. John Butcher, ANZSOG member of the ANU

E Press Advisory/Editorial Board handled the publishing with patience and sound advice.

The careful reading and incisive editorial comments of Penelope St Clair substantially enhanced the manuscript.

We have sought to provide a balanced analysis and evaluation of this organisational experiment, recognising what is innovative, but having to be selective in our coverage of a complex case.[1]

ENDNOTES

[1] The original questions and the list of senior executives who were interviewed are provided in Appendix 1.

Introduction: Centrelink as a field of study

Centrelink has attracted more sustained public attention and scrutiny (including international attention, for example, Husock and Scott 1999a; Smullen 2007)[1] than most other public organisations in recent Australian history. For the customer, it dispenses a wide range of welfare services and payments. For the government and taxpayer, it reflects a new style of organisation that emerged in the 1990s in Australia and overseas. At the same time, it differs from traditional bureaucracy and 'new-style agencies' that have become fashionable overseas because of its multifunctionality and the breadth of its role within the public sector.

The relevance of this experiment, nationally and internationally, arises from many of the core questions of contemporary public management. These include integrated service delivery, special agency and governance arrangements, measuring performance and the capacity for businesslike operations despite being close to the heart of government.

This study examines Centrelink as it emerged and underwent extensive change, seeking to build a management capacity by positioning itself and interacting with organisations in its complex environment, and aligning management systems in support of its objectives. This introduction locates Centrelink within the context of major questions[2] in comparative public management, the challenges of an organisation driven by several imperatives and the type of analysis proposed for studying a service delivery agency.

Four themes stand out in this study of public management change. The first is the departure from the conventional bureaucracy as expressed through the agency approach and more generally the organisational distinctiveness of Centrelink. The second is the relationship between the external demands and constraints on Centrelink and its claims as an entrepreneurial organisation. The public governance and policy environment shapes agency operations but questions arise as to what scope there is for the organisation to address positioning and advocacy within this external environment. The third theme concerns the development of a service delivery model and the implementation and alignment of the management systems within the agency to support this model. Fourth is the nature of transformation in a large and complex organisation that has sought extensive change under its first CEO as the means to improve service delivery in response to the imperatives outlined in the models that underlie the Centrelink concept.

The reform context in which Centrelink emerged and evolved allowed an innovative new agency to emerge, but the changing agenda of government ultimately dictated that a more conventional type of agency was wanted.

Why Centrelink? Organisational distinctiveness and challenges

Three questions arise out of the first theme—departures from conventional bureaucracy and organisational distinctiveness. The first question involves the implications of this fundamental shift from the traditional Australian model—in particular, the agency concept, separation of policy and delivery and the particular use of the agency form. The second question asks how distinctive Centrelink is and whether a new model is emerging here. The third question relates to the implications for how the organisation operates.

The traditional public service was characterised by a public administration paradigm, based on bureaucracy, hierarchy and process and centred on the multipurpose ministerial department. The focus was on vertical arrangements within monolithic departments operating their own delivery networks and subject directly to ministers (for an elaboration, see Hughes 2003; O'Faircheallaigh et al. 1999).[3]

Institutional economics and public choice gave rise to alternative conceptions, which addressed, inter alia, the questions of agency and transaction costs. From principal/agency theory comes a focus on the relationship between the purchaser and the provider. The separation of responsibilities should occur when there are conflicts (for example, commercial and non-commercial) and when different functions are involved (for example, purchaser and provider).

The separation of policy and operations raises an old question that has taken a variety of forms. One argument is about the need for separating roles organisationally in order to provide a functional focus. The concept of identifying a single function with one organisation became the orthodoxy in some countries (Pollitt and Talbot 2004; Pollitt and Talbot et al. 2004). According to this view, policy development, implementation and regulation should be the responsibilities of different organisations. There is also a long tradition of using special organisational forms for achieving different operating environments for specific activities (for example, statutory corporations and public enterprises). This principle has been revived and extended as a means of exacting demands on public organisations—to focus them on results and performance and to cultivate a business style.

These new-style agencies—leaving aside questions about how new they are (Talbot 2004; Wettenhall 2003)—encompass structural disaggregation, performance contracting and deregulation of management controls (Halligan 1998; Rowlands 2003; Talbot 2004). Centrelink has reflected these elements as a specialised delivery agency constituted on the basis of purchaser–provider principles, performance expectations and scope for operating outside conventional bureaucratic practice.

The Centrelink experiment departed significantly from the agency model in three respects. First, there was the combination of scale and the multi-jurisdictional basis of its operation. In addition to distributing close to one-third of the Commonwealth budget outlays, it has delivered services for a range of departments and all states and territories. Second, it has been an important deliverer of integrated public services. Centrelink was created as a 'one-stop shop' or 'first-stop shop' for government services with the raison d'être of linking services for the citizen. Third, there was the capacity to operate entrepreneurially. As well, Centrelink has shared features with agencies internationally—for example, in operating as a government agency under special governance principles.

There is also the question of its operation (as opposed to its conception). The organisation evolved rapidly, seeking to define and reinvent its approach during its first eight years. Centrelink was also under pressure to adjust constantly to a changing environment. Originally envisaged as an organisation that was on notice to perform,[4] Centrelink had to address how to ensure that it was a sustainable enterprise (Vardon 1998a).

Organisational imperatives for a new agency

In contrast with the past approach that often combined several functions, modern public organisations have tended to be established to achieve one distinctive purpose such as policy, delivery or regulation. Centrelink's principal task is service delivery, but in its conception and execution as a public organisation, several different organisational imperatives have been apparent. Four models underpin Centrelink and each provides a different lens for viewing the organisation's functioning and thus a basis for considering the potential conflicts identified between them (Halligan 2004).

The first model, the political, derives from being directly or indirectly subject to ministerial direction, despite operating under special governance arrangements. Centrelink must adhere to the top-down authority relationship with ministers and government agendas and function as a public service organisation subject to public service legislation as a statutory agency. This model is ultimately grounded in traditional, but still central, ideas about responsible government (Aucoin et al. 2004).

The second model is of Centrelink as an agent and service provider in a purchaser–provider relationship in which it is expected to behave in specified quasi-contractual ways. Its operations are grounded in relationships with client departments: the purchasers of its services. The link to new public management is strong (for example, disaggregation and contractualism), but it is influenced specifically by principal-agent theory and particularly the concept of executive agencies (James 2003; Pollitt and Talbot 2004; Pollitt et al. 2004).

The third model is that of an entrepreneurial organisation, which must compete in the market to secure existing core work as well as seeking new work. Under this conception, Centrelink is concerned with market share and with competition in the public and voluntary sectors, and even with extending its operations to the private marketplace. This imperative derived from the government's injunction to the Australian Public Service (APS) to operate more like the private sector and reflected new public management and entrepreneurial government dictums in vogue in the mid-1990s (Halligan 2003).

The final model conceives of Centrelink as a customer-driven organisation that is responsive to recipients of its services and thus driven by customer relationships and satisfaction. Feedback is gathered through surveying and benchmarking with the aim of stimulating continuous improvement and realignment within the organisation.

Each model captures an organisational imperative that is externally grounded and usually has a basis in the agency's empowering legislation. Each has a different external driver: politicians, clients, competitors or customers. They reflect top-down authority and contractual relationships and environmentally determined pressures from quasi-markets in which choice operates.

A further imperative can also be distinguished. A public sector agency that operates within the core public service is subject to the budgetary and administrative requirements of central agencies such as the Department of Finance and Administration (DOFA) as well as the strictures of external accountability from, in particular, the Auditor-General, the Ombudsman and parliament. An agency this large with extensive dealings with the public invariably attracts continual scrutiny from external organisations.

Changing management and policy environments

In examining the implementation of major change, the Public Service environment needs to be considered—in particular, changing agendas and how organisational capacity absorbs new policy and management priorities. There are also the routine policymaking and political preferences and the difficulties that agencies could have in the sphere of social security, in adjusting to changing requirements with time (Derthick 1990; McNulty and Ferlie 2003).

Public sector reform: new public management and beyond

Centrelink's creation reflected the mood of the mid-1990s. The past 25 years have been remarkable for the level of public sector change in Australia, which has been a foremost exponent of the new public management in the reform era that emerged in the 1980s (Halligan 1997). The wave of reform was characterised by its magnitude, experimentation with new organisational forms and attention to system design. Reform was rapid, systemic and comprehensive as a range of specific measures was applied across the public sector (Halligan and Power 1992).

These reforms arose from societal pressures on governments to improve public services. There were demands for more cost-effective and high-quality services, increased consumer awareness and higher expectations of services tailored to individual needs and distrust of command structures and hierarchies with overheads that were administratively obstructive compared with devolved arrangements in which decisions could be made at the point of delivery. Further factors included advances in information technology (IT), which automated or facilitated many clerical tasks, and a changing international environment. In the search for solutions, governments turned to the private sector in the belief that a more businesslike public sector would rectify past difficulties and improve performance (Wills 1999).

The reforms can be seen through the changing agendas covering political control, management, markets and reorganisation. The Hawke–Keating Labor Government (1983–96) favoured the public sector while pushing it heavily towards the private sector. The conservative Coalition government that followed favoured the private sector but recognised the need to maintain a strong core public service. Later directions that emerged in the 1990s were fundamentally different from those in the initial decade of reform, in particular the shift from management reform to market-based change. The election of the Coalition Government in 1996 accelerated the emerging trends, initially focusing on cutting the budget deficit and the level of public sector staffing, and then on other fundamental changes.

The four terms of the Howard Government can be viewed as coinciding with different reform phases. The first term supported a neo-liberal agenda that emphasised cost cutting, markets and the private sector. The second and third terms provided opportunities for the reforms to be tested through implementation and then refined. In the process, the hard-edged focus of the 1990s emerged as less appropriate in the 2000s. In the fourth term, new agendas emerged such as reviewing corporate governance, a whole-of-government agenda and a strengthening of central processes (Halligan and Adams 2004; Halligan 2005, 2006a, 2008; Hamburger 2007).

What was significant was that the reform environment surrounding the formative years of Centrelink was characterised by devolution, privatisation, contracting, consumer choice and an intensification of cutbacks and the promotion of the private sector over the public sector. The second half of the period under consideration was dominated by different government agendas that favoured reintegration and reviews of non-departmental organisations.

Policy environment of social welfare developments

The refocusing of policy agendas for social security has also been important. Since the creation of Centrelink in 1997, there has been a number of changes to income support and welfare programs. For the first few years, these were limited in scope, but in 1999 another rethink of the welfare system was announced (details in Appendix 2), which had a significant impact.

The first strand of this round of welfare reform focused on working-aged people who were unemployed and receiving support. 'Work for the Dole' programs began in 1997 and involved local communities in activities of value to them that provided work experience for the unemployed. 'Youth Allowance' was introduced in 1998 and represented the rationalisation of income-support arrangements for the young unemployed and students.

The Job Network introduced from 1998—a result of the dissolution of the Commonwealth Employment Service (CES) as part of the Centrelink solution—completely changed employment placement assistance arrangements for the unemployed. After clients registered with Centrelink for benefits, they were referred to the Job Network—mostly voluntary agencies outside the Public Service that were contracted to assist the unemployed to find work or undertake training. Selected job seekers aged between 18 and 34 were required to meet mutual-obligation activity requirements.

A second major strand of reform involved reviewing welfare policy. The government launched a welfare review based on a set of principles that included establishing better incentives for people receiving payments, creating greater opportunities to increase self-reliance and capacity building and expecting people on income support to help themselves and society through participation in a mutual-obligation framework. The government response, 'Australians Working Together' (AWT), was intended to strike a new balance between incentives, obligations and assistance in welfare. AWT implementation occurred in stages through budgetary decisions and legislation that allowed a package of incentives, assistance and extra requirements to be introduced, and which impacted on Centrelink's service delivery.

Three major implications for Centrelink emerged from these agendas: the commitment to welfare reform and major policy change, the overall momentum of environmental change and the regular policy adjustments to service delivery.

Engaging the external environment

The importance of the external environment is well understood but the form of interaction with external actors varies from conceptions that view the environment as the determinant of organisational behaviour (for example, conformity with the market produces the best results) to those that recognise that the environment can be influenced, managed and can be 'pliable and responsive' (Light 1998:14). The capacity to influence the environment, or rather significant actors in the environment, recognises a more dynamic relationship that will vary across issues and actors.

All organisational imperatives for Centrelink can be regarded as external, but the two primary relationships are those with the political executive and its client departments. The interaction between Centrelink and its external environment is where institutional tensions are potentially strongest. Centrelink has the attributes of a department of state but is positioned within contractual relationships with a range of departments for which it provides fixed and variable services.

The need to 'position for opportunities' has been identified by studies of the US Social Security Administration and Air Force (Derthick 1979; Barzelay and Campbell 2003). Public organisations operating in potentially constraining environments can, through positioning themselves, implement their objectives. Centrelink originally emerged from a combination of personalities, agendas and opportunities after the election of a new government. The concept was shaped by a compromise reflecting political expectations and the interests of existing departments. This compromise had long-term consequences for operations and relationships between client departments and Centrelink (Halligan 2004).

The continuing constraints took the form of the general reform agenda under a neo-liberal government, specific agendas such as welfare reform and the various imperatives discussed earlier. These constraints imposed different types of discipline on Centrelink, in particular where potential conflicts arose among the different stakeholders. The basis for subsequent debates about the roles of purchasing departments and provider agencies was laid by the combination of models that could be discerned in Centrelink's organisational imperatives (such as different interpretations about the relative importance of purchaser–provider principles, partnerships and political direction).

These differences were also established by the bureaucratic politics attendant on the entrance of a new type of agency. Unlike the United Kingdom and New Zealand, where the separation of policy and implementation was applied systemically, in Australia, Centrelink was an exception as a new delivery agency.[5] Despite being the largest organisation in the APS and undertaking work for a number of departments, Centrelink was excluded from the departmental club.

Obstacles, however, need not preclude the creation of opportunities, if an agency can lever off other attributes. Centrelink was an innovation of a government that conformed to the neo-liberal agenda. The ambiguity and conflicting imperatives also provided scope for initiative. The mandate to seek new business was a spur for entrepreneurial initiatives and the language of 'positioning' featured in Centrelink documents. Through advocacy and smart practices, opportunities could be turned to advantage as long as organisational longevity was ensured. The original mandate as a delivery agency designed to provide services to purchasing departments and its unconventional character provided bases for Centrelink to position itself within the Public Service. The positions advocated, in addition to the one-stop shop, were the 'provider of choice', premier broker of information and solutions and 'inclusive service delivery' (Vardon 2000c; Zanetti 1998).

The advocacy of an agency position was clear in various operational contexts involving different types of inter-agency interaction. One was about competing for policy and contributions to the process; another examined using entrepreneurial and advocacy skills to consolidate and expand the agency's role while evolving a distinctive service delivery focus. A more intriguing development was the way the agency addressed inter-agency conflict and moved towards a more integrated alliance with its main client. This ultimately meant building inter-agency capacity to bridge organisational divisions.

Implementing new service delivery models

Service delivery is the core rationale of Centrelink as a specialised agency. The original policy problem for the Federal Government was that two departments had developed an overlapping network of offices that provided similar types of service—primarily social welfare payments and unemployment benefits. This was seen as wasteful duplication and confusing to recipients, many of whom were customers of both departments. The solution was intended to reduce government costs, to remove confusion for service recipients and to increase efficiency. The new agency was to provide services for both original departments, which could establish purchasing agreements for the services delivered.

Redesigning and modernising a large organisation for service delivery is a complex task. It was to be a customer-focused agency operating in a contested environment. Insights into the response of an agency specialising in service delivery can be found in the concept and operation of its core responsibility—namely, how it engages the customer and the design of its service delivery structures. External and internal dimensions—specifically, the policy context of service delivery already discussed and the management support for this function—need to be examined.

How did Centrelink respond to these challenges? In short, it developed a clear and systematic approach to service delivery models. In time, this involved moving from the original diverse and individual government programs towards a more holistic, integrated customer service. As the organisation developed, the delivery model moved through several stages (Vardon 2000b).

Important issues faced by Centrelink included how to achieve organisational goals (which could be conflicting), such as customer responsiveness, improved service quality and the demands for cost efficiency. The achievement of goals requires the building of management capacity. To transform an organisation from a traditional departmental and bureaucratic form, however, and to sustain performance, requires careful consideration of an appropriate process for change.

Leading and managing major change

Transforming a large organisation

The traditional literature on reform and change emphasises unsuccessful initiatives and resistance to change (Halligan and Power 1992). In the reform era, however, the success rate has been notably higher, and there has been a new emphasis on factors that stimulate and support change. These factors include strategic thinking, acting according to core values, customer focus and the development of human resources. Factors determining success in organisational change include the level of acceptance of the need for change, leadership communication, support from senior management and politicians, institutionalisation and alignment of management systems (Rainey and Fernandez 2004:36).

The scope of change ranges from a more limited focus on innovative practices to transformative or fundamental change. Is it in fact possible to produce transformation in organisational change in large public sector organisations and, if so, what is the result? According to McNulty and Ferlie (2003), the discussion of organisational transformation is vague because of the lack of empirical evidence to assess the impact of these planned transformations in the long term. The question of whether to view Centrelink as a transformative case derives in part from its own depiction of its development. After the set-up stages, Centrelink anticipated change at the level of transformation, particularly with the delivery of government services (Vardon 1998d, 1999b).

Vardon's conception of transformation was informed by Kotter's (1995) examination of why it failed and this influenced her thinking about organisational change. There was also a broader dimension that located Centrelink within international pressures on organisations delivering public services facing transformational change, which reflected thinking about the future 'transformation of the business landscape' (Vardon 1998a). The drivers of change were globalisation, consumer power and technology. The conclusion was that 'the public sector cannot escape the impact of such transformational change' particularly through the interface with customers: 'Centrelink's communication with our customers will be the first and most visible area of transformational change [of] the ways of doing business' (Vardon 1998a:1–3).

Two stages of transformation emerged: the original transition from the departments (Social Security and Employment, Education, Training and Youth Affairs) that focused on branding, customer service and cultural change; and the re-engineering of service delivery and entrepreneurship to create a new organisation.

Leading change

Successful change requires leadership and its significance in organisational change and public agency performance is reaffirmed by a number of studies (Rainey 2003; Nutt 2004). In reports on large-scale public sector change—the cases of the US Air Force, Internal Revenue Service and the Social Security Administration—leaders played crucial roles in the change processes (Barzelay and Campbell 2003; Rainey and Fernandez 2004; Thompson and Rainey 2004).

A number of propositions about leadership are well understood. During the life cycle of an organisation, or at different stages of development or for specific processes, different types of leadership can be appropriate (Stace and Dunphy 2001). There is evidence to indicate the need to think beyond individual leadership to concepts such as the 'mutualist' (Nutt 2004), who draws on broader patterns of support, or the model of integrative leadership as a more comprehensive means of viewing these processes (Moynihan and Ingraham 2004). Transformational change also requires the attributes of transformational leadership involving interaction with the external environment and building management capacity through internal management systems.

Effective leadership is shown 'through actions that build and improve organisational abilities and…governmental capacity, represented by management systems' (Moynihan and Ingraham 2004:429). In the well-known distinction between management (planning, budgeting, organising, staffing, and so on) and leadership (establishing direction, aligning people, motivating, and so on), there is, however, advice about the need to fulfil multiple leadership roles. Successful transformation is argued to be mostly about leadership and secondarily about management (Kotter 1996:25–6).

In the case of Centrelink, the CEO was the pivot, with the governance oversight mechanisms of the board (including the chair) and the minister playing roles; but how was a large and complex organisation to approach a model of integrative leadership? Distinctive roles also needed to be adopted by the CEO and complemented by the different roles of members of the most senior management group (covering responsibilities for the key management functions).

Building management capacity is a core element based on internal management systems such as finance, human resources and IT. These provide the levers for leaders to produce the organisational capacity that drives and improves service delivery. For Centrelink, the focus was on the importance of strategic direction and planning in supporting the objectives of the organisation. Policy management and implementation were carefully crafted for service delivery. The development of human resource management and an organisational culture over time was important. Performance improvement was to be achieved through focusing the management capacity to achieve service delivery results and to be facilitated through using the balanced scorecard for oversight of performance.

Articulating strategy and seeking internal alignments are important precepts for action (Spicer et al. 1996; Stace and Dunphy 2001). A crucial factor in successful change is 'the implementation of a set of mutually reinforcing changes' (Rainey and Fernandez 2004:36; Moynihan and Ingraham 2004). The connection between these elements can be handled through a standard management approach, starting with strategy and looking for conformity from management systems and organisational fit with the environment. For Centrelink, certain leverage points were significant for moving the agenda on, such as the relationships between strategy, delivery models, performance and human resource planning and implementation.

Overview of book

Balancing conflicting imperatives

The existence of four models based on politicians, clients, competitors and customers within one organisation creates challenges in satisfying a range of interests and values. The incorporation of conflicting models in a complex approach to institutional design is well recognised as potentially problematic (Aucoin 1990). In the case of Centrelink, several of these models had to be either reconciled or resolved in order to address the sharper conflicts and contradictions.

This balancing act also profoundly affected the governance and management of Centrelink, particularly its planning and internal capabilities. Moreover, these imperatives can lead the organisation in different ways, which makes the achievement of internal alignment particularly challenging for a public organisation. They can emphasise continuities and suggest path dependencies or departures and change. The fundamental question for Centrelink under these circumstances is how does it handle the multiple demands on it in practice, particularly when they are in conflict? Reconciling the models and the fit with internal capability provides a basis for analysing this question.

The main issues derive from Centrelink's origins as a reconstituted organisation, which was designed to be original, and the ways in which it can confound existing stereotypes about public organisations (cf. Kaufman 1985). The external relationships are complex, involving client departments, the board, the government, the minister and customers. The governance relationships encompass detailed contractual obligations, partnerships, direct authority relationships and public accountability. As a 'one-stop' organisation, Centrelink represents a complex experiment with integrated service delivery for a range of policy clients.

Within this overall concept there were potential conflicts. Centrelink was a public organisation subject to political demands and pressures, which sought to operate as a business within a competitive environment. It was a large and complex organisation at a time when disaggregation and single-function agencies were favoured. It was also a delivery agency accountable to client departments that had differing policy expectations, requirements and standards.

Chapter coverage

Chapter 1 examines the origins of Centrelink within the policy nexus of ideas and the management reform environment of the 1990s, and their influence on the design decisions for Centrelink. This leads into an overview of the organisation in Chapter 2 that provides a historical and descriptive context, including how Centrelink evolved.

The strategies and frameworks that have been developed to focus and integrate Centrelink's approach are addressed in Chapter 3. The next chapter, on leading and managing change, analyses and explains how change has been managed in Centrelink, focusing on the chief executive, Sue Vardon, and her leadership style.

Chapter 5 examines how delivery systems have been transformed in response to the changing policy environment and new conceptions of how to respond to customer needs.

The next two chapters focus on external relations with the political executive and clients. Chapter 6 addresses Centrelink's governing arrangements, and in particular the role of the political executive and the board of management. Chapter 7 explores the range of relationships between client departments and Centrelink and how they have evolved towards more collaborative arrangements. In Chapter 8, the agency's relationships with other significant stakeholders are viewed from its perspective, and in terms of the organisational imperative to be entrepreneurial and to constantly seek repositioning of the organisation within its environment.

Chapter 9 provides an overall evaluation of the formative years of Centrelink against the questions raised in this introduction. The impact of an organisational life cycle is considered as Centrelink continues to be subject to a changing environment. Centrelink is the product of the 'new public management' environment of the mid-1990s that provided opportunities for a new agency to be entrepreneurial and innovative. With the different public management agendas emerging by the mid-2000s, a more conventional departmental approach has replaced the initial Centrelink experiment. The final chapter, by Margaret Hamilton, a former Centrelink executive, provides a postscript to Centrelink's first eight years and the departure of Vardon, and addresses changes to the organisation after its incorporation into a new, integrated Department of Human Services.

ENDNOTES

[1] For references to Centrelink as a case of integrated service delivery, see Kernaghan (2005) and WBI Leadership Development Program and IPAC (2007).

[2] The original questions are in Appendix 1.

[3] The pragmatism inherent in the British tradition encouraged statutory authorities to flourish at times as specific solutions to problems.

[4] Of course, no conventional department can expect to be immune from changes by the government, but in Centrelink's case it was advised of the need to perform in order to retain functions, and there was a sense that its very existence was not guaranteed.

[5] A few other cases existed, such as the Australian Taxation Office, which was not a product of the move towards new-style executive agencies, but simply a conventional pragmatic solution for implementation.

1. Designing a delivery agency

Explaining organisational innovation

The creation of a large public organisation is a significant event because such a major institutional commitment is rare.[1] Democratic governments normally have limited capability for radical design (Olsen 1998) as the conditions for major change occur infrequently, but a window of opportunity occurred in Australia in mid-1996.

Australia has had large public organisations before and the progenitor of Centrelink, the Department of Social Security (DSS), was large in the departmental pantheon. There was also the 'mega-department' experiment from 1987, which resulted in agencies of greater complexity but not necessarily of more substantial scale (Halligan 1987). In Centrelink's case, the concept that emerged after its inception was for a new type of Australian organisation: a generalised delivery agency that could handle several major functions. In moving towards the combination of elements, as discussed in the Introduction, a number of considerations were involved.

The interest in reform origins derives from the process of conceiving a distinctively different public organisation and the early decisions about the range of design features that came to be embodied in it. Why did the Commonwealth Services Delivery Agency (CSDA), the precursor of Centrelink, emerge at this time and why as a new type of organisation? These questions require interpretations of organisational origins and institutional change based on the historical evidence.

A perspective on management change within the rational instrumental tradition assumes that reform is the product of deliberate choices between distinctive organisational options. How much freedom of choice do reformers have, however, when they decide whether to reform or not and then when they determine reform content, implementation and consequences (Brunsson and Olsen 1993)? Existing solutions are often applied to problems when the conditions for change arise, but the results are shaped by institutional values.[2]

One study that has successfully integrated a set of elements for handling the complexity is Kingdon's (1984) depiction of three distinctive streams in agenda setting: problems, policies and politics. These streams operate independently: the recognition of problems that require attention, the policy ideas that eventually produce alternatives and the political arena covering, inter alia, changes in government. The confluence of the streams through the merging of politics, problems and solutions provides an opportunity for an item to be promoted to the decision agenda.

The second consideration was the process of deriving a set of design choices for a delivery agency that articulated and developed the concept that was launched in September 1996. The issues covered structural questions about the decoupling of policy and delivery, the integration of delivery roles and the choice of agency features at a time when the international reform movement was at its peak. More practical options involved the division of responsibilities between departments and agencies, governance arrangements and the delineation of relationships under purchaser–provider arrangements.

This chapter examines the confluence of trends, ideas and agendas that led to the establishment of a new type of service delivery agency and considers the design decisions that shaped the development of the organisation before its inauguration in 1997.

From traditional bureaucracy to new delivery options

The Department of Social Security and the two-network question

The DSS represented the traditional face of Australian departments of state. It was monolithic and multifunctional, covering policy and delivery responsibilities. It was a very large department by Australian standards that was slowly modernising.

A longstanding issue was the existence of separate networks of regional offices directly serving the public for the DSS and the Department of Education, Employment, Training and Youth Affairs (DEETYA). The maintenance of two networks by these departments—the DSS to claim benefits, DEETYA to register for employment—was regarded as duplication in some quarters (but not necessarily within the departments, as they perceived themselves as serving different customers: the DSS, the unemployed, who were the labour-intensive component of a broader benefits system; and DEETYA, the employers). In addition, there were client and customer problems including 'people falling between the systems', uneven liaison between agencies and other delivery problems,[3] hence the observation that 'there have been many plans to combine employment registration and employment benefit payments in Australia but they didn't happen—it seemed too hard' (Vardon 2000b).

The committee report of the House of Representatives (HR SCEET 1988) entitled *Getting to Work: Report of the Inquiry into Training or Return to the Workforce by Social Security Pensioners* concluded that '[c]loser liaison between CES and DSS is essential in ensuring that beneficiaries have access to counselling and/or employment advice even when they are unable to travel to the relevant office'.

There was a historical antecedent to the Centrelink arrangements: the series of attempts over the years to join DEETYA's unemployment, youth and student assistance arrangements with the DSS's unemployment and youth payment arrangements. Acknowledgment of their related nature led to co-location of the Commonwealth Employment Service (CES) and the DSS offices in some areas. A series of meetings in the mid-1990s between departmental secretaries Tony Blunn and Derek Volker was aimed at improving coordination between the DSS and DEETYA, but a new service agency was never contemplated. Otherwise, the intentions to improve coordination failed (Briggs 1996). There had also been a long history of 'turf wars' between the two organisations, reflecting departmental territorial imperatives. That rivalry was to have a strong influence on the ultimate structure and governance of Centrelink.

Delivery modes

The 48-year monopoly the CES had on the provision of services to unemployed people had been challenged by an experiment begun under the previous government. The Labor Government had sought to contract out case management to a variety of private and community bodies (Donald 1996:24) and wanted greater freedom of choice and competition through extending the market share of the non-government sector.

At the time of the election, Coalition policy on employment and training focused on employment assistance and case management. It mentioned duplication in service delivery between the Commonwealth and state governments as an object for scrutiny by a commission of audit. It also accused the then case-management system of being overburdened because, inter alia, of functional duplication. There was no mention of a perceived overlap between the DSS and DEETYA or of possible restructuring. The document mentioned income support explicitly and committed a Coalition government to administering unemployment benefits through the Department of Social Security. It also promised that the CES would be asked to make public its standards of service in each office and its performance against targets in its immediate area (Liberal Party of Australia 1996).

A senior Commonwealth public servant, at a conference on competitive tendering and contracting, queried the CES's capacity to deliver services effectively and expressed surprise that there was 'still a belief that very large government bureaucracies can do a good job of delivering complex services to clients in Australia...the Commonwealth Employment Service is one body that will no doubt get some questioning in that regard' (Moran 1996:19). It was expected that the new government would scrutinise the CES, and this was understood by DEETYA's senior management (Rowlands 2003).

There was also a growing consciousness of the connections between the social policy departments (DEETYA, DSS, Health and Veterans' Affairs). These departments were developing policy that impacted on the same group of people.

Policy ideas and options

One-stop shops

The concept of the one-stop shop or 'retail government store', and specifically the one-stop welfare shop, had been discussed since the mid-1970s (Wettenhall and Kimber 1996:15–17). The idea of creating a one-stop shop appeared explicitly in the report of the Royal Commission on Australian Government Administration:

> The object of a 'one stop shop' is to provide as nearly as possible a complete service (including if possible the power to make decisions) in one place, at one visit, and with members of the public having to deal with not more than one or two different officers. (RCAGA 1976:161)

The commission sponsored an experiment with a one-stop shop, the Northwest One-stop Welfare (NOW) Centre in Coburg, Melbourne. It was unable to evaluate the experiment satisfactorily but it considered NOW to be an excellent example of intergovernmental cooperation (RCAGA 1976:163) and recommended that the experiment be continued for at least two years. It further recommended that the Commonwealth Government indicate its willingness to help establish other one-stop shop centres experimentally where local and regional organisations wished to sponsor them, and where the relevant state government was willing to participate.

There were also experiments at other levels: local government, the 'shopfronts' established in the Australian Capital Territory from 1987 and cases that crossed sectors and levels of government (Wettenhall and Kimber 1996).

One other echo of this interest was Prime Minister John Howard's address at the official launch of Centrelink, which traced the one-stop shop idea to the 1970s (Howard 1997):

> From the moment I entered Parliament in 1974...I began hearing complaints about the number of agencies you had to visit...And what focused my mind at the time was that so many people felt that if only they could go to one place and have all their business done in that one spot it would be a lot more efficient, it would be a lot more human and it would make a great deal more sense.

Politicians had already picked up the notion of a one-stop shop several years earlier. It emerged from Liberal Party proposals for public sector reform contained in the 1993 'Fightback' policy statements that promised to 'combine the Department of Social Security and the Commonwealth Employment Service and devolve responsibility for administering employment and training programs from government agencies to Local Employment Boards with an increased investment on [sic] the community' (Hewson and Fischer 1991a:39).

There was explicit reference to creating a one-stop shopfront and further discussion of amalgamating the delivery functions of the DSS and the CES, citing an Australian National Audit Office (ANAO) report on the merits of closer working relationships between them (Hewson and Fischer 1991b). The Fightback documents painted a picture that resembled Centrelink—that is, collapsing the CES into the DSS network to create a one-stop shop for the unemployed and contracting out the job-placement function.

Trends in service provision and diffusion

By the early 1990s, Australia's public administration reforms had been consolidated and the first decade officially evaluated (TFMI 1993). There were unfinished agendas. The first was the evolutionary acceptance of market principles that were assuming centrality by the mid-1990s as competition and contestability became the currency of reform. The second was the acceptance of more flexible approaches to delivery systems for public services and the need to move beyond the traditional monolithic departmental structure.

New trends were appearing that influenced the direction Centrelink would eventually take. These included:

- the concept of entrepreneurial government; although the underlying ideas were familiar to Australian reformers, they were given impetus by the 'reinventing government' movement that was stimulated by the popular US writers Osborne and Gaebler (1992)
- purchaser–provider—which was among the related options, such as contestability and new contractual relationships, being appraised by the Department of Finance (1995), which was producing reports on these subjects by the mid-1990s
- the development of specialised agencies—pioneered in New Zealand and the United Kingdom, the best known being the latter's executive agencies.

A pivotal influence on the DSS was exposure to the New Zealand system of decoupled policy (ministry) and implementation (agency), which occurred during the six-country (Australia, the United Kingdom, Canada, Ireland, New Zealand and the United States) annual meeting of social security departments in the mid-1990s. One view was that Centrelink was born on a visit to New Zealand, where Tony Blunn was exposed to delivery arrangements that went beyond the boundaries of what was thought possible. The experience produced a 'sea change' in terms of what was seen as operationally attainable.

Three ideas were now in circulation. The first was the growing realisation that service delivery could be a form of specialisation that went beyond arrangements internal to a department. The second was the acceptance of the focus on the 'customer' as a primary objective. The third was the movement away from the traditional DSS office layout by using open-planning principles in branch offices that encouraged better access for customers. The confluence of these complementary (and contending) ideas provided the opportunity for an organisation design that envisaged some combination of service delivery, purchaser–provider and integrated services.

The agency trend internationally

One of the most interesting developments internationally at this time was the experiment with separating policy formulation from implementation, which included the creation of new executive agencies (Halligan 1998; Rowlands 2003). The diffusion of these ideas internationally was one of the strongest public sector trends of the 1990s, making the decade an age of 'agencification'. The cases from New Zealand and the United Kingdom were well known to senior staff of the DSS and the central agencies.[4]

In Australia, these ideas were not accepted either rapidly or enthusiastically. During the reform period, three positions were important: an attachment to traditional views regarding the handling of policy; the horizontal consolidation of departments; and the shift in attitudes in the 1990s towards separating policy and operations. Until the early 1990s, Australia was attached to combining policy and implementation roles within a department because it was thought essential to maintaining effective feedback from those delivering services. Of the anglophone countries, Australia remained closest to the tradition of maintaining integrated policy and administration. This tradition also reflected the firm belief that there must be close interaction between policy and execution and that integration within one department was the best means of securing this. Australia not only resisted moving in line with the United Kingdom and New Zealand, it followed a different approach in 1987, when it sought policy coordination and portfolio rationalisation through the horizontal consolidation of departments.

At the same time, however, the doctrinaire belief of the APS in the superiority of integrated policy and implementation was being eroded. The British executive agencies and New Zealand's decoupling now seemed less unpalatable. In 1994, the option of experimenting with new-style agencies was raised at a conference by the former head of the Department of the Prime Minister and Cabinet, Michael Codd (1996:179):[5]

> The extension of the principles of business enterprise reform into the delivery of programmes and services in core government functions, through the establishment of agencies for that purpose, has also attracted increased interest in recent years. The central part of the rationale is that, by drawing a boundary around a discrete administrative function (such as payment of pension cheques in accordance with entitlements) and giving the task to an agency, the responsibilities and expected performance can be clearly specified, and people with the appropriate

skills recruited or assigned and held accountable for achieving that performance.

Moreover, what Codd considered was a reasonable approximation to the arrangement was later instituted for the DSS and Centrelink (albeit in the context of questioning the merits of agencification, as befitted the ambivalence that still existed at that time). He argued that social security entitlements were defined clearly in the law and that the boundary between exercising administrative authority and policy work should be capable of being drawn with sufficient clarity without invoking an agency arrangement (Codd 1996:180). The benefits of agencification might therefore be realised without requiring a major organisational change.

There were other signs of change. Blunn, the head of the DSS, reflected on his conversion: '[W]e'd previously been trying to integrate service delivery into the policy structure so that it was sort of seamless because [the] view…was that if you separated service delivery from policy then you created the potential for failure. But in my view it wasn't working' (Interview).

Impetus from a new government

The emerging consensus on new and possibly more integrated solutions for delivery, which might employ purchaser–provider principles, needed an impetus. This was provided by the Howard Government's reform agenda for the public sector, which included a commitment to make the provision of government services open to competition (Vardon 1998a). This commitment conformed to the broader move towards the use of market-like mechanisms in the public sector (Rowlands 1999).

After the Coalition's victory in the 1996 election, APS attention was dominated by how best to respond to the expectations of the new government. In particular, this meant focusing on the government's intention to address a substantial budget deficit. The Treasurer, Peter Costello, announced that the government would review all measures agreed to by the previous government between the 1995/96 budget and the beginning of the caretaker period preceding the election.

The Minister of Finance, John Fahey, also proposed that action begin to reduce government costs, starting with an across-the-board 2 per cent running-costs reduction from 1996/97.[6] He also proposed that the National Commission of Audit (NCA), created by the new government shortly after taking office, undertake a major review of the management and financial activities of government and establish what additional efficiencies might be achievable in later years through, inter alia, the adoption of more cost-effective personnel practices; developing a framework and strategy for IT; greater use of competitive tendering and contracting out; benchmarking; and rationalisation of client contact networks between and within agencies. The new government considered these proposals early in its first term.

It is also apparent that the impending changes had their origins not solely at a political level but among central agencies, especially Finance, which generally took a professionally conservative view of public spending.

Anticipating the new government's agenda

The specific idea of creating Centrelink and the associated arrangements flowed from the two departmental secretaries most involved, Sandy Hollway (of the newly formed DEETYA) and Blunn (DSS). The duplication of the DSS and DEETYA networks was an obvious target for savings options for the Department of Finance. Blunn and Hollway recognised what was coming and moved quickly to achieve at least some control over events.

Blunn approached Hollway with the idea of creating a combined 'shopfront'. According to Hollway, 'it took us approximately 15 minutes to agree in principle that we wanted to head in this direction' (Husock and Scott 1999a:3). In late March 1996, the secretaries arranged a meeting of their senior staff at which the third agenda item was '[c]o-operation in client service delivery, including property co-location and rationalisation; reciprocal placement of DEETYA and DSS information/desk officers in each department, and scope for [a] joint approach to realising savings' (Husock and Scott 1999a:3). One participant commented after this meeting that Blunn and Hollway appeared to be 'falling over one another in the struggle to appear to have the broader view and the grander vision' (Interview with senior Centrelink official).

Blunn and Hollway, having anticipated the issue, used the available intellectual concepts (in the form of the agency or purchaser–provider models of government activity) to shape events. Those models were not at the forefront of the thinking that inspired this change; its basis was a 'savings option'. As can be seen from the NCA report (1996), however, such thinking was not far away and was likely to have influenced the final reform.

The considerations that were influential included the following.

- The need for the two departments to consider better integration of service delivery and program design because the two would be forced to undertake something along these lines, in view of the budget deficit and the need to find savings in expenditure. If the two departments could not formulate an approach to achieving substantial savings in running costs, they could expect to face less palatable options, most likely proposed by the Department of Finance.

- For the same reason, the ideas of one-stop shops and the integration of service delivery had to be addressed even though they raised fundamental issues about the architecture of the system.
- The question of whether there should continue to be two separate networks of regional offices, each responsible for carrying out the work of its portfolio only.
- There were only two obstacles to having a single delivery agency: accountability arrangements and how these were 'policed', and the possible loss of the 'profound connection' between those who developed policy and those who designed and carried out its implementation (see Rowlands 2003).

Conceptually, the DSS and DEETYA could be thought of as two organisations, each with shared ownership of a delivery organisation. There was a range of possible variations and substantial potential savings. There were also concerns, in Blunn's view. First, he did not want to confuse or destroy roles. Second, he did not want to separate delivery and policy roles. There was, however, little choice. If the DSS and DEETYA did not take the initiative, others would. It was clear from subsequent events that the idea was then fed into the early decision-making processes of the new government, particularly its decisions focused on reducing expenditure.

One of the DSS division heads involved in the early process summarised it as follows:

> The recent change of government provided the Secretaries of DSS and DEETYA [with] the opportunity and climate for fundamental and innovative change. They agreed within a month of the election that it made good customer service sense to integrate the two networks under new purchaser–provider arrangements, thereby establishing an agency with a community side rather than [a] low income customer base. They presented their vision to Ministers and senior managers of both Departments and by 'merging' rather than 'taking over' functions and maintaining Departments they were able to take their managers and other Departments with them. (Briggs 1996)

It is generally accepted that had the DSS and DEETYA not come up with the proposal, the government would have taken action (as evidenced by the report of the NCA). Indeed, there was an element of satisfaction in Blunn's (1997b) later comment, as part of a reflection on life in the first year of the new government, that he felt comfortable with the NCA. The government

> zeroed in very quickly. It said: 'We can achieve big savings in the DEETYA and DSS area. We can crunch together the delivery mechanisms and make huge savings'. And it was great to be able to say, 'Ah! We are there before you'. We had actually started that process. (Blunn 1997b:35)

Interpretations: opportunities, events and personalities

An announcement was made in the 1996 budget of the decision to create the Commonwealth Services Delivery Agency (CSDA), later renamed Centrelink. The decision was consistent with the findings of the NCA, which reported to the government in June 1996. It recommended rationalising the delivery of income and employment services and raised the idea of opening the provision of those services to the private sector (NCA 1996:107).

A chapter in the NCA report entitled 'Best practice in government activities' (NCA 1996) listed a range of techniques that could be employed to improve the delivery of Commonwealth programs (a list similar to that proposed by Finance Minister Fahey in the new government's initial weeks in office)—in particular, the discussion of 'cross-program approaches' that focused directly on DEETYA and the DSS. AusIndustry was cited as an example of a 'cross-program approach to service delivery', and 'rationalising the delivery of income support and employment services' was mentioned as the only potential case. The report observed that two departments were the major agencies delivering income support services:

> DSS has a service delivery network of 19 area offices, 217 regional offices, 69 smaller outlets and 16 teleservice centres. DSS employs 20,850 staff. DEETYA has a network of 19 area offices, 186 large offices, 134 smaller offices and 88 CES agencies. DEETYA employs 11,500 staff. (NCA 1996)

There was seen to be significant scope to rationalise service delivery through developing a network of shopfront offices. There was also thought to 'be scope in the long term to contract out the delivery of these services to the private sector' (NCA 1996:107, 115).

Translating the concept

In March 1996, the new Commonwealth Government was keen to address a substantial budget deficit. Some senior public servants believed that ministers thought that reducing APS staff numbers could generate a substantial proportion of the desired savings. An early decision (in April 1996) was made on strategies for securing a reduction in APS staffing.[7] About this time, the government agreed that the Minister for Social Security, Jocelyn Newman, and the Minister for Employment, Education, Training and Youth Affairs, Senator Amanda Vanstone, should develop options for a one-stop shop for beneficiaries. In conjunction with the Minister for Finance, the two ministers were to bring forward a proposal on this matter for consideration by the government. The government also decided that the Minister for Employment, Education, Training and Youth Affairs should examine the scope for further privatisation of employment-placement services and report back to the government.

There were therefore two processes operating simultaneously, but the outcomes were shaped by two stipulations: the general brief from the two key secretaries (Blunn and Hollway) and the government's expectation that initial savings of 10 per cent would be achieved. This required the merger of the employment side of the CES and the payment side of the DSS. The stage was set for the full development of proposals for a service delivery agency and associated changes to the CES and employment services.

Three models were initially offered: a super social security department, an independent statutory authority and a middle-ground service delivery agency. In terms of setting the agenda, the DSS preference was for social security to assume a broader delivery role that encompassed other departments. As this was unacceptable to DEETYA, the concept became one of policy coordination through a delivery agency. The third model was the preferred option, which derived from the original concept of a new agency emerging from the policy–delivery split.

The refining of the concept for implementation proceeded through two main stages: the initial approval by cabinet and the subsequent approval of the CSDA in the 1996 budget (before the public launch of the CSDA in September 1996). Again, two processes were operating: the first, influenced by considerations of rational design, was concerned with exploring the options for the development of a multipurpose CSDA. The basic concept was of an agency with two major clients but with the potential to serve others. There was also a 'blue-sky' dimension that reflected the open-ended potential of a large agency serving multiple policy departments. A range of possibilities could be envisaged for a multipurpose, one-stop shop. Ross Divett, the subsequent first deputy CEO of Centrelink, eventually incorporated the concept of an agency that could provide services in the draft legislation. In addition, there were the new governance arrangements under which it would operate. The other key element of the delivery agency refined at this time was a separate agency with a chief executive and an executive board of management (which would offer the government opportunities to appoint members with private sector experience).

The second process, paying heed to bureaucratic politics, addressed the question of pinning down the concept in a meaningful way for final approval by the government and laying the basis for the implementation of a viable organisation. This required recognition of the constraints on choices and the need to balance political expectations and the interests of departments.

The actors involved in these processes extended across the relevant departments and central agencies, with key secretaries and members of task groups most important. Of strategic importance were the head of the DSS, Tony Blunn, and a new leader of the task group, Carmen Zanetti, who was appointed fresh from exposure to the US environment during study at Harvard University.

The original concept envisaged a policy–delivery split that would produce a large agency with several small, high-level policy departments (each with perhaps 150 staff). The small policy department reflected organisational thinking at that time in New Zealand and the United Kingdom. Other models, such as the Treasury–Australian Taxation Office relationship had also been considered.

Blunn, however, had second thoughts about being left with a small department confined to policy and sought a clear demarcation of the interface between the two new organisations. Blunn's reformulation was to add a middle area between policy formation and delivery that essentially represented program management or operational policy. This meant that the DSS would keep product design of delivery and control of the program—retaining as much as three-quarters of the program area. Under this revised concept, Blunn envisaged that the department and the agency would compete in the middle ground and the challenge would therefore be to 'get the interface working properly' (Interview). The use of purchaser–provider relationships was to be a core element in this process.

This compromise over the distribution of responsibilities reflected the dogma of the Commonwealth system, but had long-term consequences for operations and relationships between client departments and Centrelink.

Conclusion

Centrelink was a product of the mid-1990s. A new organisation emerged from a combination of personalities, agendas and opportunities as the political stream became actively engaged through the election of a new government committed to rationalisation and cutbacks. Policy options became more concrete as a solution was sought for the problem of APS departments confronting a government with a cost-cutting agenda. Out of the convergence of the streams came an organisation that was quite different from the most prominent international experiments with new-style agencies.

The next step of the process was formulating options that would be accepted by the government and could be given organisational form. In explaining the changes, Blunn was pivotal and could claim as much responsibility as anyone for the concept of some form of agency, and then exercised decisive influence over policy options for the government and hence Centrelink's eventual form. Choice (Brunsson and Olsen 1993) was constrained by the government's agenda and by reformer preferences that reflected existing institutions, however, conditions were sufficiently propitious for significant organisational innovation to occur.

The rationale for Centrelink derived from cost factors and integrated service delivery (Rowlands 1999; Mulgan 2002). The source of later debates between departments and the agency was the structural features of Centrelink and how to define the roles of purchaser and provider.

ENDNOTES

[1] A US example was the creation of the Department of Education (Radin and Hawley 1988).

[2] As envisaged by the 'garbage-can' approach. Under the 'logic of appropriateness', rules and routines influence actions and produce conformity (March and Olsen 1989).

[3] A related but different idea was the removal of responsibility for social security operations from the DSS, which was referred to much earlier by Carlton (1986:202) in expressing concern about the large proportion of public employees engaged in 'major operations such as paying pensions' in a management environment 'not suited' for such purposes. The context for the remarks was the debate about privatisation (Rowlands 2002).

[4] Some DSS executives had participated in the design and implementation of the UK Benefits Agency, while on exchange with the British DSS.

[5] In its extreme application, Codd argued, all administrative tasks of government could be assigned to agencies. In these circumstances, core government functions would comprise only policy formulation, advice and determination.

[6] 'Running costs' was the term then used for the operating costs of departments, to be distinguished from the costs of benefits, grants and so on distributed by them—a much greater proportion of the Commonwealth budget. The terms 'running costs' and 'program costs' were replaced with the introduction of output-based budgeting by 'departmental' and 'administered' items.

[7] Minister Peter Reith's press release (1996) said that the government's approach had been settled earlier that week.

2. Centrelink's development

Centrelink was established in July 1997 as a statutory agency within the social security portfolio with a simple and quite original task. This was to enter into arrangements with department heads to carry out functions and to be responsible for delivering federal government services and benefits to Australia's unemployed and social welfare recipients. The Prime Minister, John Howard, called the establishment of the new CSDA 'probably the biggest administrative reform of recent times', with its combination of 'efficiency with sympathetic and responsible service' (Howard 1997:6).

This chapter examines how this administrative reform has been played out since its creation by providing an overview of the main dimensions—including the challenges and achievements—and serving as a bridge to the more specialised treatment in subsequent chapters. It expands on the ideas behind Centrelink's creation touched on in the previous chapter—an efficient organisation; a customer-centric one-stop shop separating policy from delivery; a modern public agency with purchaser–provider arrangements; an executive board with multi-portfolio accountability—and tracks how they developed in times of major change. It also examines how Centrelink has sought to integrate successfully staff from two departments, to re-engineer procedures and systems and to develop its own culture and business processes.

Concept and responsibilities

Presented as 'the human face of the Commonwealth government', Centrelink's mission was 'to provide easy and convenient access to high quality government and community services that improve the lives of Australians, their families and communities' (DFaCS 2003:249). Centrelink was to be the Howard Government's key administrative innovation of the 1990s. Jocelyn Newman (1997), the Minister for Social Security at the time, saw it as a new model:

> Service delivery agencies have been established overseas, notably in the [United Kingdom] and [New Zealand]…but the new agency takes the concept of single-point government service delivery further. Unlike overseas counterparts, the Agency will not operate solely as an administrative entity within a department of state or be limited to single portfolio responsibilities. In many ways the Agency represents a groundbreaking model for government service delivery at a federal level…customers will have a single point of contact—a one-stop shop—for a range of government services.

According to the explanatory memorandum for the bill creating the new organisation, Centrelink would deliver various services that were provided by a variety of departments. The second reading speech of the bill reiterated Centrelink's role as a cross-department delivery agency, and high expectations of service: 'The clear principle underlying the concept of the agency is the government's commitment to put the needs of people for high quality service delivery above the boundaries of Commonwealth departments and agencies' (Ruddock 1996:7623–4). This chapter considers how Centrelink went about responding to that responsibility in its first eight years.

The new agency immediately took over responsibility for delivering social welfare and employment-related services and income support to some 6.2 million members of the Australian community. The biggest two segments, in terms of customer numbers and payments made, were 'families and children' and 'retirement services'. Its recipients—or customers, to use Centrelink's preferred term—are set out in their main groups in Table 2.1

Table 2.1 Centrelink's customers

Customer segment	No. customers (million)
Families and children	1.80
Retirement services	2.00
Employment	1.10
Disability and carers	0.70
Youth and students	0.50
Rural and housing	0.02
Total	6.2

Source: Centrelink 1999a:2–3.

While the creation of Centrelink was partly about combining employment and welfare services in one organisation, providing employment services was always going to be a small part of the total and, because unemployment fell after Centrelink's inception, it came to make up just 5 per cent of its business. Nevertheless, the employment segment consumed a higher proportion of staff effort than other segments, primarily because each payment required more processing effort within the office. In colloquial terms, the unemployed were expected to 'jump through more hoops' to gain payments and the natural concomitant was a greater administrative effort.

A year after beginning, Centrelink estimated that it had made some 300 million contacts with more than six million customers, answered more than 20 million telephone calls in the year and processed more than 3.4 billion transactions. Information provided to customers was delivered by mail, telephone, the Internet, by personal contact at a Centrelink office and by off-site visits.

It was not just the size of this activity that made Centrelink significant in day-to-day Australian life; it was also the nature of its task. The wellbeing of most recipients of government income support has been dependent on Centrelink successfully continuing its daily operations. Many of its customers are the most vulnerable members of society and any confusion about support payments or failure to pay pensions is immediately a major issue politically and in the media. A major disruption to its services is significant to those dependent on it and an embarrassment to the government of the day. The fact that the payments it delivered amounted to a major portion of the Commonwealth budget reinforced the attention Centrelink attracted from the government.

Organisation, staff and funding

At its inception, the new agency immediately became the biggest agency in the APS—totalling one-quarter of all the APS in staff numbers. Its establishment involved bringing together 21 000 staff from the former social welfare delivery department, the DSS, and 3000 from the department formerly responsible for delivering unemployment payments, DEETYA, and consolidating their two Australia-wide, overlapping, regional networks.

The new agency not only inherited large numbers of staff from the two departments, it was funded by them. Centrelink was set up, not as a budget-funded agency, but as one funded directly from the organisations for which it delivered services. Because Centrelink's funding came principally from these departments and agencies (with only a very small percentage—in 1997, just 5.17 per cent—as direct appropriations from the budget), each organisation negotiated a purchase price for the services Centrelink agreed to provide and, using resources appropriated to it in the budget, paid Centrelink for its work. Centrelink was responsible for using these funds to meet the negotiated outcomes when delivering each program.

These relationships with its clients—because they purchased its services through purchaser–provider arrangements—were governed by negotiated contractual agreements with each department. Initially known as Strategic Partnership Agreements, short documents containing comparatively little detail, they subsequently evolved into more comprehensive documents renamed Business Partnership Agreements (BPAs).

The BPAs gave details of the services, the funding arrangements, agreed performance outcomes and allied reporting mechanisms and outlined arrangements for the sharing of information and for dealing with unforeseen issues. The BPAs therefore established the scope and provided the detail for a formal purchaser–provider relationship between two organisations and were used to manage and review the operating and performance relationships between each organisation.

The use of BPAs was a fairly new experience for Commonwealth government agencies. They required all parties to understand fully what services were to be provided, when, how and at what cost, without making the relationships between the organisations too rigid in a politically and publicly sensitive environment. They took the form of a memorandum of understanding—as the Commonwealth was unable to enter a contract with itself and the purchaser and provider organisations were, in the main, Commonwealth agencies. The requirement for Centrelink to report to its client departments on its performance against a series of detailed indicators in the BPAs became the centre of Centrelink's network of accountability for the money it received.

At its inception, Centrelink acquired a new governance model (see Chapter 6). Accountability was managed through a board of management, an executive board appointed by and reporting to the Minister for Family and Community Services.[1] This in itself was a rare occurrence as few public service agencies worked with a decision-making board rather than one with a purely advisory role. Moreover, the secretaries of the two client departments were members. The board established the overall objectives, gave strategic direction and set broad business rules for the organisation. Centrelink reported to the minister through the board on administrative issues relating to the minister's portfolio.

Administrative imperatives

The initial task required the new organisation to bring together the staff of two departments with different expectations and cultures into one organisation, and to rationalise the delivery services of these two departments that were now responsible for overseeing the delivery of their policy program outcomes by one new agency. These departments had a long history of rivalry and turf warfare so the potential for tension, conflict and dispute was considerable.

The different cultures and expectations of each parent department would gradually lead to different relationships developing: one more contractual, the other more of a partnership or strategic alliance. Within this structure, Centrelink was subject to more than one minister, with a decision-making board appointed by and responsible to the minister of its largest client portfolio department, yet without control of its budget or staffing numbers. These were the prerogative of its client departments, which determined its outputs and performance measures through purchaser–provider agreements. In time, Centrelink would extend service provision to other clients, federal and state.

There was a range of issues that could create tensions. Centrelink was established as a customer-focused agency, which offered new levels of integrated customer service and was promoted as the human face of government, but it was also required to save money through the amalgamation of the two service networks of its parent departments. It would, as Sue Vardon put it, need to adopt a businesslike approach that was 'harmonious with the aspirations of human service' (Vardon 1998d).

As the Prime Minister (Howard 1997:2, 3) said when he launched Centrelink in September 1997:

In the past we have encouraged people to go from one location to another and we have often confused them with a lot of administrative duplication. And in one very big stroke Centrelink cuts through that duplication. Centrelink consolidates in an efficient, modern fashion the major service delivery activities...The consolidation in Centrelink of so many of the services of the Government that interact with people will provide, of course, a more human face. It will provide a more efficient service. It will lead to far less public dissatisfaction...Because Centrelink is carving out a new horizon and a completely different horizon. And it is a demonstration that there is...a unique Australian way, of delivering service support to those in the community who deserve and need our help and assistance.

Improving services for customers became a high priority. The initial emphasis was placed on improving staff attitudes and shopfront offices, and later on developing clearer options for customers and broadening technological access.

An agency through which such a large proportion of funding was transmitted and with such a large, and often economically vulnerable, clientele was always going to be of interest to politicians. Any weaknesses, errors or failures would be noticed and reported in parliament and the media sooner and louder than failures in smaller organisations with less vulnerable customers. Centrelink became an agency whose every move was scrutinised.

There were also possible tensions in being a public service agency. Minister Philip Ruddock (1996:7624) indicated that Centrelink would be a statutory agency with public service responsibilities and subject to the mainstream legislation for agencies as well as the *Audit Act* and finance regulations and directions. As a statutory agency, like the Australian Public Service Commission, Centrelink has operated under the *Financial Management and Accountability (FMA) Act 1997*, which brings with it a high level of accountability. The chairman of its board of management was the chief executive for the purpose of the *FMA Act* and was given specific powers in the legislation establishing Centrelink. This included direct accountability to the portfolio minister.

These accountability and reporting mechanisms were quite complex, with the CEO, appointed by and reporting to the board, also reporting directly to the minister (or ministers) of the client departments while also being responsible for delivery of programs for which their departmental secretaries were funded and accountable. Ministers had the power under Centrelink's legislation to intervene directly in Centrelink's affairs. Attendance at Senate Estimate Committee hearings was therefore a joint activity with officials from Centrelink and the Department of Family and Community Services (DFaCS) in attendance to respond to questions. There were also potential tensions for Centrelink as a public service agency staffed by people transferred from its parent departments, but also expected to be an agency able to operate in businesslike ways that were entrepreneurial and alert to expanding its business.

A further challenge was the separation of policy and service delivery, which was unusual in Australian public administration. Another example of where the two had been separated, the service delivery organisation of the Australian Taxation Office, had just one policy department, the Treasury. Centrelink began with two clients and had three after one year, with the expectation that this number would grow in time.

Governments invariably modified and amended social welfare and employment policies during their tenure so a degree of policy change was anticipated, but not the radical changes that occurred soon after Centrelink's inception. The government undertook a wholesale review of social welfare, and the policy decisions taken in 2001 flowing from that review substantially changed how Centrelink needed to operate and significantly extended its core business. These changes galvanised Centrelink's role in designing the implementation of the new policies. They also obliged the policy departments to take into account and modify policies when given feedback from Centrelink about how policy changes were affecting recipients or community service providers. Managing the policy/service-delivery balance was always likely to be difficult, even more so in times of a complete overhaul of social welfare and employment policies.

In time, these administrative issues and varying expectations would drive Centrelink to behave and develop in particular ways. There were opportunities for conflict between the different objectives set for the new organisation. Moving in one consistent direction was going to be difficult as there were several imperatives to be attended to. These were worked through in several stages.

Developmental stages

Centrelink evolved with time in a series of stages. They are based on a number of dimensions with dominant tasks being important—transition and implementation, productivity and service delivery—and reflect Centrelink's, in particular the CEO's, developmental aspirations.

Creation and establishment (1997–98)

The initial focus was to establish effective governance structures, bring the disparate staff of the organisation to one culture and set of goals and create an easily identifiable brand for the organisation and customers. One of the earliest challenges for the new CEO was to develop an organisational culture to meet the new expectations of Centrelink as a one-stop shop with heightened responsiveness to customer needs. The legislation establishing the new organisation aimed to set up 'an administrative framework for integrating access to Commonwealth services by consolidating services so that...people can get the help they need in one place' (CSDA 1997c:1). It was to be an agency 'focussed on, and specialising in, customer service' (Ruddock 1996). Although initially it was to administer all the services provided by the DSS, plus some from DEETYA and, a year later, from the Department of Health and Family Services, it was anticipated that the provision of other services would be added in time.

The new organisation also required a readily identifiable public profile that differed from its predecessors. A name and corporate identity were needed with extensive advertising to inform the community of the changes. The agency was launched officially on 24 September 1997 with new goals, livery and a name: Centrelink. At the same time, it was necessary to address the concerns of staff about job security and fears that their functions could be opened to competitive tendering. The public service reform agenda at the time supported contracting out and emphasised the superior efficiency of the private sector. Staff had seen the government decide to split the functions of the CES and place some with Centrelink and others, through the Job Network, with contracted job-placement agencies. Many staff feared that their jobs could go. Melding together an effective organisation was also complicated by the initial difficulties of bringing together groups from two departments, with the smaller group—outnumbered seven to one—feeling overwhelmed.

Developing a common approach to customers took time. Those who had previously worked with employment services were used to finding innovative solutions to maximise the help they could provide; those with a social security background were more concerned that the applicant was really eligible, that they met all the criteria and complied with the legislation being administered. Not surprisingly, the first staff survey showed that fewer than half the staff members were satisfied with their jobs.

The new industrial agreement focused on customer services. National and local surveys of customer satisfaction had begun to identify what customers valued and a program of value-creation workshops attended by staff and their customers 'had a powerful impact on the people of Centrelink and generated an impetus for change' (Vardon 1998d:2). A decision by the executive that Centrelink offices would be redesigned with open-plan layouts contributed to the culture change. 'There had to be symbols, symbols that this was different' (Vardon interview).

Another symbol was the reduction of hierarchies within the organisation and the use of new cultural language, such as the collective phrase 'the guiding coalition' to identify all the members of the senior executive service (SES). Flatter structures and teams headed by an SES officer replaced traditional divisions and branches. Within the boundaries determined by the board of management, the guiding coalition constituted Centrelink's internal management committee, setting the direction and taking key decisions, while establishing a culture for the future and acting as an educative forum (Centrelink 1999a:85).

During this time, the governance arrangements were gradually worked out. The minister appointed the board members, many of whom had a strong private sector background. There was initially some uncertainty about the roles of the board members, the ministers and the CEO. During this period, Centrelink also identified four primary stakeholder groups as having major interests in its operations: the portfolio ministers, client departments, internal customers (board of management and agency staff) and people who used Centrelink services and their representatives.

To assess its performance against Centrelink goals, in late 1997, the board decided to adopt the balanced-scorecard technique derived from Kaplan and Norton. The scorecard became the prime performance-management tool and key accountability instrument tracking Centrelink's performance towards the goals in its strategic framework by measuring performance directly against these goals. The scorecard underwent several iterations but continued to be the main reporting mechanism to the board of management. As a public service agency, Centrelink was subject to the Auditor-General's early investigation into how the implementation was carried out. The ANAO report provided some third-party support for Centrelink's administration.

The creation of Customer Relations Units in all Centrelink's area offices in 1997 provided a contact point for customer complaints to Centrelink and the Ombudsman soon referred more than three-quarters of all the complaints received in his office back to Centrelink for resolution.

During this phase, no attempt was made to change the structure of Centrelink services. They continued to be based on the delivery of specific programs—the result being multiple queues and reception counters for separate customer segments, program-specific telephone numbers for customers and Centrelink teams organised by customer segments. While a person seeking help from the government now had just one organisation to approach, they might, depending on their circumstances, still need to deal with different parts of Centrelink.

A year after its launch, Centrelink had established a clear image in the Australian community, was making headway in developing a customer service culture in its staff, had built a new set of relationships—with client departments, the board and ministers—had achieved the efficiency dividend required by the government and had begun to find new ways of working. During this phase, customer satisfaction levels remained stable despite the changed agenda and the difficulties that customer service and call centres experienced in meeting demand. It also began to attract some new business, extending its work for the health department, winning a competitive tender to provide services to veterans and providing some farm-relief payments on behalf of the Department of Primary Industries and Energy. While some believed that Centrelink's existence would be up for review at the end of three or four years if it did not perform, initial staff fears of imminent privatisation abated.

The lessons learned during the transition from a conventional government department to a service delivery agency, according to Vardon, included: the value of communication, the need to temper business approaches with service requirements, the importance of determining the real costs of operations and measurement of real performance, the need for organisational leaders to articulate visions at the local level for staff and the necessity of evening out the implementation of change to reduce peak workloads in the service network (Vardon 1998d).

Consolidation and design (1998–2000)

The second phase of Centrelink's development focused internally on a restructure that led to about 5000 staff being invited to 'take a package' to reduce the total workforce, and on productivity improvements. The theme for this period, 'Doing our current business better', was aimed at achieving best practice in the organisation's core business by adopting the best-practice achievements of the most productive offices throughout its network. A target for the end of 1999, based on the performance of the top-50 offices, would, it was estimated, result in a 28 per cent increase in productivity across the network.

Striving for efficiency was a high priority for Centrelink from the beginning. The NCA report (1996:115) had recommended that a saving in the annual budget—an efficiency dividend—of about 20 per cent was achievable in certain areas of government business and particularly through the amalgamation of the service delivery functions of the DSS and DEETYA. In practice, an efficiency dividend of 10 per cent was imposed, in increasing steps, over the first three years of operation. An additional 1 per cent was included, matching the standard efficiency dividend for the rest of the APS, and a further levy was placed on IT in anticipation of savings from outsourcing.

An audit report recommended that Centrelink and the Department of Finance and Administration (DOFA), in consultation with purchaser departments, agree on the processes for determining future efficiency dividends. The identification of the efficiency dividends was to be undertaken. While supporting this recommendation, the DSS noted that 'under its Strategic Partnership Agreement with Centrelink, responsibility for discussion and negotiation with the Department of Finance and Administration of future efficiency dividends for Centrelink rests with DSS. Any such consultations and negotiations will be undertaken with the full involvement of Centrelink' (ANAO 1997b). The ANAO (1997b:4.31–4) responded that 'responsibility for these negotiations is not explicit in the Strategic Partnership Agreement. Responsibilities should be clarified, taking into account that in the future, Centrelink rather than the DSS will be in a stronger position to identify achievable efficiency savings.' These differences in perceptions typified much of the early period when relationships and responsibilities were still being clarified.

In terms of customer service, the aim during this phase was to improve the integration of services between call centres and customer service centres, re-engineer work flows and processes, introduce technological improvements to facilitate customer self-service and staff assistance and to improve services to rural and remote areas. Above all, the organisation had to retain its current business as well as expand its alliances.

Information technology was central to Centrelink from the beginning. This was recognised by the initial planners when they decided to transfer the computer system from the DSS with the staff who maintained it. In contrast, the employment department had retained its own computer equipment but gave Centrelink access to it. Nevertheless, there was always the threat that Centrelink's IT would have to be outsourced to meet the government's IT outsourcing agenda—an agenda that did not change until the Humphry Report to the government. The board of management had made it clear that it did not support this agenda and managed to hold off taking action until the agenda was discredited.

A new IT platform was created in 1998 bringing together into one common database information from the full range of social welfare and unemployment programs. It allowed Centrelink staff for the first time to view a full customer record and helped them to determine eligibility for benefits. It was introduced at the same time as, and was crucial to, a new welfare program: the Youth Allowance. Testing and training was cut short to meet program deadlines and the result, according to the press, was 'chaos' (Husock and Scott 1999b).

The new IT interface completely changed how Centrelink's front-desk staff operated. For the first time, the IT system was 'live' and customer eligibility could be determined on the spot. With the earlier system, customers could be registered and issues of eligibility could be sorted out later; now incomplete information or ineligibility meant that staff had to tell customers to their faces that they did not qualify for benefits. The effect was slower processing of customers, longer queues and impatient and in some cases disgruntled customers being told they were not eligible for benefits. As noted by the deputy CEO, Ross Divett, 'it made the front line a very unpleasant place to work' (quoted in Husock and Scott 1999b:3). While the system itself was considered to be working reasonably well, the shortage of time for testing and acculturation put people under real pressure. There were accounts of 'absolute chaos in Centrelink offices around the country' (Husock and Scott 1999b) and of customers taking out aggression on staff.

At the same time, the Youth Allowance was initiated with short deadlines for Centrelink. While many young people benefited, the new parental means test meant that more than 50 000 people lost payments or had them reduced because of their parents' income. The media reported these cases avidly. While Centrelink was not the policy agency, as the deliverer, it was often blamed.

Vardon (Interview) described the position when the Youth Allowance was introduced with a tough timetable:

> We had five youth payments that had to be introduced on the first of July. There were huge technological changes, loads of staff training. Young people in the community didn't know what was going on, there was no real community education about youth allowance. I couldn't believe that governments could work this way. Then I'd go into Minister Kemp, and he'd say, 'Sue, you know you're not getting the referrals out' and I said to him, 'We are going as fast as we can, we have to change everything'…But we could not have gone any faster, it was a massive change, and they expected miracles in five minutes. So we had a huge organisational change, we had to make everybody feel loved and wanted and part of this new thing, and then came a massive amount of policy change. And I think that the fact that we did it was a miracle, but we didn't ever do it fast enough for the government of the day…But I don't know that anybody could have done it much faster…So there was [a] certain amount of 'Oh, we shouldn't have given it to the public service, they're too slow'.

Centrelink's annual report (1999a:11) put it more circumspectly: 'The introduction of the Youth allowance…put considerable pressures on Centrelink, particularly its Call Centre and Customer Service Centre networks. This was a difficult time for customers and staff alike and from it Centrelink learned some valuable lessons.' The Youth Allowance program was just one example of a regular feature in Centrelink's life: rapid policy change with little time to plan implementation of service delivery changes.

The bad press was exacerbated by huge delays in call centre responses. Centrelink had chosen to develop the call centres it inherited from the DSS as an accessible option for customers and a cheaper option for Centrelink, but the creation of so many policy changes at the one time had expanded its customer base and created confusion. The number of calls a day rose from an average of 200 000 in March 1998 to more than one million in July. Centrelink's call centres could not cope. Again, the media and talkback radio reported the chaos as people told of trying unsuccessfully to get through numerous times and one media outlet reported that an internal document showed that 90 per cent of calls to Centrelink received an engaged signal. As noted in Centrelink's annual report (1999a:38), 'while Centrelink Call generally achieved its contracted performance standard of an average speed of answer of 210 seconds, consistently high demand presented a very real challenge to maintaining quality customer service'. The call waiting time in July 1998 reached an average of 325 seconds.

The substantial expansion of call centres from 1999 significantly reduced the call waiting time of customers. A 2002 review of Centrelink's cost efficiency showed that call centre workload almost doubled in four years. The number of calls had risen from 19 million to more than 23 million and the duration of calls from an average of 5.4 minutes to 7.8 minutes (BCG 2002:21, 23); call waiting time dropped to 108 seconds. A year later, the 4500 staff in 23 call centres were responding to about 300 000 emails a year and taking more than 25 million calls with an average duration of 8.8 minutes. Despite the fact that call waiting times were a primary driver of customer satisfaction, average waiting times increased by one-third—to 144 seconds. Nevertheless, customer satisfaction with these services rated consistently between 85 and 90 per cent. The call centres became the largest single-purpose call centre operation in Australia (Centrelink 2003a:114–15).

Centrelink did have warning and was involved in the policy development process of the biggest welfare and employment reform initiative to take place during these years. In October 1999, the government appointed a high-level Reference Group on Welfare Reform, chaired by Patrick McClure, CEO of Mission Australia, to guide the development of a comprehensive review of welfare reform. After extensive consultations and numerous submissions and workshops, it reported in August 2000. The report showed that, while the unemployment rate in Australia was falling, six times the number of people were on income support than had been in the 1970s. In the 1970s, one in 20 working-aged people was receiving payments; it was now one in five—more than 2.5 million people. More than 700 000 children were living in families in which no-one worked. Only about 15 per cent of these non-working adults—including the unemployed, people with a disability or sickness and sole parents—were required to look for work or contribute to their communities in any way. The report called for fundamental change and suggested action in five major areas: individualised service delivery, a simple and responsive income support structure, incentives and financial assistance, mutual obligations and social partnerships. It recommended the development of a participation support system based on the principle of mutual obligation.

The report provided the opportunity for the underlying fear of the privatisation of Centrelink to resurface. In response, the Minister for Community Services, Larry Anthony (2000), declared: 'This report is not about privatising Centrelink, rather it has highlighted that a central gateway is needed to deliver the best service to all Australians...There are opportunities for Centrelink as the gateway to the new welfare system'. After the announcement of the government's response to the report in mid-December 2000, the Minister for Family and Community Services, Senator Newman (2000a), reaffirmed this: 'Centrelink will remain the main gateway to the participation support system.' This became clearer in May 2001, when the government announced in Australians Working Together (AWT) substantial changes to the social support system for working-aged people. Centrelink was to be responsible for implementation. In their joint press release announcing the initiative in May 2001, the Ministers for Social Security and Employment declared that Centrelink was to be

> the gateway to the new system. But we are asking more from Centrelink, and we are providing more money so they can get the job done, said Senator Vanstone. Centrelink Personal Advisers will provide a high level of service to people needing additional help to overcome personal or other barriers. (Vanstone and Abbott 2001a)

The ministerial statement confirmed Centrelink's role: '[A] vital element in a better, more balanced system is offering personalised assistance and support. Accordingly, improving Centrelink services will be the key to making *Australians Working Together* a success' (Vanstone and Abbott 2001a).

A series of pilot programs began to address specific groups such as the older unemployed, workless families and the long-term unemployed. Many of the initiatives were to be phased in over a number of years, but this reform agenda changed permanently how Centrelink operated. Its primary task as an income support payment agency would gradually be supplemented by helping those of working age to increase their participation in education, training, community activities and employment. This was a much wider role, which required staff to develop new skills, new knowledge, new information systems and greater understanding of the possible sources of assistance for the unemployed. Much of Centrelink's subsequent focus and development was driven by this policy reform agenda.

During its involvement with the work of the McClure Reference Group, Centrelink began the planning needed to redesign the way its services were delivered—the key feature of its next phase of development. Customer feedback and many of the consultations and submissions to the reference group called for a more personal approach. Customers indicated that approaching welfare issues in terms of programs did not correlate with the events of their lives. What was needed was to be able to tell one person their story once, not have to repeat it and to be able to understand what services were available to help with the current crisis in their life. Centrelink's response was to provide a single point of contact for the customer—a one-to-one contact officer—so each customer would have only one main person within Centrelink with whom they made contact.

For the first time, customers would be able to tell their story once only and receive a personalised response. The one-to-one officer would coordinate and integrate the products and services available from Centrelink (or elsewhere) to respond to the specific needs of the customer. Staff members were allocated a pool of customers and accepted responsibility for all continuing business relating to that group. These arrangements were expected to speed up decisions, to help staff to develop a more professional relationship with customers and to give them greater satisfaction with their work.

These one-to-one arrangements, accompanied by some encouragement for straightforward business to be directed through the call centres, were implemented in all offices by the end of 1999. They were the initial step in implementing the further response in the next phase: a new service delivery model based on a range of possible life events.

Nevertheless, a decision by the government in 2000 to establish another form of one-stop shop, the Family Assistance Office (FAO), to deliver, as part of its new tax system, a 'new' family assistance package, was surprising. It might have seemed logical that Centrelink, as the main provider of family assistance, would become the 'provider of choice', but this required political support. Instead, it was decided to establish a new 'virtual' agency within the Family and Community Services portfolio and to share the delivery of services between the three agencies currently responsible for delivery of family payments, family tax benefits and childcare benefits—Centrelink, the Australian Taxation Office and Medicare—by establishing FAO outlets in each of their networks of shopfront offices.

The decision to use three service delivery agencies increased the number of FAO outlets available to the government; 550 offices were set up. It also separated the delivery of family assistance from any association with 'welfare' payments, an association that some considered could be seen as distasteful by some people. DFaCS officers had told the senate committee examining the family assistance legislation that 'we certainly know that some people dislike dealing with Centrelink for their family assistance' (Senate CALC 1999). In practice, Centrelink managed the bulk of FAO business, but the creation of the FAO separated that business from 'welfare'.

Centrelink was never solely an income support agency, though that was clearly the core of its work. The new emphasis on 'participation' and mutual obligation significantly changed its focus. It was also gaining new business. By mid-2000, Centrelink was providing a broad range of more than 70 'products' and services that could be tailored to meet the needs of individual customers undergoing life changes. These included financial information services, social work services, passport call services, industry adjustment packages, career counselling through occupational psychologists, job seeker assistance and disaster, crisis and refugee assistance. Ten federal government departments were using its services as well as the Australian Electoral Commission, the Tasmanian Government and state and territory housing authorities (Centrelink 2000a:Figure 1). The original expectation that its services would spread beyond two or three client departments to encompass broader social services had proved correct. Nevertheless, the social welfare part of its work continued to dominate.

Centrelink's badging as a Commonwealth government agency was also important politically to a government wishing to be seen as active in rural Australia, as it provided a clear presence. Having Centrelink as a Commonwealth agency in rural areas was regarded as an asset by the government.

By the middle of 2000, there were more than 6.4 million customers and more than 1000 Centrelink offices Australia-wide; 300 customer service centres, 25 call centres, 42 local specialist centres, 400 local visiting services and 300 local agents including six rural transaction centres received about 22.5 million telephone calls a year and sent out approximately 101 million letters each year. Centrelink was ranked the fourth-largest IT user in Australia. Average call centre response times reduced from 177 to 70 seconds during the year (Centrelink 2000a).

New service delivery model (2000–02)

In its third evolutionary phase, Centrelink looked to transform service delivery (Vardon 1998d) with a new model based on a life-events methodology. It also focused on acquiring new business, consolidating staff development programs, developing more advanced electronic service delivery and closer connections with state and territory one-stop shops.

Centrelink's efforts now concentrated on becoming an easier place for customers to use, building on one-to-one service by implementing the idea of a 'life-events' service delivery model (Vardon 1998d). The life-events approach meant that

> at points of transition or crisis in peoples' lives (eg. leaving school, becoming unemployed, retiring from the workforce, separating from a partner) a range of government services will be tailored by Centrelink to meet their needs. This contrasts with traditional approaches to service delivery whereby people needed to know about and apply for a range of assistance measures, often missing out in the process. It means that Centrelink will sort out the complexities of government, not the customer. (Vardon 1998c)

To make it easier for customers, Centrelink staff would take responsibility for recognising what services would best meet their customers' needs. The onus shifted from the customer to staff to match needs with available products and services, including internal and external referrals.

> No longer will our customers have to spend their time trying to locate
> the part of Centrelink that deals with their particular situation. However
> they choose to approach us, the response they receive will be guided by
> the 'life event' which has prompted their contact with us. (Vardon 1999c)

The life-events approach was designed to ensure this shift in responsibility, so
that customer confusion no longer occurred about what support they were
entitled to within the range and complexity of Centrelink's services.

Neither of these approaches—the one-to-one approach nor the life-events
model—was unique to Centrelink. Canada, with its 'citizens-first' approach (Erin
Research Inc. 1998), and Britain, in its reworking of government servicing
arrangements (Bellamy 1998), had come to similar conclusions about the need
to reduce complexity and access difficulties for customers. The use of life events
as the way for governments to build knowledge of customers' circumstances,
and to present tailored business to them, was becoming a worldwide
phenomenon. A UK Government paper, 'The Need for a Clearer Vision', for
example, explored the potential presented by technology for the re-engineering
of government activities along completely different lines. One of the key
possibilities it had considered was to repackage government services for citizens'
life events (Vardon 1998d:10). The life-events approach was expected to take
until 2005 to implement in full (see Figure 2.1).

Figure 2.1 Centrelink Strategic Directions

Its implementation would require significant changes to IT. A decision was made to provide that support through an 'expert' system developed to help staff ascertain the appropriate services and programs for each customer. An expert system supporting the FAO payments had already been installed at several Centrelink sites. If Centrelink employees were to take responsibility for sorting out the complexities of government assistance for their customers, they would also need to expand their understanding and knowledge of government services.

In 2002, a new 'customer account' system was rolled out, displaying information about current customers in a single view and requiring updating only from the front desk to make changes to the mainframe record. In time, this was to allow customers to update their own account information.

New online transactions using the Internet began in mid-2001, allowing customers to update their income estimates from home at a time to suit them. A year later, customers had made more than 50 000 changes using the Internet.

With all these changes, Centrelink's client departments formed a view that the agency's focus on increasing customer satisfaction had been to the detriment of accuracy and protecting the integrity of outlays. Centrelink recognised the importance of being a good steward of taxpayers' funds so that the public had confidence in the social security system, but some considered this aspect of their work was not a sufficiently high priority. Attention to business assurance and an initiative called 'Getting it right' began in 2000. Two audit reports—one in 2001 on the management of fraud and incorrect payments in Centrelink, and one on age pension entitlements in 2002—brought the issue into greater focus. Mistakes had administrative and public costs for Centrelink and eliminating preventable rework became an important part of cost effectiveness.

Plans were implemented for the next phase of development: an emphasis on building mechanisms that would allow customers to take more control of their information, in which user-friendly and accessible technology would help them 'get it right'. The staff of Centrelink could thus increasingly focus on intensive help for those with complex problems.

Selective sourcing of IT was now possible after the government's relaxation of its requirements for mandatory outsourcing (Treadwell 2001).

The impact on Centrelink of the AWT program cannot be overrated. Staged introduction of this program would significantly increase the onus on Centrelink's unemployed customers to engage in their communities, particularly through employment. To achieve this, Centrelink had to build stronger relationships with the business and community sectors. A Boston Consulting Group (BCG 2002) report to Centrelink showed that the workload relating to Centrelink participating customers had increased from 12 million minutes a year (in 1997–98) to 46 million minutes (in 2001–02) as a result of job-seeker and preparing-for-work agreements. AWT would significantly increase this. From May 2002, approximately 15 000 Centrelink staff would have their jobs redesigned to ensure they were more prepared for the AWT initiatives. To achieve this, Centrelink took measures to improve the management of its referrals, to improve follow-ups and to ensure that staff had the tools, knowledge and business intelligence to meet the challenge. There was a new focus on improving relations with community organisations and business.

Review and redesign (2003–04)

The fourth stage reflected Centrelink's move beyond the formative period of development to building on and refining relationships and processes. This is clear from Centrelink's *Future Directions—2004–2009*, which provided a sense of activity in several key areas. It envisaged strengthening Centrelink's vision, improving alignment with strategic themes and simplifying planning, targets and key performance indicators to assist with performance monitoring and to improve operational planning (Centrelink 2004a:20).

There were reviews during this period of life events and of the balanced scorecard, after which a new scorecard was implemented in mid-2003 (Centrelink 2004a:21). Relationships received attention in the form of improvements to those with customers, and a special emphasis on the community level emerged more prominently. With client departments, the move towards an alliance approach was now stronger.

At the same time, there was a redesign element to this stage. The view remained that service delivery should be advanced (Vardon 2003c). The redesign element was apparent through re-engineering in conjunction with further development of the life-events model. This re-engineering envisaged a process from 2004 of bringing together all parts of Centrelink into an integrated national network to improve customer access, increase efficiencies and improve decision making. The challenges for the future centred on redesign through alignments between the community segments, channels (site, call, online or paper) and business processes through point of contact while taking into account the levels of risk and complexity (Vardon 2003c).

By mid-2004, Centrelink was handling payments of about $60.1 million on behalf of 25 client agencies. Centrelink's 6.5 million customers accounted for 9.5 million entitlements and were involved in 28 million telephone calls. The network now comprised more than 900 service centres across Australia, including 321 customer service centres, 349 Centrelink agencies, 29 separate specialist service centres, 26 call centres, 159 access points and six remote-area service centres (Centrelink 2004a: ch. 2; Appendix Table 6.1).

The composition of the staff had changed in eight years. The SES had expanded to 103; for a number of years, about 45 per cent were women and 64 per cent of Band 2 and 3 SES positions in 2004 were women. Indigeneous employment had often been high compared with other Australian organisations and was averaging about 3.6 per cent of staff (Centrelink 2004a; Appendix Table 6.2).

Centrelink was not, however, immune to the new reform movement in Canberra that favoured integrated governance rather than entrepreneurial agencies, with their associated ambiguities. The winds of change in the APS were now registering through the government's concern about issues such as ministerial direction, opaque governance and monitoring delivery (for example, Shergold 2004).

The agenda had a direct impact on Centrelink in late 2004 when new governance arrangements were introduced (see Chapter 9) thereby bringing to an end this phase and the formative years of Centrelink.

Conclusion

The four stages produced sustained change and the implementation of a new type of agency of significance in Australia and internationally. There remained challenges and issues in the mid-2000s: cost transparency for clients and for Centrelink management so that channel-management decisions were soundly based; spreading better practice within the organisation; enhancing IT systems and flexibility; improving relations with client departments; increasing feedback into the policy processes; improving staff technical and interpersonal skills; streamlining reliable processes that linked with business or community organisations; reducing call centre waiting times; reducing errors and improving compliance; further implementation of personalisation of services; improving and extending Internet transactions; and reconsidering the purchaser–provider funding model. There were also the questions about contending with Centrelink's media image and gaining the confidence of the wider community.

Whether Centrelink could call itself a one-stop shop or just a first-stop shop remained open to debate. It did refer its customers to other agencies and organisations—Job Network providers and community organisations—but it also tended to be the first point of contact. The government had created other agencies to deliver specific services that might have been expected to have been given to Centrelink, but it increasingly aimed to provide an integrated, whole-of-government approach to service delivery.

There was a change of role and language from being a one-stop shop to being a broker of services. The AWT initiative placed Centrelink in a new central role working with all those who could assist its customers to improve their integration and participation in the community: community organisations, businesses and educational institutions. It could not work alone, it could not be a one-stop shop but it could provide the bridge that helped customers participate in society.

Centrelink's unusual and perhaps unique public administration model is made up of several elements that are not necessarily original, but when bundled together in one organisation they have produced something new and worth understanding. These aspects are analysed in the remaining chapters of this book.

ENDNOTES

[1] During the second term of the Howard Government, the board reported to the Minister for Community Services, the junior of the two ministers in the Families and Community Services portfolio.

3. Strategies and management structure

From its inception, Centrelink was subject to several driving forces and constraints. Its enabling legislation (CSDA 1997a) described the new agency's functions as providing services in accordance with service arrangements, functions conferred under other legislation or under direction from the minister and anything else related to the performance of its functions. The accompanying second reading speech (Ruddock 1996:7623) noted that the organisation was expected to expand on the delivery of income security payments and services for the DSS and provide 'an administrative framework for integrating access to Commonwealth services by consolidating services so that, where possible, people can get [the] help they need in one place'. Additionally, the government envisaged better and more efficient and effective service to individuals and the community from an integrated, customer-focused organisation.

Despite its reform agenda and philosophy, the Howard Government did use this opportunity to restructure the Public Service to commercialise, corporatise or privatise the welfare service delivery function, presumably because it contained 'some of the most sensitive social responsibilities of Government' (Ruddock 1996:7623). Indeed, it described the CSDA as a core part of the government's operations. Still, it did make a significant financial impost in the form of additional efficiency dividends as well as introducing the spectre of competition through its service-wide contestability policy, which meant that the government could look at alternative providers if Centrelink underperformed.

As noted in Chapter 2, the major issues facing the new organisation included achieving government policies and outcomes, providing existing DSS services, integrating the CES and other functions, becoming more customer orientated, simplifying and streamlining services and improving performance in terms of operational efficiency and effectiveness within a purchaser–provider arrangement with departments. Implementing these changes needed to take account of organisational culture, decision-making processes, business development and long-term positioning of the agency. While the DSS had developed a comprehensive planning regime during the 1990s, this menu of change presented planning and organisational design challenges for Centrelink.

This chapter examines how Centrelink's planning strategies and structures developed in its formative years. It also reviews adjustments in strategic directions and how the organisation confronted changing circumstances and pressures.

Formulating strategies for Centrelink

From the outset, Centrelink planners implemented strategic planning concepts and processes. This meant considering political and legislative mandates and stakeholders' expectations against changing corporate environments and the newly constituted organisational resources and structures. The intention was to develop suitable corporate, business and functional strategies to ensure survival and growth. To assist this process, a Business Development Group was established early in Centrelink's existence to examine strategic options.

Viewed against the options for strategies to provide the basis for coordinated and sustained efforts for meeting long-term business objectives (Pearce and Robinson 2000), Centrelink selected a combination of strategies including concentrated growth, market and product development, innovation, horizontal and vertical integration, concentric diversification and strategic alliances. Concentrated growth involves directing resources into profitable growth areas of particular products in particular markets. It might be unusual to discuss profit in a public agency, however, the idea of market penetration for Centrelink's operations related to spin-off products or services for third parties with the potential to generate revenue apart from purchaser funding as long as those products or services were acceptable to the government. Innovative strategies were also applicable in the use of technology to provide more channels to access services as well as improving staff and systems efficiency in service delivery. Horizontal strategies for Centrelink meant consolidating support functions to create shared services or even outsourcing some corporate support, including human resources management and IT infrastructure, with the aim of reducing overheads. Concentric diversification usually involves a departure from the existing base of operations and building an internally separate business. For Centrelink, this could apply to specific infrastructure and processes for utilities that had common customers with Centrelink whose payments could be deducted from Centrelink's income support payments to those customers for a fee[1] (Pearce and Robinson 2000:251–63).

Arguably, growth for a public agency might not be a socially desirable alternative and the ideal business strategy for Centrelink might have been liquidation. Or, as Hubbard (2000:131) was later to argue, Centrelink's business strategy should focus on 'designing and delivering products and services with optimum efficiency and effectiveness. The concentration should be on improving internal value chain activities rather than concern with the development of new products and services in order to grow.' It is likely that Centrelink's purchaser departments would have agreed with this sentiment. The notion that Centrelink was immune to the policy lessons and subsequent political advantage it derived from its contacts with customers, communities and the government made it unlikely that

Centrelink would work towards its own demise. By building its knowledge base, it would be imperative that it used growth to sustain its value-added capacity.

Taking these several factors into account, the CEO and the board envisaged a corporate direction for Centrelink containing the three evolutionary stages discussed in Chapter 2: cultural change and improving customer service; building on progress, finally developing new service ideas and transforming service delivery (Vardon 1998d) with a new service model; and acquiring major new business and consolidating earlier programs. These strategic directions needed detailed planning to reset the course of the agency towards its new destination. The following discussion outlines these developments.

Planning and building the strategic framework

Precursor: DSS planning

The DSS had developed a model of strategic management between 1990 and 1997, which left numerous planning legacies for Centrelink. The DSS initially based its portfolio program on a 10-year strategic outlook, but events had overtaken the original plans and short-term issues captured or diverted the attention of executive and business-level managers. Also, the DSS retained a primary focus on annual program or business plans to coincide with budget cycles. Nevertheless, the program planning process enabled staff to develop clearer program objectives and performance indicators, which provided the benchmarks for subsequent program evaluations. The department conducted elaborate multi-level planning to translate strategic plans into shorter-term business and functional-level work plans.

Throughout this period, the DSS stressed the value and utility of technology, information and reporting systems to assist operations at all levels of the organisation. The same attention to detail was taken with organisational design to support the network; however, the DSS directed its objective setting to existing structures rather than aligning service delivery network structures with portfolio strategies. The organisation retained segmented program delivery divisions in its national headquarters through the early 1990s while operational units (areas and regions) worked to combined program structures to facilitate local customer service. This infrastructure provided a pragmatic solution to the perennial policy/administration problem but perpetuated the fragmentation and complexity of the performance-management system.

Nevertheless, DSS strategic and business-level planning in the 1990s inculcated a culture informed by highly structured procedures and processes. This awareness provided a sound base for Centrelink strategists and planners and enabled a common understanding in Centrelink and the DSS of the nature of hierarchical planning needs in the newly established agency. This understanding was critical to the development of initial output performance indicators and standards within purchaser–provider agreements. The DSS experience meant that most of Centrelink's founding executives and its staff had participated, to some degree, in formulating strategic plans for a large public policy and service delivery organisation. Additionally, the new CEO came with her own extensive background in public sector planning and practice.

This experience, combined with a clear message from the government to establish a different, more customer-oriented service organisation, stimulated Centrelink's planners to formulate a 'continuation-transformation' strategy aimed at creating a viable, long-term business entity. The *CSDA Act 1997* empowered the Centrelink board to decide the 'goals, priorities, policies and strategies' and the CEO was asked to prepare a strategic plan for Centrelink as the vehicle for meeting its legal obligations.

Centrelink phase one, 1997–98

Vardon and her deputy, Ross Divett, selected Carmen Zanetti as the inaugural chief strategist to help them set a new direction for the organisation. Zanetti (1998) had been influential in the design and development of the new agency in 1996–97. She approached strategy creation as an inclusive process, obtaining information from local and overseas sources and discussing concepts with a wide range of government and private sector operatives. She recalled that the main driver in building the strategic framework for Centrelink was the need to make the shift from a transaction and procedurally based culture to one that focused on customers, streamlining and integration and achieving significant efficiencies. The board was instrumental in bringing financial discipline and a focus on outcomes to the process and highlighting issues about managing relationships with Centrelink's clients. The pivotal architects of the framework, however, were acknowledged to be Vardon and Divett.

All existing strategic tasks and major activities flowing from the pre-agency arrangements were included in the draft CSDA strategic plan. The board agreed to a strategic framework for the period 1997–2002. The notion of local customer service improvement plans (CSIPs) within the planning hierarchy was introduced as a way of promoting strategic policy alignment throughout the organisation. The resulting strategic plan (Centrelink 1997) contained a five-year program designed to focus and guide staff efforts to:

- achieve the government's policies and outcomes
- develop the identity, culture and 'brand value' of the new organisation
- improve operational decision making and business performance
- enhance business development and long-term positioning
- establish systems to improve the quality, efficiency and innovation of customer service.

Centrelink planners envisaged the organisation operating within renewable partnerships with government departments to provide services to the Australian public. The overarching context was that Centrelink was accountable to the portfolio ministers and parliament for efficient and high-quality services, and for the integrity of its service to its customers. Centrelink was bound by the contractual discipline of purchaser–provider arrangements, as well as intra-governmental contestability and potential competition in the marketplace. To survive as a provider, Centrelink needed to deliver consistently high-quality service at highly competitive prices. In the event, because of the complex and sensitive nature of the portfolio, the government allowed some leeway in transition and announced that Centrelink was the preferred central delivery organisation for government services. This diminished the immediate threat of divestiture through contestability.

The organisation's monopoly–monopsony status was accompanied by some severe financial imposts. The agency received a special efficiency dividend designed to harvest the savings of combining the DSS and DEETYA networks amounting to more than $1 billion over five years. The obvious area for reductions was in Centrelink's running costs, with its high staffing salaries and associated costs. Centrelink instigated a program of voluntary redundancies that, when combined with natural attrition, achieved overall staffing reductions of up to 20 per cent, or about 4000 staff. To maintain service levels and quality in the wake of these losses, it was decided to adopt more efficient processes and to make more innovative use of technology, especially IT.

Against this background, the agency established a suite of strategic directions comprising corporate goals, a vision and a mission as key elements of its strategic planning processes. It also formulated strategies designed to meet increasing community expectations of government services, especially about having ready access to reliable and responsive services. Centrelink sought to link its services, personalise solutions and to broker information on behalf of the community and other agencies. It aimed to improve the convenience of services beyond the usual contact modes with customers and to provide information for a range of organisations through online facilities as well as through its offices, mobile services, an extensive call centre network and other interactive services. The master plan was to deliver services more efficiently and cost effectively, provide ethical and accountable services and observe all laws (Centrelink 1997:8).

The *Centrelink Strategic Framework, 1997–2002* was built on the understanding that the agency's principal commitments were to its customers, employees and client departments. First, the agency looked to provide guidance, to listen to its customers and to be responsive in finding solutions and to excel in service delivery through innovation and effective use of IT. The marketing language declared that customer contact would be 'welcoming, friendly, fair, courteous and respectful' (Centrelink 1997:9). As well, the organisation aimed to provide correct and current information, assessment, referral and payments to its customers, making certain that they understood their obligations in receiving services and payments. Over the years, accuracy or rather the lack of it in these areas had produced unfavourable press and parliamentary questions for DSS ministers. As an improvement measure, the organisation was looking more frequently for feedback on service delivery and Centrelink customers would need to be satisfied with the level of knowledge of Centrelink staff and be confident that staff advice and the quality of service were accurate and consistent. There was also to be a greater emphasis on customers' rights to privacy and holding personal information in confidence.

Second, in the best traditions of the human resources management maxim that 'people are our greatest asset', Centrelink wanted to keep its staff enthusiastic about the organisation's goals. Commitments to employees included creating an environment in which people wanted to come to work; providing a satisfying and effective workplace; training and staff development, recognising that employees needed appropriate skills and knowledge to meet expected performance and customer service (an area of criticism contained in previous reviews of the DSS); and continual involvement in designing and refining business practices and processes. People-management planning was to be integrated with the overall strategic directions for the organisation.

Third, Centrelink acknowledged the importance of establishing and maintaining its commitment to its client departments. These commitments were to be reflected in the BPA protocols and to include maintaining a performance-orientated organisation focused on achieving client-department outcomes, being responsible for providing value for money and cost-efficient services, being responsive to the needs of client departments with high-quality, appropriate and timely information and being available to all other levels of government and community organisations for service delivery.

The 1997 framework set out multi-phased targets to be met in 18 months, three years and five years respectively for sub-components of each of the categories: stakeholder relationships, customer and community relationships, staff culture and service delivery support. On the basis of the application of the balanced scorecard in large public and private organisations around the world (Kaplan and Norton 1992), Centrelink's executives saw this approach, discussed later in this chapter, as a useful means to help define, record and manage corporate performance across the six goals using best-practice and first-choice criteria. The strategic directions were to be reviewed annually to ensure that they provided a sound and current basis for annual business plans and programs (Centrelink 1997:19–24).

Following on from the strategic directions, and included in the same framework document, the Centrelink strategic plan spelled out key strategies and actions to implement the basic corporate thrusts. The plan detailed business outcomes and strategies centred on Centrelink becoming the 'first choice of governments for the provision of government service for the next five years' (Centrelink 1997:25). Each goal—business development, customer service, people, cost reduction, innovation and best practice—was elaborated in terms of high-level performance measures and accompanying strategies and activities to achieve the goal in the next two years.

Overall, the 1997 strategic framework was a transitional blueprint for the newly established organisation. It reflected the planning lessons of its antecedent departments, the DSS in particular, and introduced commercial concepts and content to indicate its new status as a provider agency. It was a groundbreaking publication that signalled the transformation of the organisation from a traditional public sector body to a more business-orientated agency. In particular, it demonstrated the change in strategy and culture to meet new ambitions and goals.

Consolidating corporate strategies, 1998–2003

The experience of its establishment year caused the Centrelink board to reflect on its initial performance, review its strategic pronouncements and publish a revised framework (Centrelink 1998b). The new document contained two major sections entitled 'Our business' and 'Our future' and expanded on purpose, vision, goals and other strategic direction elements for an organisation depicted as one of the 'largest business operations in Australia' (Centrelink 1998b:22).

Performance against each of the agency's six major goals and key strategies for 1997–98 was shown in Centrelink's annual report (Centrelink 1998a:43). While the organisation set ambitious targets for itself, it had built on a historical foundation of service delivery and it was not surprising that it regarded its first public report card as highly satisfactory (Centrelink 1998a:41–89).

The agency evaluated its service delivery approach and foreshadowed significant developments involving brokered solutions, service offers and other holistic means for meeting customer demands and client-department outcomes. IT solutions in the form of electronic service delivery were expected to play a major role in changing existing processes.

A major change affecting Centrelink and its relationships with clients during this period was the government's move to implement accrual budgeting. The 1999 federal budget presented appropriations in accrual budget format for the first time and required agencies and authorities to describe their planned program outcomes and to specify prices for the outputs that would contribute to those outcomes. Organisations were given at least 12 months' notice that they would be required to set out the performance information needed to manage outputs and to monitor real outcomes. Centrelink's major client department, Family and Community Services, subsequently redefined its program structure into an outcomes structure comprising three classes: stronger families, stronger communities and economic and social participation. Each outcome contained a series of output groups replacing the previous sub-program payments or service categories.

In response, Centrelink developed a simplified outcome and output structure. As a portfolio unit, the agency professed a single outcome—effective delivery of Commonwealth services to eligible customers—and a single output applicable to each of its client departments as: efficient delivery of services to eligible customers (DFaCS 1999). The 2001 annual report shows the relationship between Centrelink's and its clients' outcomes, reflecting the wide range of outputs delivered by Centrelink.

Consolidation and growth, 2001–06

In its next strategic framework (Centrelink 2001b), the organisation published a list of achievements for the previous three years as evidence of the success of its program of continuous improvement in performance and service delivery. Centrelink also expanded the scope and content of its framework.

- The strategic directions for 2001–06 (Centrelink 2001b) built on previous statements of purpose and aspiration as well as introducing notions of risk management and listing achievements of the first three years of operations. (An extract of planned strategies and outcomes for each corporate goal is in Appendix 3.)
- A three-year business plan with integrated sets of projects was included to improve organisational focus and alignment. Eight business plan objectives were presented[2] and the initiatives accompanying these were expected to lead to 17 concrete transformations of Centrelink's service delivery systems and processes (Centrelink 2001b:3). The theme for the business plan was 'delivering today, transforming tomorrow'.
- The mechanism for operationalising the business plan objectives rested with business improvement plans, which would be developed by 'each NSO [National Support Office] team, each area and the Call Centre network' (Centrelink 2001b:2). A separate booklet provided guidance on business improvement plans in linking local initiatives and operational activities and business objectives, which themselves were manifestations of the strategic plan's outcomes.

This plan revealed integrated Centrelink planning for three distinct organisational levels: strategic planning covering the longer term (to at least five years) and direction for the whole organisation and its macro and business environments;

business/tactical planning focusing on medium to short-term priorities, dedicated projects and activities for the next three years; and operational planning to assist managers with short-term business decisions in local environments (Centrelink 1998c:1, 2001a:8).

At the same time, the organisation professed a 'one business, one team' concept that encompassed team functions and shared behaviours. This combination represented an interesting conflict between the many products and services designed, developed and delivered by the agency and the need for a unified, corporate image. Arguably, Centrelink had many businesses and many teams and it was simply protecting itself from opportunists who would emerge if Centrelink were ever opened fully to competition.

The 2001 plan placed great emphasis on business planning. On the one hand, this was an admission that previous planning had been too centred on higher-level objectives and that CSIPs had not provided the hoped-for implementation or corporate alignment at the working levels of the organisation. On the other hand, introducing business or operational plans at this stage was consistent with the longer-term strategies espoused by the CEO for organisational transformation building on previous phases of establishment and consolidation (Vardon 1998d).

While previous strategic documents emphasised the need for aligning plans and actions throughout the organisation, Centrelink's planners refined processes to match the required cascading effect from goal to operational activity in the 2001 framework. There appeared to be clearer links between the planning levels and an emphasis on the importance of business improvement plans and the use of performance assessment and team and individual learning plans to contextualise and reinforce performance targets at the operational level. There was also an association drawn between a range of national supporting documents, which raised awareness of risk assessment and accountability. This created alignment and consistency between business design and delivery.

Another area of note was the inclusion of statements of corporate governance in the 2001 directions. This was complemented by the issue of a detailed handbook on Centrelink governance (Centrelink 2001c) and commentary on governance issues in the 2001 annual report.

A simplified business model for Centrelink is shown in Figure 3.1.

Figure 3.1 Centrelink business model

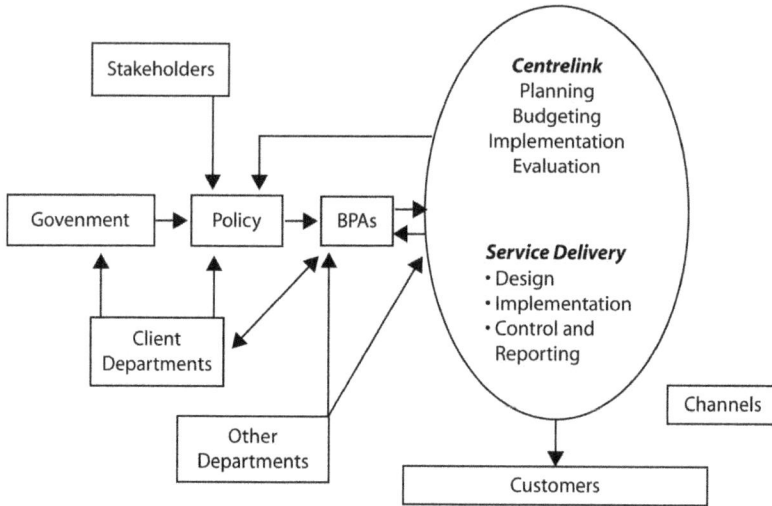

Extending the planning

In 2002, the Centrelink board commissioned a comprehensive report on organisational efficiency from the Boston Consulting Group (BCG 2002). The report noted that since 1998, Centrelink had reduced the cost of services delivered by 21 per cent per workload unit, which was represented as an improvement in cost efficiency comparable with that achieved by banks. Other findings were that:

- service costs compared favourably with the costs of processing comparable financial services products
- customer and staff satisfaction had improved and more client-agency key performance indicators had been achieved
- corporate and property expenses were lower than public sector standards and generally comparable with the private sector (Centrelink 2003b).

The report also recommended improvements through developing better performance-management information across the network, better systems for identifying and implementing internal best practice and working with client departments to reduce the cost and frequency of notifiable events (which accounted for more than 40 per cent of costs). It also suggested establishing tighter linkage between improvement projects and effective implementation.

There was a watershed in 2003, when in response to a raft of ANAO findings on payment administration and management processes (see ANAO 2001a, 2001b, 2001c, 2001d, 2002a, 2002b) as well as numerous internal reviews, Centrelink reviewed its strategic framework and strategic directions and presaged a new look in its planning. The new directions were negotiated with and approved by Minister Vanstone, who wanted an alignment with new government directions. The *Future Directions* document introduced a new mission and vision and reiterated the revised basis for local and national business planning, while concentrating on four new key themes: protecting the integrity of outlays, supporting participation outcomes, providing even more flexible services for all stakeholders and providing value for money (Centrelink 2003c). This change was intended to 'simplify the planning framework, make it more clear and concrete and to capture a "whole of Centrelink view"' (Centrelink 2003c). A complementary document on business planning was issued to assist operational teams to prepare business improvement plans as well as to identify operational issues to manage principal risks that could impede achieving the organisation's goals.

Balanced scorecard for reporting performance

Centrelink's primary tool for recording, reporting and communicating performance was the National Balanced Scorecard (BSC). Vardon had begun to develop a way of using it when head of the prison system in South Australia because she was 'worried always over measurement in the public sector…we were sick of measuring the prison system by escapes, we just knew we had to measure differently. And we'd just started when I got the job in Canberra. So I thought…we'll build a balanced scorecard' (Vardon interview).

The scorecard was introduced in mid-1998 on the basis that it:

- identified key performance attributes that Centrelink must succeed in to reach its goals
- allowed monitoring of continuing performance through a range of key measures, which recognised achievements and identified weaknesses to give opportunities to improve performance
- communicated performance results across the whole organisation to support continued planning
- provided a flexible comparison tool enabling performance information to be viewed in many formats including geographical performance mapping (Centrelink 2002a).

Although the BSC was reviewed and modified continuously, it was criticised by external recipients of its reports as being too simplistic and inadequate for the job. The ANAO conducted a performance audit of the BSC in 2002 to assess whether it was 'based on key elements of better practice principles and its use assists Centrelink to understand and communicate its performance against its strategic goals' (ANAO 2002a:3).

The ANAO concluded that the BSC focused on operational effectiveness and in particular on the purchasers' key performance indicators, which represented an equivalent bottom line for the agency. In terms of better practice, it was an integrated element of a robust planning framework based on published strategic goals, making it a useful source for monitoring and reporting results. It was used at national, area and customer support centre levels to identify performance feedback for improved decision making. Information was available to all business units on the intranet. The ANAO recommended changes to improve the system by clarifying statements of intent, linking strategic goals to business objectives and revising performance information to assist performance assessment in more quantitative as well as qualitative terms and to balance out lead and lag indicators (ANAO 2002a:3–4).

Centrelink also reviewed the BSC in 2002–03, effectively accepting the ANAO's recommendations and implementing a new scorecard from July 2003 to be 'more strategically focused, based around organisational goals and include lead and lag indicators' (Centrelink 2004a). Centrelink conducted a follow-up review of the BSC in 2003–04, concentrating on all the internally set measures and targets to ensure that they reflected business priorities, were relevant and meaningful, were strategic and assisted in monitoring organisational performance (Centrelink 2004a:21); changes were incorporated to apply from July 2004.

Table 3.1 lists the performance information that Centrelink used to assess the achievement of its outcomes during 2003–04 (DFaCS 2003:272).

Table 3.1 Centrelink balanced scorecard

Contribution of strategic goals to output one: efficient delivery of Commonwealth services to eligible customers.	
Goal	Outcome
Accountability to government and client agencies	The extent to which we achieve client-agency key performance indicators
Business and community	Increased community sector satisfaction with Centrelink
Customer	Increased customer satisfaction with their most recent Centrelink contact
Developing and supporting our people to achieve business outcomes	Increased staff satisfaction with work
Efficiency and effectiveness of our operations and processes	Achievement of a reduction in operational expenses as a proportion of program outlays

Management structure

The task of designing organisational structures to accommodate strategy can be approached in many ways. In practice, organisations prefer an incremental approach that combines components of several methodologies, which is the approach taken by Centrelink (Wills 1999).

Transition from the DSS

The DSS staff members moving to Centrelink were used to operating primarily on functional and geographical lines as a result of 50 years of political imperatives, legislation, social policy initiatives and communication and information system changes. The wide range of policies and payment types that was planned and delivered for the government made it difficult for the DSS to align its programs throughout the organisation; however, each regional service outlet had adopted a pragmatic solution over the years and settled into broad, program-based groupings at its service counters (nominally, families, pensions and benefits) on the supposedly sound basis of mutual administrative and client convenience. This arrangement facilitated technical support and maintained discreet IT platforms until consolidation practices were introduced in the 1990s.

Other structural reforms were incorporated in the twilight years of the DSS. State offices were abolished in the early 1990s and the fledgling network of area offices grew to absorb their roles as more demographically based regional groupings. Tele-service centres proliferated to provide another service channel as well as reducing or at least controlling the flow of customers into offices. Regardless of the prevailing DSS rhetoric about improving customer service, the organisational structure retained its bureaucratic character with strict lines of top-down policy and management control, a rules-based process culture and limited recognition of devolution of decision-making authority at the counter-officer level.

The one continuing experiment in structural adjustment was the centralised management of the design and layout of DSS network offices. As early as 1990, DSS property staff had been planning to replace the closed, counter-ridden, front-and-back partitioned model with open-planned offices based on successful trials conducted by the US Social Security Administration.[3] By the mid-1990s, an overall replacement plan had been formulated for a wholesale refit of DSS offices. This provided a sound basis for Centrelink planners in changing the image and environment of offices in the new network.

Centrelink inherited a customer service network of regional offices, DSS offices, Family Service Centres, Retirement Service Centres, Visiting Services and Teleservice Centres. These offices provided the front line for contact with customers seeking advice and assistance, registration, referrals, assessment of claims and determination of entitlements (Vardon 1997c). Area offices managed and coordinated groups of offices and centres with their own supported functional structure.

Designing new structures

Vardon recalls one facet of designing the organisation with Divett: 'We spent one Friday night at the blackboard designing it…a funny diagram of circles.

We couldn't think in terms of programs, we had to think in terms of customer groups' (Interview).

In keeping with its overall program of change to implement the customer-driven, service-provider strategy, Centrelink opted for a relatively flat management structure, taking note of the size and scope of its operations. The organisation renamed its offices Customer Service Centres (CSCs) and Teleservice Centres became Call Centres. Area Offices became Area Support Offices and retained their management role of geographically based groups of CSCs. Centrelink kept its headquarters in the National Support Office in Canberra.

As traditional public sector departments, DSS and DEETYA staff were organised into Canberra-based divisions, branches and sections, with equivalent hierarchies in the field. The new structure was reorganised radically.

- Customer segment groups reflected the change in relationship with the government through the introduction of purchaser–provider measures. Although the title was about customers, as the recipients of provided service, the customer segment groups were required mainly to liaise with client departments about standards, outcomes, training requirements and IT needs. They also were the conduit for informing client departments about the interaction with customers, the impact of programs and policies and defining customer service delivery practices. The initial customer segment groups reflected the pre-existing program-management groups of the DSS: aged, youth, families, unemployed and special.
- 'Theme teams' effectively segmented corporate support for the customer segment groups and everyone else, at least initially, into teams responsible for customer/quality/complaints, people management, innovation, strategic, IT, finance and communication functions.
- The Business Development Group was formed to establish working relationships with identified client departments and to negotiate BPAs with these and potential purchaser bodies.

The new structures were implemented with remarkably little fuss. Once Centrelink was formed, Vardon and Divett used the newly structured organisation to facilitate service delivery and to streamline work processes.

In time, Centrelink expanded and modified its structures to match changes in policy and to align the implementation with corporate strategies. Some area support offices experimented with structures that aligned staff skills more effectively and reduced operating costs. Romeijn (2000) notes that despite the push from Canberra for changes, some areas were reluctant to forgo hierarchical structures, possibly due to the attitudes and experience of the long-serving managers in those areas. In other, more innovative areas, clusters of CSCs were formed, taking on centralised and specialised corporate roles that supported all the other CSCs. This left the area support office with a more coordinating role and fewer staff. Areas also experimented with matrix arrangements, with 'vertical-slice' teams comprising area service office staff, CSC managers and team leaders becoming area-based leadership teams to support area-based business planning.

The role of the renamed community segment teams changed from having responsibility for the implementation of processes to the purist role of policy and research on customer segments, accountability for delivery of what was signed up to in BPAs and accountability for providing clients with feedback on policy issues (Bashford interview).

By 2004, the organisation had a clear divisional structure with four deputy CEOs responsible for customer service, business, business transformation and service management. Business referred to corporate management and performance while business transformation incorporated the roles of chief information officer, business solutions and e-business among other duties. Service management covered the area network, call centres and self-service operations (Centrelink 2004a).

There was another major element to the management structure, the guiding coalition, which is examined in the next chapter.

Reviewing Centrelink's strategic planning

The impact and effectiveness of Centrelink's strategic planning as the vehicle for presenting its corporate strategies can be considered in terms of governance, positioning, planning methodology, planned and emergent strategies, outcomes and outputs and performance reporting.

In relation to organisational governance, the continuous stream of planning documentation and announcements indicated that Centrelink planners continued to demonstrate awareness of and reporting on the organisation's strategic environment by including greater operational content that would complement the organisation's performance indicators. There was a concerted effort to achieve better governance linkages between strategy, planning, implementation and performance. The balanced scorecard was introduced as the prime means for gathering and collating data for BPAs and government reporting. Finding the 'right' measures to include in this system to reflect the desired levels of relationship, accountability and conformance was a formidable challenge for such a large organisation.

The basic governance approach was broad, top-down policy direction from the board/CEO, with executive-level managers reviewing and confirming goals and objectives and then canvassing all staff for comments and suggestions to enhance and implement the policies. The adoption of a five-year planning horizon seems to have been a direct result of the turbulence associated with becoming a more business-oriented agency combined with the inherent uncertainty of the public environment and an acceptance of the realities of three-year BPAs aligning with budget forward estimates for resource planning and allocation. The introduction of three-year business plans attempted to better align governance structures with desired performance.

Centrelink's planning methodology employed a gap-analysis process that analysed the differences between the current and desired situations for the organisation and devised strategies to reduce those gaps (Hubbard 2000). Planning was seen as complementary to strategic thinking, positioning and implementation and stressed the importance of relating environmental scanning with organisational purpose and internal capability (Centrelink 1998b:13–16; Mintzberg 1994). While Centrelink had already adopted many private sector concepts, it was seeking more commercial planning methodologies and techniques to meet its strategic objectives. Along the way, planners compiled regular strategic outlook reports containing key environmental trends of economic and fiscal outlook, customer numbers and demographics; additionally, they related these trends to agency performance trends against corporate goals and conducted comprehensive scenario planning (Centrelink 2001e). Other approaches were reflected in annual reports from 2000. As such, Centrelink combined the industrial organisation model of external environmental influence with the resource-based view of internal core competencies to derive strategic futures (Hanson et al. 2004).

Centrelink undertook considerable work in establishing its strategic frameworks by linking its vision with customer-driven purposes for its operations. This led to a corporate sense of business logic with very clear overtones of commercial interest in agency growth and profit to include such notions as price differentiation, market share calculation and the creation of market demand for organisation services (Centrelink 1998a, 2003c). This planning methodology obviously influenced the resultant corporate goals, national and area-based themes. Further, Centrelink consolidated its goal structure and derived its strategies using a 'vision for success' approach (Bryson 1995) by identifying future achievements for the various planning periods.

The organisation retained some historical baggage from its amalgamation but effectively cemented its new identity and position using continuous improvements in service and technology innovation to overcome any residual reservations or constraints. The agency's IT and communication strategies constituted a key element in this regard (Vardon 1998a). The use of extensive community consultation and feedback was pivotal in contributing to strategy development, as shown in the annual reports of the agency.

As a federal agency, Centrelink was subject to the government's 'outcomes and outputs' financial reporting framework. In complying with accrual budgeting requirements, it published explicit outcome and output statements in its budget papers. The agency also identified six corporate goals with accompanying outcomes, drivers and scheduled activities. This structure purportedly enables more targeted resource allocation against set objectives, although the lack of clear pricing information has long been an area of contention with Centrelink's purchasers and the Department of Finance (Interview with senior DoFA official).

Performance reporting provided a continuing headache for Centrelink. BPAs contained detailed performance standards for service quality and delivery for customer segment products and services, although there were continuous 'strategic conversations' with providers about the number, extent, value and frequency of these standards. Reports on customer transactions and quality indicators were prepared regularly for clients in accrual format to match budgeted output goal statements. Centrelink also reported on internal performance at local and national levels. CSIPs attempted to reflect corporate goals at the regional level and reports were collated at the area level to monitor progress. CSIPs were, however, shown to be ineffective in capturing local performance and were replaced with business plans and business improvement plans. The key performance indicators in the National Balanced Scorecard reflected national performance objectives and progress reports were prepared for the board each month. The balanced scorecard mirrored corporate goals, which covered customer and community involvement and satisfaction, staff, partnerships and client departments, efficiency dividend to government and innovative and personalised solutions. Collectively, the scorecard indicated achievement against a separate goal entitled 'benchmarked as best practice and first choice' (Centrelink 2001a:13). Balanced scorecard results were available to staff on the agency's intranet, but the system's usefulness was subjected to close scrutiny over the years, resulting in significant changes in its coverage and outputs.

Risk-management and evaluation processes have been significant in the planning, implementation and conformance aspects of managing the organisation. The tightening and consolidation of strategic planning reflected in the *Future Directions* series and heightened emphasis on business planning showed a growing maturity and awareness of the socio-cultural environment in which Centrelink operated. Indeed, they showed a degree of responsiveness to political oversight with big changes occurring in 2003 with a new mission, vision, goals, strategies and key performance indicators (Centrelink 2003c, 2004c).

In summary, Centrelink continued to institutionalise proactive planning, including basic financial and corporate planning. The Centrelink board and executive provided corporate direction within the legislative mandate and communicated their longer-term intentions to the rest of the organisation. The agency's planning developed rapidly and appeared to incorporate a better understanding of the purchaser–provider environment as evidenced by its growing list of clients

Conclusion

Centrelink established comprehensive planning processes drawn from the private sector to develop and maintain its strategic framework. It pursued an aggressive mix of strategies to ensure its survival in a hostile and contestable environment. The introduction of more detailed business planning acknowledged the need for a stronger approach to align corporate and functional-level strategies. Its business model and processes remain subject to close scrutiny in performance-laden, purchaser–provider relationships with an increasing number of clients. Managing these relationships required clear lines of communication and accountability throughout the organisation and its structures needed to match its strategies to produce the promised performance of its BPAs. The BSC, after initial problems, became a useful performance-monitoring tool for the organisation.

Centrelink experienced some lag in adjusting to the revised set of organisational designs instituted earlier in its life. The National Support Office in particular underwent substantial structural adjustment in adapting to the realities of liaison and alliance with the agency's clients, as discussed in Chapter 6. The parade of ANAO reports and internal reviews generated strategic and shorter-term adjustments in organisational direction and goal setting. Notwithstanding other changes in governance discussed later, Centrelink evolved under the tenets of new public management into a trusted body with improved service delivery performance and a more businesslike management in keeping with the Prime Minister's statement at the organisation's 1997 launch foreshadowing efficiency with sympathetic and responsible service.

ENDNOTES

[1] This arrangement was the basis for Centrepay, which was convenient and cost effective for utility companies and provided a revenue stream for Centrelink.

[2] The eight were: access, business, correctness and accuracy, delivery, efficiency and effectiveness, focus, governance, helping and supporting employees to achieve business objectives.

[3] Several prototypes were installed, which received mixed responses from staff and customers. Some DSS and CES offices combined as part of these experiments, reminiscent of the Coburg trials of the 1980s.

4. Leading and managing change

This chapter examines how change was managed in Centrelink. As the origins of Centrelink were in government decisions and legislation, there were high political expectations that the new agency would produce improved performance and administrative savings by combining the operations of the DSS and DEETYA. Centrelink was a risky experiment for the Commonwealth, with its separation of policy from 'customer' service and the introduction of purchaser–provider agreements to maintain accountability. Centrelink also faced many obstacles—external and internal. The transitional management challenges included ensuring the government's policies and directions were complied with; effective coordination between stakeholders; developing a unified culture to progress the new agency based on staff from different agency cultures; gradual implementation to build on successes and minimise risks; and maintaining customer service (ANAO 1997b:11).

Managing major organisational change requires structures, processes and systems that are mutually supporting. There needs to be a clear strategic direction, alignment of organisational structure, reshaping of employment relations and changes to organisational culture (Spicer et al. 1996).

Leading transformational change

Leadership is highly significant in organisational change and performance and particularly in large-scale public sector change processes. During an organisation's life and at different stages of development, different types of leadership are appropriate. Transformational change requires the attributes of transformational leadership, which involve interactions with the external environment and building management capacity through internal management systems. As Kotter (1996:25–6) observes, 'Effective leadership is exhibited through actions that build and improve organisational abilities and management systems expressed through interactions with governmental capacity, represented by management systems.' Successful transformation, it is argued, should be mostly about leadership (establishing direction, aligning people, motivating, and so on) and secondarily about management (planning, budgeting, organising, staffing, and so on).

Ultimately, successful change has to be registered at the level of culture. Cultural change 'requires the mutual interaction of new symbols and definitions and of changed structures, expectations, and rewards. New attitudes need to be demonstrated in new behaviours and expectations' (Spicer et al. 1996:180).

The watchdog of APS processes and performance, the ANAO, considered that an important factor in successful organisational transformation was 'the employment of strategic leadership to provide the vision and drive for change' (ANAO 1997b:6). This form of leadership was defined as 'the ability to anticipate, envisage, [and] maintain flexibility and empower others to create strategic change as necessary', which was exercised by determining strategic direction, exploiting and maintaining core competencies, developing human capital, sustaining an effective organisational culture, emphasising ethical practices and establishing balanced organisational controls (Hanson et al. 2002:427–36).

Strategic leadership has been particularly important in developing and transforming Centrelink. The board and the CEO exercised strong leadership to determine the changes in the organisation. As part of their responsibilities, they needed not only to manage organisational improvements and have stewardship of individual functions, they had to manage strategy by 'defining and communicating the company's unique position, making trade-offs and forging fit among activities' (Porter 1996:77). This involved interacting with a range of strategic management elements, including organisational processes, people and control systems. The ultimate test of meeting these multidimensional requirements would be whether the organisation performed to internal and external performance standards and met its output and outcome objectives.

Agents of change and their roles

The Centrelink board appointed Vardon as the founding CEO of CSDA/Centrelink. The preference was for someone not associated with either the DSS or DEETYA. Vardon was headhunted from her position as chief executive of the South Australian Department of Correctional Services, where she had successfully implemented reforms to reduce costs, develop a new corporate culture and improve customer service.[1]

Vardon arrived at the DSS in February 1997 to prepare for the creation of Centrelink in July 1997. She was the single determining figure in change and overall direction. Other significant actors—in particular, ministers, the chairman of the Centrelink board and key staff—had roles and specific responsibilities, but none approached Vardon's influence. The CEO needed to adopt distinctive roles, which were complemented by the different roles and functions of members of the most senior management group.

Vardon, like most CEOs, had never managed an organisation as large as Centrelink and was not familiar with the Canberra environment. In this regard, she was supported by her deputy, Ross Divett, who was able to offer astute strategic intelligence and advice to a new CEO versed in state government practices. Divett was also an experienced and effective public manager who had been a deputy secretary in the Department of Administrative Services during its commercialisation program. When he became deputy secretary of the DSS, he brought across many of those lessons and attitudes, particularly about marketing and business concepts, and introduced major planning and structural change in the department. In moving to Centrelink, he provided Vardon with this experience and a working knowledge of the history of the CSDA development concept and processes from his involvement under DSS secretary Blunn. Vardon worked very closely with her deputy, whom she regarded as her co-leader in the organisation, characterising their partnership as 'a double-headed energy source' (Interview).

She was also supported by her board, which endorsed her approach to quality service to customers through good staff management, as expressed by board member Don Fraser's concern with the people who served the customer and all that went behind customer service, particularly leadership development and succession planning. The board developed an initial set of operational ground rules in consultation with the CEO and her deputy during the first crucial months of organisational transition.

As noted earlier, Vardon saw herself as an agent of strategic change and could be characterised as a leading public entrepreneur in her transforming efforts at Centrelink in terms of leadership, creativity and innovation, opportunism, risk taking and facilitating and synthesising (Forster et al. 1996:11), noting especially that her personal view of leadership was 'a set of processes that creates organisations…and or adapts them to significantly changing circumstances' (Vardon 1998c:2).

With many of the transitional management details being assigned to the deputy CEO and his team, Vardon saw her leadership role as giving the organisation 'a shape, a face, a design, a style' (Interview) and travelling around the network to sell the vision. In her view, the traditional DSS/DEETYA leadership patterns, expectations and mores in the new agency would not meet the challenges of successful top-down change.

Vardon found an organisation fraught with risk-averse managers, fiefdoms, traditional vertical communications and limited horizontal coordination and ownership of work (Vardon 1998c).

Leadership and philosophy of change

Vardon responded to the perceived leadership vacuum by introducing team-based management with new working groups and non-APS titles. Vardon flattened the SES structure, imported new SES staff and, significantly, introduced the concept of the guiding coalition.

These changes in power arrangements created consternation and resentment among some senior staff, particularly within the IT groups, who were used to controlling the means of delivering entitlements and were confronted by the seeming lack of recognition of their contribution and importance. The later introduction of an outsider, Jane Treadwell, a former colleague of Vardon's in South Australia, as the new chief information officer added to their discomfort.

Kotter's (1995) management change process—an eight-stage framework for creating and implementing change in organisations—was very significant in Vardon's thinking about change (Vardon 1998c, 2001, 2003b).[2] The first stage in Kotter's process is to establish a sense of urgency after examining the external environment and to then identify possible crises or major opportunities. Next, the leader needs to create a 'guiding coalition', a powerful group working closely as a team to lead and provoke change. The third phase is to develop a vision to encompass and direct change efforts and devise strategies to accomplish that vision. Communication is the key element here and Kotter argues that managers should use every possible means to market the new vision and strategies; the guiding coalition is meant to provide the role model for the expected behaviour of staff.

As part of the process, there is a need to empower what Kotter deems broad-based action, meaning to overcome obstacles, to change systems or structures that undermine the vision of change and to encourage risk taking and non-traditional ideas, activities and actions. Importantly, change is dependent on generating quick success or short-term wins. Kotter recommends planning, creating and recognising obvious improvements in performance. Consolidation and generation of further change is a necessary part of the process to embed new, compatible systems, structures and policies that support the new vision. This can mean injecting new staff and introducing new projects into the organisation.

Finally, successful change is achieved by anchoring new approaches in the culture—that is, creating better performance by concentrating on customers and productivity, improving and expanding leadership and management, spelling out the links between new behaviour and successes, developing leaders and ensuring succession.

Vardon chose this model for the Centrelink transition on the basis of its comprehensiveness and applicability.[3] The model was almost tailor made for the Centrelink transition and beyond, and Vardon used it to great effect. It contained highly relevant guidelines for a CEO faced with the external and internal environments of a public service agency in transition. At the same time, Vardon was also influenced by 'emotional intelligence' (Goleman 1996; Higgs and Dulewicz 1999) as a contributory model of personal leadership, building on her social-work background and her previous experience in senior public sector positions. This model encourages participants to become willing leaders or agents of change and employs exhortations for self-awareness, emotional resilience, self-regulation, motivation, empathy, influence and intuitiveness.

Vardon's corporate philosophy also distinguished clearly between management and leadership, accepting the prevailing wisdom that managers—particularly in large organisations—were required to cope with complexity through judicious planning, budgeting, organising, staffing, controlling and problem solving to ensure organisational maintenance and survival. On the other hand, leaders deal with change by direction setting, aligning people to the vision, motivating and inspiring to ensure not only longer-term survival but effective competition and growth (Harvard Business Review 1990). These concepts and intellectual frameworks were critical in shaping Vardon's approach to management change and developing a new organisation.

Leading organisational change

Reconstituting and reshaping an organisation with more than 20 000 staff is a formidable task and requires considerable leadership skill and perseverance. Organisational change was not new for DSS and DEETYA staff, but the scope and responsibilities for developing and implementing change strategies in Centrelink rested heavily on the executive managers acting as a team under the direction of the CEO. Acting as an executive team requires a shared understanding of the tasks of change, an ability to set priorities and systematic monitoring and adjustment of performance implementation. The breadth of change facing Centrelink needed imagination, innovation, professionalism, communication and close collaboration for programs to succeed.

Vision and strategies

The CEO and the board designed a new vision and corporate directions for Centrelink and, as discussed in Chapter 2, endorsed three evolutionary stages for the agency to become a viable one-stop shop for government services (Vardon 1998d).

The first stage was to establish the organisation during 1997–98, concentrating on implementing transitional processes to integrate staff and business activities. The major challenges of this phase were cultural change and improving customer service. Comprehensive surveys of customer and staff satisfaction were conducted and the results used to facilitate program changes.

The second stage was to consolidate initial developments and achievements and to build better service delivery while introducing new service concepts. The aims were to create a seamless service for customers, re-engineer workflows and processes, introduce technological improvements to facilitate customer self-service and staff assistance and to improve services to rural and remote areas. The organisation also had to retain its current business as well as expanding its alliances.

This stage sought to introduce a 'one main contact model' with case-management processes to reduce effort and eliminate duplication for customers. There were significant technological challenges associated with this stage in preparing for even more ambitious change in the next stage. A strategic IT plan for business architecture and processes was needed to accommodate the construction and testing of extensive decision support systems ('expert systems') while allowing for the potential disruption of the 'Y2K' problem (Vardon 1998d).

The third stage aimed to 'transform the delivery of government services' (Vardon 1998d:8) with a new service delivery model based on a life-events methodology, the acquisition of major new business, consolidation of staff development programs, more advanced electronic service delivery and closer connections with state and territory one-stop shops.

Centrelink's strategic positioning for the future was predicated on winning competitive advantage over potential rivals in the government and market sectors by first acknowledging the inevitability of a contestable environment. Its strategies aimed to consolidate its performance by forming strategic alliances with other service organisations and particularly with community groups. With its substantial customer database, it identified its niche as the community broker for all government agencies and their networks, which was seen as a logical extension of the one-stop shop concept in an electronic knowledge and service society. It constantly considered better ways of marketing its products, improving internal skills and competencies and providing better service and choice. At the same time, it had to satisfy its clients as their service provider. It is interesting to compare the changes in the basic tenets of the organisation's strategic framework from 1997 until the first CEO departed. The changes reflect pragmatism in embedding organisational competencies to improve the probability of surviving as an entity as well as preparing the ground for more ambitious ventures away from Centrelink's (traditional) core business.

Aligning organisational structures and the guiding coalition

The establishment of the new agency brought together about 20 000 ex-DSS staff and 3000 ex-DEETYA staff, consolidating two regional networks and developing service purchasing agreements with the client departments while maintaining existing government services to a large customer base. Faced with a myriad consolidation, transitional and reform issues, Vardon (1998a:1) decided that the

> traditional management structures and ways of management would not give me the capacity to create a sense of urgency and to bring real change to an organisation of 23 000. I needed to create a different type of organisation, an amoebic organisation, one that could readily move and change to meet a rapidly changing environment.

The organisation had to divorce itself from the DSS and absorb CES staff within its new structure. Its leaders had to start operating in a more businesslike manner and hence convince supervisors, staff and unions to accept different organisational directions, attitudes and structures. The agency faced problems of setting up new operating frameworks, rules and understandings with client departments and the government, while simultaneously maintaining existing systems and the flow of payments to customers. Throughout this transition process, Centrelink also had to face the threat of contestability and potential 'cherry picking' by the private sector of attractive organisational functions.

How was a large and complex organisation to approach a model of integrative leadership? The main internal mechanism chosen was that of the guiding coalition, a group of senior managers advocated by Kotter (1996) as one of Vardon's precepts for successful change, as outlined earlier in the chapter.

While executive teams supporting the CEO were part of normal internal governance practice in the APS, the introduction of the Centrelink guiding coalition was unique to public agencies at that time. The guiding coalition was a top team that had to address a number of initiatives concurrently, such as formulating strategy, managing performance and stakeholder expectations and renewing talent pools. This executive gathering was expected to welcome external challenges and set high performance and effectiveness standards for themselves. Finally, the group was to work to improve the organisation by instituting short-term cycles of action and reflection by accelerating the pace of change and applying their combined business experience and judgment to problems as a team.

Another symbol was the reduction of hierarchies within the organisation and the use of new cultural language, such as the collective phrase 'the guiding coalition' to identify all the members of the SES. Flattened structures and teams headed by an SES officer replaced traditional divisions and branches.

> The one thing that I learnt in South Australia is that it's all very well to say you want to go from here to here, but you actually have to say why, [and] how you're going to go from here to here. So we set a level of expectation...of the SES [and] introduced this notion of less hierarchy.

> [We] enjoyed building the guiding coalition...They didn't like the name of it but couldn't think of a better word either...But I didn't want to have executive, senior executive or any of those words...I tried to introduce as many new languages to create the culture as I possibly could—a long term, cultural language. (Vardon interview)

Vardon considered that the guiding coalition concept would be valuable for Centrelink because it would allow senior managers to discuss strategies and monitor progress while evaluating performance trends against expected internal and external outcomes. She had already tested a variation of this arrangement: 'Every place I've been, I made a co-linking of the senior executives.' In this case, she resolved that we would all speak with the same voice…we had a big agenda to sell, and I had to have everybody selling the same agenda. And because of the size of it, I had no choice but to go with part of the decision making process, because I wanted them locked in. (Vardon interview)

The CEO formed the guiding coalition to create a sense of shared ownership and governance of the organisation, to increase the leadership capacity and create a force to sustain and drive change; to process more information more quickly and speed up the implementation of initiatives; and as a vehicle to eradicate the 'destructive competition between respective patches' (Vardon 1998c:1, 2). The aim was for the coalition to be a form of matrix consultative management that consulted horizontally and vertically and that sought to unlock the 'old command and control style' (Divett 2002:56) and replace the functionally based hierarchy of committees dominated by senior executives and divisional heads of Centrelink's predecessors. As a strategic management group, the guiding coalition comprised all SES officers and the executive, and included national and area managers. It merged the business and functional levels of the agency and was at the peak of the executive committee structure, as indicated in Figure 4.1.

Figure 4.1 Guiding coalition and other key Centrelink committees

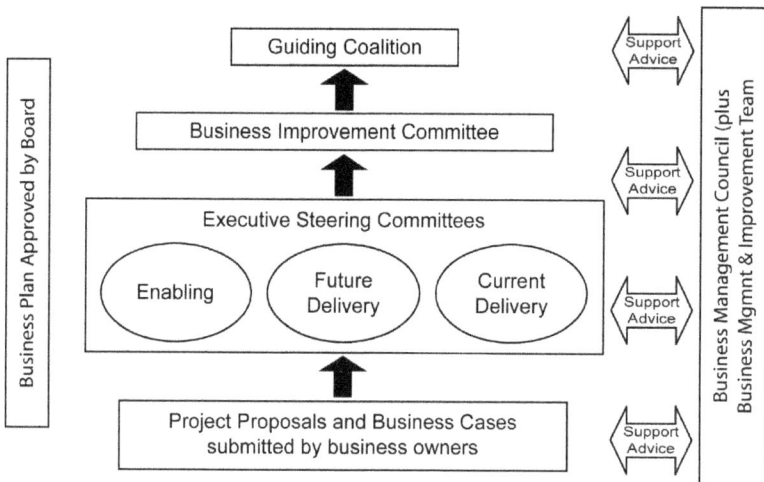

It was also intended to reinforce the shared vision and accountability of its managers and the vision of the agency. Vardon saw the body as communicating the corporate vision as well as generating short-term wins from a myriad improvement projects and 'anchor[ing] new approaches and behaviours in the organisational culture' (Vardon 1998c:3). Within the parameters set by the board of management, the guiding coalition took on setting the direction and taking key decisions, while establishing a culture for the future and acting as an educative forum (Centrelink 1999a:85).

The management group met about every six weeks for two days to manage the agency's internal governance and strategic agenda and to discuss business-level issues. The meetings provided a forum for operational feedback from area staff on the implementation and management of programs, and allowed national support officers to report on forthcoming events and the status of development projects. The wide-ranging and forthright discussions involved a sharing of responsibility and ownership based on achieving the strategic goals of the organisation. Everyone was expected to participate. These occasions represented a group dynamic that reinforced the leadership ethic of the agency's SES while updating its knowledge.

In an early evaluation of the guiding coalition concept, Vardon (1998a) asked members what they thought of the operation of the idea and its functional performance. The responses were mixed in terms of its role, the role of the CEO, the coalition's relationship with the board and the efficiency of such a large decision-making body; the group began with 55 staff (Divett 2002) and expanded in time to about 80, then to almost 100. Some members thought that the issues being discussed were not significant and that participants were either unprepared to contribute or reticent in this type of forum. Others valued the inclusiveness and the building of a corporate sense of network that forced senior officers to come to grips with strategic and operational issues.

Vardon credited the guiding coalition with setting key agendas for reforming the organisation as well as fostering a shared understanding of its new roles and responsibilities. She saw the team as a significant factor in building Centrelink's success and was heartened by healthy changes in the coalition itself, such as a greater maturity of members, manifested in part by the fact that people were starting to disagree (Vardon 1998c). In her view, critical disagreement contributed to strategic decision making in the organisation, but also strengthened group collegiality. Divett (2002) observed: 'It took us nine months to turn this big and geographically dispersed group into an effective team, but payoffs have been substantial. We're creating an entirely new organisation.'

The process of development of this innovative structure paid off in the formative years of Centrelink. By 2003, the annual report noted that this body was responsible for guiding the organisation, setting direction and leading change, establishing a culture for the future, providing an educative forum and communicating decisions (Centrelink 2004a).

Changing organisational culture

Vardon had outlined the scope of change in a welcome and orientation package for staff in April 1997 (CSDA 1997b). In it, she presented the reasons for establishing the agency, its responsibilities, how it would be formed and the number of changes already under way. She characterised the nature of the agency's business as assessment services, information giving, referral services and payments. The document also identified the four main customer groups or stakeholders as the DSS portfolio minister, client departments, internal customers (the board of management and agency staff) and 'people who use our services and their representatives' (CSDA 1997b).

Vardon adopted a highly personalised approach in building a new staff culture and bringing together staff from the DSS and DEETYA. She was acutely aware of past tensions and competition in the DSS–DEETYA relationship as a result of following different and at times conflicting procedures and processes. She saw the new agency as providing an 'opportunity to combine our services into one organisation without barriers for us as staff in attending to customer needs and without the frustration our customers feel when dealing with two separate agencies' (CSDA 1997b:18).

Vardon stressed the necessity for transformational and transactional change through a continuous stream of messages to staff, but she also recognised individual reactions that could accompany these seminal changes. She acknowledged a range of likely emotional responses including feelings of loss, resistance to change, denial, uncertainty, resentment, frustration, indifference, caution or indeed increased energy for those who would embrace change wholeheartedly (CSDA 1997b:18–19). Staff counsellors were made available to support staff during the changeover. These communications to staff were highly optimistic and positive in tone but they also dispensed practical ideas in trying to assuage understandable staff concerns. Those staff members who were unable to accept the new workplace culture were invited to 'reassess their career goals' and to consider possible moves either within or outside the agency.

During the initial period, Vardon visited most offices in the network to explain the new roles and responsibilities of Centrelink and to answer questions from sometimes anxious staff. Her previous experience in introducing change and her confident manner, combined with her formidable communication skills, provided an obvious focal identity for staff and facilitated her task.

Creating a customer-focused organisation required more than keeping the customers happy. It raised significant concerns for staff about issues of job security and the prospect of their functions being opened up to competitive tendering, compounded by the initial difficulties of bringing together a large number of staff from two different organisations. Because of the tight financial constraints imposed by the additional efficiency dividends, the question of cost cutting through staff reductions was high on the list of priorities; indeed, it provided the major driver for long-term strategy formulation for Centrelink's future. Most of the initial savings could be obtained only through voluntary redundancies. Because of the historically confrontational approach between the DSS and the Community and Public Service Union (CPSU), the relevant APS union, a new staff employment agreement—seen as an essential for reinforcing the management of change—needed to be negotiated carefully and quickly to ensure that remaining staff were coopted into the new organisation with assurances of continuing status as public servants and promises of productivity-linked staff pay rises.

A Centrelink Development Agreement (CDA) was drawn up during the organisation's first year of operation to improve the working environment. Centrelink staff members were consulted in developing the agency's vision and culture and given incentives and opportunities to achieve the requirements of the Customer Service Charter and the BPAs. In 1999, a revised CDA paid particular attention to the job classification structure and introduced a broad banding of classifications. This effectively provided staff in the frontline service centres with pay rises matched to improved work skills and productivity. The aim was to encourage staff commitment and development and to reward improved performance based on service rather than a more generic public service administrative function. Vardon played a central role in first smoothing and then reforming previously acrimonious relations between the CPSU and Centrelink management.

An early challenge for senior management was to develop a new Centrelink culture that reflected those elements of the previous departments that managers wanted preserved and to develop values deemed important for the emerging organisation. A number of shared behaviours were identified and defined through five shared values: listening to customers and the community, mutual respect for customers and each other, behaving ethically and with integrity, addressing innovative ways to provide the right outcome, and problem solving and developing opportunities (Centrelink 1997:8–10, 2003c).[4]

The first value was listening, because Centrelink wanted to share and apply a culture of listening throughout the organisation, drawing on the strength of CES staff, who were regarded as listeners because they gathered information about customer skills and life experiences. Social security staffers were thought to lack such skills because they were less integral to their work. The second value, respect for customers and colleagues, emerged from studies undertaken by Centrelink on the culture of the organisation in which staff and customers perceived that they were not respected. The third value focused on behaving with integrity and in an ethical manner.

The fourth value centred on exploring innovation, which Vardon (O'Donnell 2004; Interview with Vardon 2002) attributed to a comment by a senior executive from the DSS about the need to learn how to explore...this was a journey we were going on. He used the early pioneer experience and you get this wonderful visual image of somebody lifting up the bottom of a building, the bureaucracy, and looking out and seeing different ways of doing things.

The final value, solving problems, was selected because DSS front-desk staffers were not regarded as possessing such skills. The DSS staff did not

package things up for people. You said yes or no if they were entitled. There was a strong cultural value which says only answer the questions that people ask. So the customer was expected to know things they wouldn't know. There was a legal argument for this, an administrative law argument, that said that...you are there to provide a range of information, and if you fail to, you could be sued for failing, they might be able to claim or recover in a payment area that they missed out on. (O'Donnell 2004; Interview with Vardon 2002)

Vardon regarded the five values as statements about the future, which had been chosen to reflect a distinctive philosophy. The values and associated behaviours became a significant element of the organisational culture that was reflected in staff interaction and external behaviour (O'Donnell 2004). The shared values reflected a special insight into the nature of the organisation and its priorities.

Strategic human resource management

A strategic approach to human resource management was developed over several years. Centrelink had a number of frameworks to address human resource development directly or indirectly, such as the strategic framework, business plan and the National Learning Strategy 1998–2001 (ANAO 2001c:16). Vardon, however, lamented in 2002 the absence of a focused framework:

[W]e've done lots of things really well, but having an integrated package which says what we stand for, believe in, what things are important to us, how we look after our staff, what we're going to measure, what the most important drivers are for performance—having a framework for all of that, we just didn't have one. (Interview with Vardon; O'Donnell 2004)

By 2002, the integration of human resource practices into business planning processes remained limited, according to O'Donnell. A national people manager, appointed early that year, observed that when he arrived

the people effort was completely disconnected from the business. We had a little goal in the business plan on a piece of paper but there was nothing living and breathing behind it in my view. And even [in] major initiatives that were underway, the people issues were absent. (Interview with National People Manager; O'Donnell 2004)

A National People Plan (Centrelink 2002a) was developed in 2002 to improve integration between people management and business. The strategy emphasised six business-improvement focus areas: adding value to business decisions; leaders leading and managers managing; encouraging talent for success; commitment to safety, health and wellbeing; focus on learning, an investment in business; and fostering a culture committed to values, outcomes and innovation. Several major projects for implementing the plan included CDA initiatives, strengthening workforce planning capability and implementing the leadership framework. The National People Plan was fitted into the broader framework of strategic directions and business plans and the balanced scorecard. It was connected also to business-improvement planning processes at the team level and down to personal performance plans.

Integrative leadership

Centrelink emphasised the importance of organisational leadership and developed a set of normative national elements and associated performance criteria and measures for the leadership qualities it deemed necessary to contribute to the success of the organisation. The list represented a compilation of trait, situational and transactional theories with generalised and specific characteristics. Each quality described its elements with a set of examples of processes: for example, in the leadership quality covering innovation, leaders were expected to demonstrate their innovative abilities when creating a vision, solving problems or planning and facilitating major change. Performance criteria then described further activities that provided a checklist for leadership. Finally, each quality had performance measures segmented into leadership groups at various organisational levels—for example, the National Support Office, area support offices and CSCs.[5]

Vardon sought to foster these qualities in applying herself to transforming Centrelink and its leaders into a very different government agency. Her impressions of the impact of leadership on change were that: 'We have learned that we need dynamic and cohesive leadership...an executive who acts as advocates [sic] for collaboration and organisational change, shaping organisational structures and processes and promoting the concept of one business' (Vardon 2001:10).

The competing demands of manager/leader were difficult to reconcile but the organisation had at least attempted to outline a leadership philosophy that was being matched to the demands of current and future performance-related officers. Mentoring leaders involved nurturing self-confidence by allowing staff to try to succeed at new things, and valuing employees.

Learning culture and the virtual college

The overall reason for establishing a virtual training college was that the elements of the new entity existed but needed to be pulled together, according to the CEO (Hamilton 2007:103). Centrelink had inherited a tradition of staff training from the DSS, but this new stage reflected Vardon's 'vision for an organisational learning culture' (Hamilton 2007:111). The virtual college was to support the steering of Centrelink 'towards a learning culture'.[6] According to Vardon:

> From time to time I didn't get the balance right and there was a perception that she cares more about the customers than she does about us. And out of that came this big drive from me to get the college going and the upgraded qualifications so that our staff could see that we actually cared about them. (O'Donnell 2004; Interview with Vardon 2002)

The Centrelink Virtual College was established in 2001 to provide a facility for staff to acquire accreditation for the training they were undertaking. With the introduction of the college, many of the two-day courses that were previously offered to staff were replaced by accredited qualifications (Centrelink 2002a:19).

Culture and change

According to O'Donnell (2004), elements of a best-practice model of human resource management—regarded as significant for organisational success (for example, Pfeffer 1998)—were in place. These included the work of the Centrelink Virtual College, the promotion of teamwork and the handling of performance and recruitment. There was 'evidence of the emergence of a more strategic approach to [human resource management] whereby human resource policies are increasingly integrated with the organisation's approach to business planning via the development of Centrelink's National People Plan' (O'Donnell 2004:19). O'Donnell also observed that these initiatives did not yet represent a coherent and complementary set of human resource practices. The experience suggested a

> contingent and organisational specific response to the challenges and pressures involved in creating a large integrated service delivery organisation employing almost 25,000 employees operating under strong market pressures and under intense scrutiny from the federal government and other government departments. (O'Donnell 2004:19)

Changing culture is essential for major organisational change, but it is regarded as difficult to accomplish. The requirements include 'the mutual interaction of new symbols and definitions and of changed structures, expectations, and rewards. New attitudes need to be demonstrated in new behaviours and expectations' (Spicer et al. 1996:180). In Centrelink's case, the challenges of pre-existing cultures were dealt with as the organisation was infused with a distinctive new culture that was aligned increasingly with strategic directions. The leader played a pivotal role in communicating the new order and investing 'spirit' to produce change in staff attitudes and behaviour. As a consequence, the organisation was able to claim that, in time, it became more customer centred, service delivery conscious, client oriented and performance focused.

ENDNOTES

[1] Vardon had previously served in local government and in senior positions in the NSW Department of Youth and Community Service and the South Australian Department for Community Welfare. She had also been South Australian Commissioner for Public Sector Employment and head of the Office of Public Sector Reform. During this hiatus as a consultant to the DSS, she worked closely with the transition team to address marketing, legal, structural, procedural, accommodation and relationship issues. In 1995, she was named the Inaugural Telstra Business Woman of the Year.

[2] Despite Centrelink providing an international exemplar of the Kotter approach, Centrelink's contribution to a subsequent Kotter publication authored by Ross Divett (2002) was presented as a 'down under' case and not even from the public sector. Divett's position was not identified, unlike about 50 employees of Deloitte's, who were acknowledged.

[3] This model of change has also influenced departmental secretaries—for example, Metcalfe (2007).

[4] This discussion draws on a paper by Michael O'Donnell and material derived from an interview that he conducted with Sue Vardon in October 2002.

[5] An example of the emphasis placed on the practice of leadership was the area leadership team in northern central Victoria, a middle to operational-level version of the guiding coalition, which used global leadership expectations within the organisation as a means to improve staff performance in the area. The *Leadership Expectation Statement* was comprehensive but simple in its format. It was published as a wall poster and provided to staff as a small fold-out pamphlet. The statement was separate from the national *Leadership Qualities* papers and had three sections: operational standards, attendance, and image and behaviour. The document represented an amalgamation of many disparate pronouncements and directions that had been distributed throughout Centrelink. The area conducted extensive consultation with staff and managers to use the final product to rectify the 'poor performance' of staff in the network. In identifying relationship and management issues, it emphasised the pivotal role of staff in providing service rather than concentrating only on customers.

[6] There were other factors involved, such as an audit inquiry into the systems and strategies for ensuring customer service officers had access to appropriate skills and knowledge, but the report was published after the creation of the virtual college (ANAO 2001c: no. 9).

5. Reinventing service delivery

One reason for Centrelink's creation was to improve the quality of service for the unemployed and those on income support. This chapter examines how Centrelink sought to achieve this, considers how its services changed from the customer's point of view and identifies some of the successes and difficulties. The focus is on the customer's perspective of Centrelink and its services.

The rationale for a service delivery agency can be found in how it conceives of and handles its core responsibility. This involves how it engages the customer through its conception of the customer relationship and the design of service delivery structures. Customer-oriented service design includes the service concept and the service delivery system covering physical aspects, staff and access processes (Flynn 2007). Recognition is necessary of the policy context of service delivery on the one hand and of management support for it on the other—in particular, service culture. Important issues arise from balancing the conflicting demands of cost efficiency against responsiveness and, importantly, service quality for the customer.

Centrelink's role and priorities were defined in terms of service delivery and evolved with time. The political executive had clear views, with the Prime Minister observing that Centrelink would achieve 'a balance between compassion and responsibility', be 'a more human face' yet 'more efficient' and 'lead to far less public dissatisfaction' (Howard 1997). The Minister for Family and Community Services, Jocelyn Newman, agreed: the change 'was the result of long term public dissatisfaction with the existing arrangements...Centrelink was set up not only to maintain, but [to] improve, services to the Australian people' (Newman 2000a).

Centrelink's own conception became 'service delivery as the right services provided to the right customer through the right channels' (Vardon 2002c:9, 1998d). It was expected that by 2005 'the key elements of service...for Centrelink customers will be access, choice, value, integration, connecting and brokering' (Vardon 2002c:11). According to Paul Hickey (2004:1), deputy CEO with responsibility for service delivery, the arrangements were reviewed to meet several aims: 'maintenance of quality customer service principles; better access to services for customers; improved quality in decision making; and greater efficiency in operations'.

The policy context of Centrelink's growth and other external pressures affected its service delivery role with time. The early political climate placed a strong emphasis on the new Centrelink becoming more efficient and effective. Later, Centrelink would redesign its services in response to the government's agenda for welfare and other reforms. This chapter explores Centrelink's response to these challenges in moving from the supply of diverse but individual government programs to more holistic, integrated customer service. As the organisation developed, the delivery model evolved through stages, becoming more streamlined as challenges arose with system and customer relationships.

Challenges and constraints in a customer focus

Government support for its new agency gave Centrelink leaders the opportunity to create an organisation able to meet its expectations of being the government's 'human face' and to design delivery structures for programs that would assist customers. Centrelink's focus on customer satisfaction was clearly supported by the government's wish for less dissatisfaction, yet there were significant constraints on achieving this goal.

The two fundamental tensions were between efficiency and customer needs—the former a particular focus of the government and departments, the latter a foremost concern of the specialised delivery agency. A subsidiary tension was with the process of administering programs, which had (selective) customer relevance and efficiency implications.

The first major constraint was the equal emphasis of the government on the need for Centrelink to be efficient and effective. The efficiency dividend required by the government as part of the Centrelink solution meant heavy staff reductions early on and a strong emphasis on productivity improvements through staff behaviour and technology. Furthermore, almost all the staff of the new organisation had come from two public service departments with attitudes based on an older, more regulatory culture. Their willingness and ability to change were unknown and untested.

A third constraint was that departments previously responsible for delivery of the services were now paying Centrelink for its services. They continued to design the policies, and the programs that flowed from them, and could specify how and at what level the services were to be delivered. In the early days, they tended to micromanage Centrelink activities. While Centrelink could decide the environment and the culture of how each service was delivered, at times it had a limited role in designing the service itself.

Fourth, there was a need to find a balance between improving customer services and meeting the expectations of client departments to deliver the programs for which they were accountable, with accuracy and assurance. When the Audit Office questioned the accuracy of payments to some customers and a study of errors two years later attributed most of them to Centrelink, what were the repercussions?

Fifth, a frequently changing policy agenda required constant changes to processes in Centrelink, requiring staff to develop new skills and knowledge and adopt new ways of working. Training and development became high priorities for the organisation. The capacity of Centrelink's IT managers to implement new policy programs quickly, to make the needed changes to meet government expectations and legislative requirements and to develop staff capability in the changed arrangements became a major issue.

Finally, there were issues of contestability and seeking new business. How much energy should be expended on tendering for new business and what impact would it have on existing customers? Most crucially, finding a workable balance between the costs of spending time with customers to ensure their needs were understood and met and developing and encouraging cheaper forms of customer service became a key determinant of Centrelink's redesign of its services.

Customer satisfaction survey results provide one indication of Centrelink's relative success in managing these opportunities and constraints.

Customer satisfaction

Despite considerable effort, Centrelink experienced difficulty for much of its early life in improving its customer satisfaction ratings much above those of the DSS in 1996. Apart from November 1997, when the results could have reflected the promotion of the organisation as well as the quality of its services,[1] it was three years before the overall customer satisfaction levels reached the level recorded in November 1996 (69 per cent). In November 2000, they rose significantly to 76 per cent and remained close to that level for the next two years with a new high of 81 per cent reached in 2003 (customer satisfaction surveys data).[2]

Table 5.1 Quality of Centrelink people, services and information*

Nov. 1996	May 1997	Nov. 1997	May 1998	Nov. 1998	May 1999	Nov. 1999	May 2000	Nov. 2000	Nov. 2001	Nov. 2002	Nov. 2003
69**	67**	72	67	65	65	70	66	76	75	76	81

* percentage rating good and very good
** Department of Social Security

An independent evaluation in 2002 by the Boston Consulting Group (BCG) of Centrelink's cost efficiency found that customer satisfaction dipped as efficiency gains were sought between 1997 and 1998, largely through staff reductions and technology-driven productivity gains. Satisfaction rebounded to better levels as costs per unit of workload stabilised in 2000–01 (BCG 2002:24). The BCG also reported that '[b]eneficiary representatives interviewed over the course of the project support the view that service levels have increased over time and that, relative to other agencies, Centrelink's customer service is good'. It concluded that 'almost all stakeholders acknowledge Centrelink's achievements in merging two service delivery networks, creating a new, customer focused organisation, achieving "huge cultural change"' (BCG 2002:26).

Overall satisfaction with CSCs reached 85.5 per cent in 2002 and 83 per cent in 2003, and, for call centres, the level rose to 87 per cent in 2002 and 88 per cent in 2003 (Centrelink 2003a:46; CSS November 2003:38).

Creating a service culture

The government wanted an agency 'focussed on, and specialising in customer service' (Ruddock 1996) and Vardon, who came to Centrelink with a reputation for a customer-focused approach—even when, as head of Corrective Services in South Australia, her customers were reluctant ones (*Australian Financial Review*, 19 June 1995, p. 12)—was determined to create one. The immediate emphasis was on creating a stronger customer ethic in the agency's staff: 'they were shocking...the cultures of the organisations that they'd come from were so terrible' (Vardon interview 2001). Before developing a good customer service ethos, the staff had to feel that the organisation supported them. A study was undertaken using a series of focus groups of the culture of the staff's previous organisations. The data were analysed as a basis for determining the kind of culture for the new organisation (see Chapter 4).[3]

The former DSS had begun a trial of a fresh approach to its office layout and design to support a customer-friendly environment. This approach was adopted throughout Centrelink and played a large part in changing staff attitudes to customers and changing customer attitudes to Centrelink. Vardon stressed the importance of the environment as symbolic of change to staff and customers alike. It was crucial to establishing a team atmosphere and culture, she argued (Vardon interview 2001). A program of office refurbishment began to produce cheerful, open-plan offices, in which staff were required to wear name tags and many more were brought forward to work at the front desk instead of processing in back rooms. A focus on queue management attempted to reduce waiting times for customers and those seeking information rather than an interview were able to obtain it without queuing. Service by appointment started.

Developing a common approach to customers took time. Staffers who had previously worked with the employment services were used to finding innovative solutions to maximise the help they could provide; those with a social security background were more concerned that the applicant was really eligible, met all the criteria and complied with the legislation being administered. 'So at every level we had cultural changes, cultural differences between the two' (Vardon interview).

Negotiations with the CPSU in relation to staff employment conditions focused on customer service issues and gradually extended the hours that Centrelink offices were open.

Before the formal launching of Centrelink, Divett, the deputy CEO-in-waiting, indicated in Senate Estimate Committee hearings that the one-stop shop was headed towards a concept of more personalised service. Minister Newman said of the shift (already taking place in some 60 combined DSS–CES locations in June 1997): 'It's almost like a meeter and greeter in a hotel.' The secretary of the DSS, Tony Blunn, balanced this image with a reference to the savings made possible by amalgamation and the placing of Centrelink on a business model to achieve efficiencies and effectiveness (Senate CALC 1997b:214).

The impact of staff on customer perceptions was, however, highly significant. Surveys consistently showed that 'while other aspects of Centrelink performance were found to influence customer perceptions of Centrelink, the impact of staff [42 per cent] was found to be four times greater than the next most significant predictor' (CSS May 2000:4). The impact of staff remained almost constant in the surveys. Other service aspects that had a significant impact on customer perceptions of Centrelink overall (in order of priority) were identified in 2000 as: the payment process (14 per cent), ease of making a complaint (12 per cent), Centrelink forms (11 per cent), Centrelink letters (10 per cent) and ease of accessing Centrelink services (7 per cent) (CSS May 2000:4). While the order of these other aspects changed with time, the contents of the list remained almost constant.

The quality of Centrelink staff was also rated and showed a general improvement, particularly after mid-2000 (Table 5.2).

Table 5.2 Quality of DSS/Centrelink staff overall (per cent)

Nov. 1996	May 1997	Nov. 1997	May 1998	Nov. 1998	May 1999	Nov. 1999	May 2000	Nov. 2000	Nov. 2001	Nov. 2002	Nov. 2003
74*	73*	79	76	76	76	78	77	81	82	*	**

* not seen
** no overall figure

Nevertheless, not everyone was keen on the direction Centrelink was going and many considered the use of the term 'customer', which had just begun to be used in the DSS and was adopted by Centrelink, to be inappropriate given that the recipient had no other place to go. The response was that if Centrelink did not perform adequately the government was likely to seek other administrative options.

Understanding customer attitudes

The national and local surveys of customer satisfaction begun by the DSS were continued and were supplemented by a program of 'value-creation workshops' to identify what customers valued. These workshops were attended by office staff and their customers and involved groups of customers ranking what they considered to be the 10 most important components of good service and rating their Centrelink office on how it performed on each, while employees listened and watched and rated themselves. Major customer irritants were also identified and, together with the list of what customers valued, formed the basis of a customer service improvement plan for that office. The workshops were regarded as having 'a powerful impact on the people of Centrelink and generated an impetus for change' (Vardon 1998d:2).

Programs to make listening to customers a continuing part of the culture beyond Centrelink's early days were continued. Almost 10 000 customers were engaged in the value-creation workshops with Centrelink staff during its first two years, with more than 20 sessions run in non-English languages. In 2002–03, 165 workshops were held. What became clear was that few customers knew or cared about governmental structures, but they did care about being able to relate their problems once rather than many times, prompt and efficient service and being dealt with accurately by friendly, caring and knowledgeable staff. They also appreciated choice of access and a welcoming and comfortable office environment. Much of Centrelink's service delivery redesign and many service improvements, locally and nationally, were based on the messages from these workshops and the national and regional satisfaction surveys.

Centrelink customers were also given a service charter. The government reached the view that the Public Service needed to be more accessible to the community. Drawing on the newly introduced service charters in the United Kingdom, the government introduced Client Service Charter Principles for Commonwealth agencies in 1997 (Department of Industry, Science and Tourism 1997). By late September 1997, Centrelink's Customer Service Charter was in place and displayed in all its offices. The charter established a range of agreed service standards for staff and customers. A broad range of customer surveys assessed the effectiveness of the charter. As in earlier charters, these principles were broadly expressed and lacked specificity about service effectiveness. Nevertheless, they reflected a new notion of reciprocity and mutual responsibility between citizen and public servant. This notion was to become a key theme in the development of Centrelink.

Designing the delivery structure

A clear sequence of service delivery models was explicit in Centrelink's planning and developmental pathway.

Phase one: service integration

Before Centrelink, several federal departments provided a range of social, family and employment services and the possible recipient of any service needed to know which department provided what service. Service suppliers were not always co-located, they could have different opening hours and, outside cities, could require recipients to travel from one town to another to obtain assistance. The creation of Centrelink changed all that, as service delivery for a range of policies was transferred to Centrelink and recipients no longer needed to understand specific departmental responsibilities, as Centrelink became the central provider. Nevertheless, within Centrelink, each type of payment and service—families, pensions and employment—was delivered separately for several years (Figure 5.1).[4]

Figure 5.1 Post creation: Centrelink with payment streams

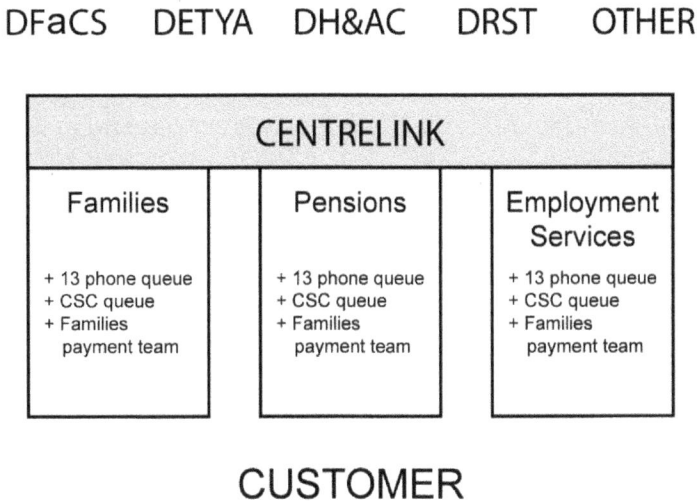

DFaCS   DETYA   DH&AC   DRST   OTHER

CENTRELINK		
Families	Pensions	Employment Services

+ 13 phone queue
+ CSC queue
+ Families
  payment team
	+ 13 phone queue
	+ CSC queue
	+ Families
	  payment team
		+ 13 phone queue
		+ CSC queue
		+ Families
		  payment team

CUSTOMER

Source: Vardon 1998d.

As well as now visiting or accessing by phone one office for most of their needs, applicants could expect to have requests and advice supplied by a range of service officers with specialist knowledge. Customers could see staff at work, use touch-screen facilities and access privacy areas for consultation and interviews. In practical terms, an immigrant who formerly had to deal with DEETYA for employment and training issues as well as the DSS for income security matters could be assisted in one place, and expect interpreter services. Recruitment targeted a more culturally diverse and multilingual employee base, with particular attention to Indigenous staff.

In spite of these significant changes, Centrelink retained multiple reception counters and queues, program-specific phone numbers and teams organised by customer segments. Customers still had to identify their own needs and join the right queues. While customers were now able to come to one office, called customer service centres (CSCs), within that office service was provided in silos. Sometimes this was convenient for customers—for instance, services for retirees or veterans were separated from those for job seekers; other times, it was not, as customers with complex problems often had to join multiple queues and retell their problems to several people. At times, particularly in large CSCs, backlogs ran close to 10 per cent.

A further area of development and refinement involved call centres. The aim in the initial two years was to improve the integration of services between the call centres and the CSCs and to re-engineer workflows and processes to improve service delivery. Telephone services, inherited from the DSS, were increasingly heavily used. In the May 1997 customer satisfaction survey of the DSS, just before Centrelink was officially created, the survey revealed that the telephone service, and each of its attributes, was the weakest area of operations. Reducing the length of time customers were kept on hold and making it easier to get through without being cut off were key priorities. By November 1997, some improvements had been made but these were offset by the chaos that accompanied the introduction of youth allowances (see Chapter 2) the next year. Customers surveyed expressed impatience with not being able to get through.

In 2001, DBM Consultants surveyed service-related expectations of Centrelink customers through 60 in-depth interviews. Customers were shown to have different time expectations for the two services, with an expectation of quicker service when telephoning Centrelink than when dealing with staff face-to-face (DBM Consultants Pty Ltd 2001). Those using the telephone expected to reach a point of service within five to 10 minutes; waiting on hold for five to 10 minutes was acceptable. A wait of 15 minutes was too long but still acceptable, while a wait of more than 20 minutes was considered unacceptable. In contrast, customers visiting Centrelink offices considered it acceptable to wait in a queue for 10–15 minutes.

The growth in calls continued and, by the close of 2001, Centrelink was handling 22 million calls of increasing duration a year. This increase was disproportionate to the growth in call centre staff. Free-call facilities were offered in 11 foreign countries and Centrelink's call centres were benchmarked as best practice within the industry. Because the call centres shared a platform with CSCs, callers could gain access also to particular sites or specialist officers. Streamlined voice prompts were designed to assist self-servicing of personal information and applications. As a further refinement, by mid-2001, Centrelink's interpreter services had increased to 2000 on-call interpreters, representing more than 60 languages and providing close to 46 000 interpreter services.

More generally, the work of Centrelink was changing and broadening from transaction-based assessment and entitlement to include planning and referral activities and continuing customer support. Managers were encouraged to seek staff suggestions and solutions and to ensure these were seen to be valued. The changes in work required the building of organisational knowledge and learning and staff needed new and improved workplace and customer skills.

Phase two: one-to-one service approach

By the middle of 1998, Centrelink had decided on a new service delivery model. Announced by the new minister, Warren Truss, in November 1998, it was a plan that was to take seven years to be fully implemented. The first stage of what was called the 'life events' model—because it was focused on the events customers experienced during their lifetimes—was the introduction of the one-to-one service. At this time, much of what customers said they would value was not yet available. Many customers still had to queue several times, provide identification more than once and repeat their problems to staff members before they could be fully addressed. No single staff member knew their full story or could be referred to again when situations changed. In the next two years, however, the separation of services into silos within Centrelink gradually began to change.

By the end of 1999, customer service officers were being allocated responsibility for a pool of customers. They were linked electronically to each customer's record and would generally handle all business relevant to them. Customers had, in theory, to tell their story only once—to their one-to-one officer. Those who required this more personalised approach could make appointments with their one-to-one officer through a special phone line. Not all Centrelink's six million customers could be given one-to-one service, and many did not want it, but it was an attempt by Centrelink to see whether it could enhance the quality of service it provided to those who needed it. Additionally, a stronger emphasis was placed on brokering solutions across payment streams and linking customers to other government and non-government agencies as necessary. A collateral benefit for the organisation was seen to be a more even spread of work, greater staff satisfaction, reduced customer traffic and reduced arrears and reviews (Vardon 2002b:50). A once-only proof of customer identity through an identity number was designed to reduce service time and promote customer profiling and risk assessment. Risk was assessed contingent on the level of payment and its expected duration.

While Centrelink had promoted one-to-one contact since 1999, the national customer satisfaction surveys from 1999 to 2001 indicated that usage was quite low—about 20 per cent of customers surveyed said they had used the service in the previous six months. Many of those who had not used it had not known about it. The other main reason for not using the one-to-one contact was that they had no need to do so. Respondents from Austudy and Youth Allowance segments were least likely to know about the service. Those who did use the one-to-one contact service were very satisfied with it (93 per cent in 2000 and 90 per cent in 2001). The most common reasons given for customers preferring to see their one-to-one contact was that staffers knew their case history, they preferred a familiar face and could deal with matters too complex to handle over the phone.

The Customer Expectations Survey reinforced Centrelink's view that one-to-one was an important service for those customers who had experienced continuing problems with Centrelink and repeated contact with staff. Conversely, many customers who had little contact with Centrelink saw no benefit in having a single point of contact. In general, the one-to-one contact was seen as a desirable expectation (DBM Consultants Pty Ltd 2001:58–9). The development of one-to-one service, however, significantly increased the cost of service delivery.

One-to-one remained the most expensive service offered by Centrelink. Alternative, cheaper methods of service delivery had to be found if Centrelink was to remain within its budget.

Phase three: life-events model of service delivery

Centrelink looked to transform the delivery of public services with a new service delivery model based on a life-events methodology. This notion was a key mechanism by which Centrelink was to deliver on the one-stop shop (Vardon 1998d; Centrelink 1999b: Appendix B, p. 9).

The range and complexity of the services provided by Centrelink and its predecessors had confused customers about the system and the support they were entitled to. The life-events model identified the key times of change or crisis in people's lives and designed services around them. To make it easier for customers, they would be asked to identify only their problems; Centrelink staff would then take responsibility for recognising what services would best meet their customer's needs.

The onus would be shifted from the customer to Centrelink staff, supported by their IT system, to ask questions of the customer that would enable a complete and accurate matching of needs with available products and services, including internal and external referrals. Customers would no longer 'have to spend their time trying to locate the part of Centrelink that deals with their particular situation. However they choose to approach us the response they receive will be guided by the "life event", which has prompted their contact with us' (Vardon 1999c). The challenge was to provide staff with the training and understanding to enable them to handle the new approach.

Figure 5.2 Life-events framework for the new service delivery model

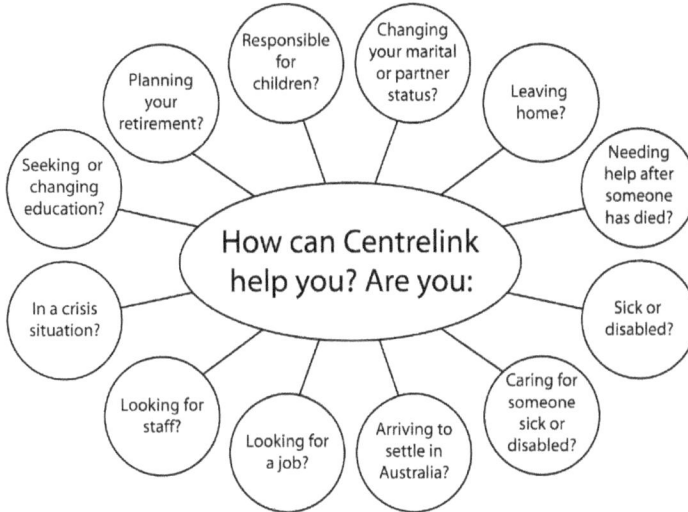

Source: Vardon 1998d.

The model aimed to support a more intuitive, logical approach and be immediately recognisable to customers, thus facilitating the transition in time to self-assessment.

Centrelink tried particularly hard to provide improved services to at-risk groups. Information on the life-events model was successfully delivered in 34 languages in communities in regional Queensland in 2003 (Innisfail Advocate 2003). In Victoria, community-based programs for those customers who experienced severe need, or who formed the most at-risk group, were designed to reach into the community where customers could be met on their home turf rather than in the more formal circumstances of a Centrelink office and without the normal time constraints on interviews (Vranjkovic 2003). Further outreach services were planned in sensitive rural areas to minimise aggression between customers and Centrelink staff (Centrelink interview). In this instance, it appeared that cost drivers were secondary to effectiveness, but overall cost efficiencies remained the key to the provision of improved services.

Figure 5.3 An example of mapping for one life event

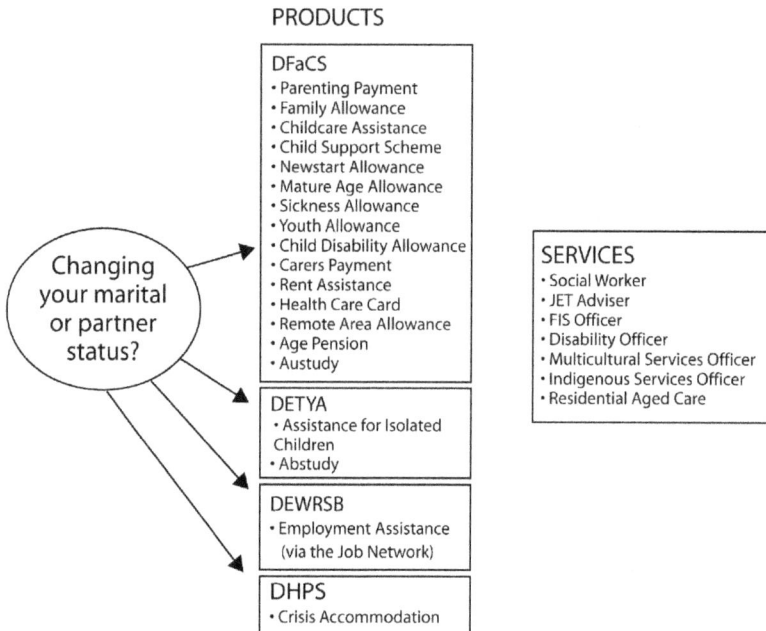

PRODUCTS

DFaCS
- Parenting Payment
- Family Allowance
- Childcare Assistance
- Child Support Scheme
- Newstart Allowance
- Mature Age Allowance
- Sickness Allowance
- Youth Allowance
- Child Disability Allowance
- Carers Payment
- Rent Assistance
- Health Care Card
- Remote Area Allowance
- Age Pension
- Austudy

Changing your marital or partner status?

SERVICES
- Social Worker
- JET Adviser
- FIS Officer
- Disability Officer
- Multicultural Services Officer
- Indigenous Services Officer
- Residential Aged Care

DETYA
- Assistance for Isolated Children
- Abstudy

DEWRSB
- Employment Assistance (via the Job Network)

DHPS
- Crisis Accommodation

Source: Vardon 1998d.

Phase four: re-engineering

The fourth phase, of re-engineering, operated in parallel with the further development of the life-events model. It involved a three-year process (2004–07) of bringing together into one integrated national network all the parts of Centrelink to gain increased efficiencies, improve decision making and improve access for customers. Customer Services Support Centres (CSSCs) were created to specialise in those areas of work that did not require face-to-face contact with customers and to assist the call centres when telephone demand was high. Processing services would be consolidated and rationalised in the CSSCs. The aim was to increase the capacity of CSC staff to spend enough time with those customers who needed greater help with meeting the participation agenda and to reduce the problem of peak call centre demand. Much of the processing of allowances and assistance, reviews and data-matching programs was to be transferred to the CSSCs where expertise could be brought together and developed.

A high priority of the re-engineering was to develop improved customer self-service options over the Internet or by telephone in selected accredited locations, so that, through the Customer Account, customers would be able to complete what were high-volume transactions for Centrelink, such as amending personal details and receiving advice on changes (Hickey 2004).

Customer access through IT and channel management

Information technology was crucial to Centrelink from the start. DSS computers and IT staff were transferred to Centrelink to enable the payment of income support to continue. In contrast, the department responsible for employment chose to provide access to Centrelink to its computer network but to retain ownership of it within the department.

The size and scope of Centrelink's IT were significant. By 2004, it was considered to be the fourth-largest IT operation in Australia, with more than 35 000 personal computers in its network processing 14 million transactions a day. Centrelink's provision of income support was regulated by more than 80 000 rules. Every small policy change involved rule changes and associated coding changes. Each major new policy created and changed rules about eligibility and payment and generated new and revised coding. Each change had to be made, tested and documented, with new or revised forms and letters generated, and the changes explained to the staff on the front desk responsible for implementing the policy with customers. Bringing together six programs into one Youth Allowance program created delivery problems for Centrelink in meeting the government's policy start-up deadlines.

Centrelink extended the call centres inherited from the DSS to become an increasingly important part of its business with customers. Each year, the demand for services grew and, by the end of 2002, there were 4500 people working in Centrelink's 27 call centres. By integrating all its electronic and telephonic systems, Centrelink was able to offer a seamless service to its staff and customers throughout Australia. It had connected its mainframe systems to software able to receive and interpret incoming inquiries from any device, such as a personal computer, kiosk, telephone or palm pilot, as well as remote-access laptops around Australia, selecting the appropriate database to conduct the transaction and respond to the inputting device (Vardon 2002c:14). By using this switching capability through its call centres from Queensland to Western Australia, it was able to use Australia's time zones to extend its hours of operation to eastern state callers up to 10pm on weekdays without requiring extensive shift work.

This was a significant improvement on what Centrelink's customers rated poor access in its early years. The ease of accessing Centrelink's services was rated 'good to very good' by only 40 per cent of respondents in 1998 (CSS November 1998). A year later, this rating had risen to 58 per cent, and stabilised at 60 per cent in 2003.

Views about access in 2001 were influenced primarily by perceptions of telephone accessibility (35 per cent), limited ways of dealing with Centrelink (13 per cent), lack of staff at Centrelink (12 per cent), location of offices (10 per cent) and other issues, such as transport and phone-line operating hours. While the morning was the time preferred by most customers to contact Centrelink, the 2000 survey report noted the 'growing demand…to transact business after hours using non-office channels (such as the internet and telephone)' (Millward Brown 2000:20). One in five customers said they would prefer to contact Centrelink after hours (mainly Austudy, families and Youth Allowance customers, and those who were studying, employed full-time or living in rural areas).

Nevertheless, most people continued to prefer to visit a Centrelink office (a reversal from the apparent trend towards preferring the telephone before the call centre difficulties of mid-1998). The reasons given for going to a Centrelink office in 2001 were, first, the need to talk to a person face-to-face (87 per cent) and second, the ability of office staff to deal with the problem straight away (35 per cent). Those who preferred the telephone did so because it was easier (54 per cent), quicker (38 per cent) or more convenient—a particular preference of rural customers. The few who preferred the Internet gave similar responses.[5]

After the delays of 1998, a substantial expansion of call centres had significantly reduced the call waiting times of call centre customers. A review of Centrelink cost efficiency showed that call centre workload almost doubled from 1997–98 to 2001–02. The number of calls had risen from 19 million to more than 25 million in 2002–03, with the duration of calls about 8.8 minutes, a continuing trend upwards from the 5.4 minutes of 1997–98 (BCG 2002:21, 23; Centrelink 2003a:115). Call waiting time, a primary driver of customer satisfaction, dropped from a high of 325 seconds in July 1998 to 144 seconds in 2002–03, well within Centrelink's target of 210 seconds and identified customer expectations. As already noted, customer satisfaction with these services rated consistently between 85 and 90 per cent. The call centres had become the largest single-purpose call centre operation in Australia (Centrelink 2003a:114–15).

As Centrelink moved its service model away from the initial separation of programs, it was necessary to integrate all program information and customer records into one record. The one-to-one officers, assisting their customers with problems that went across several programs, needed one complete, coherent customer record. Centrelink aimed to establish a 'customer account' for each of its customers, providing a clearer display of customer data. This reduced training for the staff required to update the information and allowed customers to see their own information and, eventually, to be able to update their own records.

The growth of the Internet required a further sustained response. Like other federal government agencies, Centrelink was required to respond to the government's whole-of-government initiative to have all appropriate services available through the Internet by 2001 (Commonwealth of Australia 1997). Centrelink had already developed a web site, signalling an extension of its operational boundaries, and now undertook a new range of initiatives to guarantee service delivery online to designated special groups, and, by 2001, to be accessible 24 hours a day, seven days a week. Rural and regional communities were being targeted as well as special groups.

After this, and particularly after the life-events service model was initiated, the web site was extensively redeveloped and enhanced. The passing of the *Electronic Transactions Act* and the *Social Security Administration Act* removed legislative barriers to Centrelink conducting its business with its customers electronically (Bashford 2000). Nevertheless, while customer access to the Internet rose, largely in line with that of the general community, this did not translate into greatly increased use of the Internet for Centrelink business. In 2001, while 44 per cent of customers had access to the Internet, only 5 per cent had visited the Centrelink web site in the previous three months—most (76 per cent) to get information or access job search facilities (24 per cent). Part of the problem was that many of the transactions customers wished to do on the web site, such as checking eligibility or lodging a form, required a signature or other identification that was not yet achievable through the web site. Nevertheless, the proportion of customers who claimed they would be interested in dealing with Centrelink via the Internet in the future rose from 1997 to 2003. Acceptance of voice-recognition and keypad technologies also rose (CCS November 2003:80).

By early 2004, 80 000 customers a week were using Centrelink's self-help services, although this represented only 2 per cent of all Centrelink transactions—a figure that Centrelink wanted to see grow quickly (Senate CALC 2004:52). There was potential for Centrelink to expand communications and provide customers with convenient services while lightening the load of call centres and CSCs.

Despite this limited acceptance and use of technology, Centrelink customers were experiencing improved convenience. In the November 2003 survey, 86 per cent agreed that their Centrelink office was conveniently located and 83 per cent agreed that they could usually do business with Centrelink at a time that suited them (CCS November 2003).

As Centrelink broadened its boundaries beyond social income payments to new business and greater connectivity with the community, it developed new options for its customers. CentrePay, for example, allowed social welfare recipients to have deducted directly from their welfare payments essential bills such as rent and electricity to state or local government agencies.

Beyond these approaches, Centrelink was trying to harness leading-edge technologies to enhance the quality, improve the accuracy and/or reduce the cost of their service delivery. Not all were successful. Perhaps most innovatively, but least successful, were attempts to develop a decision support, or 'expert', system, to help customer service staff by guiding them through the technical rules and assisting them to determine questions of eligibility (for example, an expert system supporting the FAO payments was installed at several sites but by 2004 Centrelink had withdrawn from further development). Another initiative that failed in the short term was the web post office for Youth Allowance customers. The idea was to deliver email letters through the Internet. It failed because recipients wanted to reply through the same means, but problems of authentication made web replies unacceptable to Centrelink.

Other initiatives were more successful. In 2003, a multimillion-dollar speech-recognition project was trialled in which students could report key information on lifestyle changes relevant to their benefits; a 30 per cent take-up of this option led to the extension of this service to other welfare recipients. A trial in 2002 of SMS text messaging to students to convey information reflected the fact that 78 per cent of Youth Allowance customers had a mobile phone and they were the group of Centrelink customers who most used SMS in their daily lives. Using SMS messages was a more cost-effective method than the use of either paper or other phone messages (Senate CALC 2002:16).

In spite of these developments, the BCG report noted that Centrelink's spending on IT had been declining at a time when that of 'comparable' organisations (that is, banks as large networked organisations) was increasing, and that a large proportion of the spending was 'geared to keeping the lights on', by which it meant the operation of the IT system. As Hickey noted at a Senate Estimates hearing, a large proportion of total IT spending was 'targeted at maintaining...existing service delivery networks...the ongoing effective operation of the IT systems is absolutely critical to making the $6\frac{1}{2}$ million payments each fortnight' (Senate CALC 2003:28).

The allocation in the 2003/04 budget of $312 million over five years for Centrelink to enhance its IT capability would enable Centrelink's IT to be upgraded. Called 'IT Refresh', it was to be used to ensure continuing IT reliability, allow Centrelink to deliver online self-services to customers, enter partnerships with community organisations, increase payment accuracy through automated data matching and information exchange with business, government agencies, banks and others (DFaCS 2003:255).

Channel management: extending and managing customer access

For some time, Centrelink's customers had been using each of Centrelink's four service channels: visiting a Centrelink office or agent or using a kiosk, phoning a call centre, using the Internet site, or writing to Centrelink (colloquially called on-site, on-call, online and on-paper). By 2004, 72 per cent were using the telephone, 76 per cent using face-to-face contact, with 20 per cent using other means (and many using more than one channel) (Centrelink 2004c:23).

There were significant variations in the cost to Centrelink of the use of each channel. As Vardon (2002b:59) noted, '[O]ne-to-one service is at the most expensive end of the range and we want to develop it for people who need intensive help.' Others, such as students, 'would prefer to do business electronically and for the government, cheaply'. Vardon added, however, that 'we have learnt that as tempting as it is to open an interactive internet channel, the resources required to do so are prohibitive. We have to go self-service' (Vardon 2002c:13). There were also challenges for many Centrelink customers in gaining computer access and developing confident usage.

The cost of different channels and different activities was reviewed by BCG, which argued that Centrelink should seek to reduce the frequency with which it contacted customers and customers had to contact Centrelink. It estimated that 'notifiable events' (the requirement by the government that customers who were seeking work must report to a Centrelink office every two weeks) accounted for 40 per cent of Centrelink's costs, and recommended that Centrelink campaign to reduce the frequency and cost of these 'events' by using risk profiling, shifting the processing to lower-cost channels, such as call centres or self-service channels, and changing its channel economics to drive down the cost of processing notifiable events (BCG 2002:34–7).

Some of this activity took Centrelink into the realm of policy change and negotiation with its client departments, illustrating how policy decisions influence costs and service delivery. Customer satisfaction surveys showed that Centrelink customers were using more resource-intensive channels, such as face-to-face, for simple transactions such as receiving information and checking payment details. The 2001 customer satisfaction survey found that 53 per cent of respondents had visited a CSC in the previous three months. In terms of Centrelink costs, it was preferable to shift these service transactions to the Internet channel. After these surveys and the BCG report, Centrelink began to manage its multiple channels more actively—for example, it placed a new emphasis on gaining as much information as possible from customers during their initial interview to reduce repeat visits or follow-up calls.

In examining the different costs of each channel and working out which channels were best suited to respond to the range of tasks, Centrelink used a 'service response framework' that identified three main approaches from its customers, each associated with a channel.[6]

In balancing its customer needs and its own costs, Centrelink had to integrate its multiple channels to ensure that customers could use the channels most convenient for them, move smoothly from one channel to another through a common interface, experience reliable data recording from one channel to another and be confident in terms of security and privacy. Centrelink underwent a significant program of business process re-engineering. In association with this channel-management project was the project looking at where work was done in Centrelink and arguing for greater consolidation and specialisation—the creation of the CSSCs. The aim was to drive down costs and lead to 'better quality decision making and more timely and more efficient service delivery' (Hickey 2004).

The management of channels required greater flexibility within the organisation in the use of organisational resources, development of broader staff skills and understanding how customers viewed particular channels, in terms of trust and privacy, and whether these views could be changed (Moore and Flynn 2004:5). It also involved Centrelink in seeking customer advice and feedback on the design of the services they used.

The issue of channel management was closely related to customer satisfaction levels. A Service Integration Survey in 2003 on call centre and CSC service concluded that customer satisfaction was lowest when customers had to deal with multiple staff and/or channels (DBM Consultants Pty Ltd 2003c). It was also shown that those who had repeatedly used call centres for one piece of business had a more negative view of Centrelink, while those who made repeated visits to CSCs were among the most positive of those surveyed. For more complex matters, all categories of respondents (except those who had used only call centres) expressed a preference for dealing with Centrelink in person at a Centrelink office (DBM Consultants Pty Ltd 2003c:41, 44).

The research also showed that customers had more confidence in the CSCs than they did in the call centres. At the same time, another survey showed Centrelink staff believed that most payment problems were the result of office staff, not call centre staff, who were considered to be better trained and more up-to-date with legislative changes (DBM Consultants Pty Ltd 2003c:43, 48).[7] This was not good news for Centrelink in terms of reducing costs, as visits to CSCs remained the most costly of all service channels.

The IT Refresh initiative to increase the stability and capacity of Centrelink's IT systems and to make self-service more easy and interactive was regarded as crucial to Centrelink shifting from high to lower-cost services. The $312 million program over five years was designed to improve service delivery and to provide customers with greater choice, particularly through technology that supported self-service options (Centrelink 2004c).

As Centrelink increasingly linked its services with those of other organisations—business, educational and community—its customers often received services from a group of organisations working through the Centrelink gateway. The capacity of the IT systems to capture data and make them available to other channels in an accurate and consistent way was regarded as critical to customer satisfaction and seamless service.

Assurance and accuracy

Despite the DSS's reputed emphasis on accurately interpreting and administering social security legislation, its May 1997 customer satisfaction survey reported that its lowest ratings for regional and counter staff overall were for 'accuracy of advice/recording and consistency of information' (63 per cent) and 'decision-making/responsible for getting things done' (62 per cent). By November, both of these had risen to 65 per cent. The telephone centre staffers were rated higher on both counts (69 per cent on both in May 1997, and 71 and 70 per cent, respectively, in November 1997).

Centrelink's strong emphasis on satisfying its customers led to concern in client departments that insufficient effort was being made to achieve high levels of accuracy and to protect the integrity of government outlays. This was not just an issue for Centrelink clients, but was important for customers. Accurate decision making is an essential component of good customer service and is as important as friendly, helpful staff or good queue management. The customer satisfaction surveys indicated that the main concerns of customers regarding the payment process were 'regularity and timing' and accuracy of payments. In these areas, Centrelink had performed well, rating 89 per cent for regularity and timing and 78 per cent for accuracy in 2000 and 93 per cent and 79 per cent, respectively, in 2001. Nevertheless, there had been numerous occasions when the media had reported stories of Centrelink errors that highlighted problems related to the capabilities of staff, IT systems and management systems. Centrelink's public reputation was affected by these incidents.

An ANAO report in 2000 highlighted issues of accuracy. It examined Centrelink's assessment of new claims for the age pension and questioned the validity of the accuracy measures. The ANAO judged Centrelink's performance against its own performance indicators, as well as gauging the accuracy of Centrelink's own reporting on compliance. The audit did not question the reasonableness of the standard or its achievability. The ANAO (2001a:20) concluded that Centrelink 'could not assure payment at the right rate, from the right date, to the right person with the right product for approximately half of new claims for the Age Pension assessed during the audit sample period'. It also asserted that Centrelink

> did not report accurate data to…[DFaCS] under the Business Partnership Agreement [BPA] on the level of accuracy of its assessments of such new claims for the audit sample period; and…did not employ adequate preventive controls to ensure the accuracy of new claims for the audit sample period. (ANAO 2001a:20)

It estimated the real error rate for new claims at 52.1 per cent, not, as reported by Centrelink to DFaCS and parliament, 97 per cent and 98 per cent accuracy in the two years between 1998 and 2000. The error rate estimated by the ANAO indicated a level of performance well below the 95 per cent accuracy standard agreed in Centrelink's BPA with DFaCS.

In response, Centrelink redoubled its efforts to achieve the accuracy of decisions and processes expected by the government and its purchaser agencies. Centrelink scrutinised and tightened its quality-control processes under the general banner of 'Getting it right'. This included independent checking, applying minimum standards, building decision support systems to assist Centrelink officers (although these, on the whole, were not successful), testing technical competencies of staff and delivering a national training strategy via satellite technology.

The ANAO audit also served to highlight the level of complexity of this and other welfare policies, such as the 200 rules governing applications for age pensions. In response, the Minister for Family and Community Services, Senator Vanstone, announced an initiative aimed at simplifying the existing administrative requirements and arrangements for new customers when they first accessed pensions, allowances and ancillary benefits (ANAO 2001a:24). The Rules Simplification Taskforce subsequently reported to the minister in August 2001 on simplifying Centrelink processes and guidelines. Its 20 recommendations included the creation of a customer account, streamlined processes, shorter forms, greater use of electronic information transfer and reduced duplication, and establishment of working groups to further investigate policy simplification (ANAO 2002b).

The ANAO report revisited age pensions in 2002. In the intervening period, DFaCS and Centrelink had developed a new BPA in which a distinction was made between correctness and accuracy: correctness related to decision-making processes within Centrelink's control that were required for a correct payment outcome; and accuracy included this, but also recognised the obligation of customers to advise Centrelink of changes in circumstances that could affect payment entitlements. Correctness resulted from interactions between Centrelink staff and customers that led to 'paying the right person, under the right program, at the right rate, for the right date, using the information supplied by the customer. Accuracy requires that these requirements are satisfied every time a payment is made to the customer' (Centrelink 2002a:89).

The ANAO analysis confirmed a previous finding that no more than 3 per cent of the errors were attributable in whole or part to incorrect processing by Centrelink and concluded that 22 per cent of cases could be attributed to customer error—mostly customers not informing Centrelink about changes in their circumstances, as required by law (ANAO 2002b:17). The government approved a subsequent public relations program to encourage customers to notify Centrelink of changes.

A series of surveys of customers to ascertain their expectations noted the importance of accuracy. Customers generally felt Centrelink met customer expectations in 'making accurate and timely payments. However, those who have experienced incorrect payments tended to feel an overall lack of trust towards Centrelink' (DBM Consultants Pty Ltd 2001). Subsequent results showed that this continued to be a problem for Centrelink. In terms of how customers saw Centrelink, in 2001, only 62 per cent of customer survey respondents said 'it can be relied upon to get things right'. Two years later, this view was held by 66 per cent of respondents. In contrast, customer satisfaction with the accuracy of the advice and information provided to them on their most recent contact was much higher. In 2002, it reached a new high of 80.4 per cent for CSCs and 88.6 per cent for call centres. The overall figure for 2004 was 86.2 per cent (Centrelink 2004a:108).[8]

Centrelink's 'Getting it right' strategy continued to be developed to improve payment correctness and eliminate preventable rework. Checklists of 'must dos' supported minimum standards by setting out the essential steps to be followed to improve accuracy in decision making. New assurance arrangements were developed and incorporated into new BPAs with DFaCS, the Department of Employment and Workplace Relations (DEWR) and the Department of Education, Science and Training (DEST). In an attempt to reduce errors and improve consistency, Centrelink was, during 2004, identifying members of its staff with high levels of specialised knowledge and developing specialised teams able to deal with some of the complex and detailed policy implementation tasks. As already noted, it was moving towards greater consolidation and rationalisation of functions and developing 'centres of excellence' for particular specialised services.

Mistakes are costly for Centrelink, administratively and publicly, because they affect the trust customers have in the organisation, impose additional work on staff and use resources better applied to helping customers. Eliminating preventable rework has become an important part of cost effectiveness in the agency. In its first full year, 1998, Centrelink's customer survey reported that almost 25 per cent of respondents said the purpose of their most recent visit to a Centrelink office was to correct a mistake. By 2003, that percentage had dropped to 15 per cent (Senate CALC 2004:36). To find ways of reducing this further, Centrelink surveyed customers who had contacted Centrelink to have a mistake fixed in the previous four months to find out about the cause and nature of the mistake. Vardon reported the key results to the next Senate Estimates Committee: '13 per cent were not mistakes at all. Fifty-five per cent of the mistakes were assessed by one of our staff as Centrelink mistakes' (Senate CALC 19 February 2004:41). For the remainder, 18 per cent of the mistakes were the result of errors on the part of Centrelink and the customer (so Centrelink was partly or wholly responsible for 73 per cent of errors), 25 per cent were wholly the result of customer error and 2 per cent were primarily third-party errors (DBM Consultants Pty Ltd 2003b:22).

Meanwhile, another report by DBM Consultants into service integration found from a random sample of customers that 14 per cent had contacted Centrelink because of a perception of a mistake, confirming Centrelink's survey results of 15 per cent as reported to a senate committee in 2004.

In 2004, the issue hit the press with headlines such as 'Millions of mistakes by Centrelink' (*Australian*, 14 February 2004), 'Centrelink hit by errors' (*AAP*, 14 February 2004) and 'Centrelink's "victims" turn to food charity' (*Australian*, 16 February 2004). According to a reporter, who obtained reports through freedom of information provisions, 1.13 million mistakes had been made over four months in 2003. Centrelink responded with a statement that its customer satisfaction level was at 86 per cent and its accuracy in payments was 96.7 per cent, with only about 20 per cent of the 3.3 per cent of errors directly attributable to Centrelink (*AAP*, 14 February 2004).

The problem for Centrelink was that the first report had taken the 14 per cent who had perceived a mistake from their random sample of 1065 customers in the Service Integration Survey and extrapolated them across the whole Centrelink service, indicating that more than 700 000 customers would be affected by payment errors (DBM Consultants Pty Ltd 2003b:24). Once multiple contacts to fix the mistake were added in, the media concluded that Centrelink had had to address 1.13 million mistakes in the previous four months. Inevitably, talkback radio had several days of lively debate and the reputation of Centrelink was damaged because it was not able to effectively communicate its side of the story.

Underlying this media scrutiny was a serious story: 14 per cent of all customers had experienced a mistake in the previous four months, equating (said the DBM consultants) to more than 700 000 customers, with some experiencing multiple mistakes. Almost one-third of the mistakes were seen as 'very serious' by the customers surveyed, with half the mistakes relating to problems with payments, 23 per cent to inconsistent advice relating to eligibility and 18 per cent to misplaced documentation. While customers attributed the majority of mistakes to the CSCs, most customers (65 per cent) attempted to have the problem fixed by contacting a call centre rather than visiting their CSC. Only 21 per cent initially approached their local Centrelink office. Because there was a range of problems that the call centres could not fix, however, more than one-third of customers were then required to go to their CSC anyway. In all, 22 per cent of customers had to make more than three attempts to have the mistake fixed before this was achieved (DBM Consultants Pty Ltd 2003b:39).

The number of mistakes being made—more than one million in the four months—created a significant and expensive workload for Centrelink, and concern and distress for customers. Customers and Centrelink staff suggested to the consultants a range of initiatives to change problem-creating practices and staff culture. A new emphasis on accurate documentation, increasing the scope of the changes call centres could make and training was instituted.

Centrelink's customers had a much more positive image of Centrelink and awareness of the services it provided than the general community. Centrelink has struggled at times to win the public relations battle in Australia's media. The 2004 media frenzy about Centrelink's error rates was one example illustrating the vulnerability of the agency charged with administering a complex range of benefits programs and services. One chink in the armour was enough to open the floodgates on stories detailing alleged capricious and heartless treatment meted out by agency staff to deserving beneficiaries. It is difficult in the public arena for an agency to communicate the full background of the behaviour of recipients and privacy protocols make it difficult to explain the quality of the relationships they maintain with the agency.

Centrelink was also associated with examples of what was often seen in the community as unpopular, poor or rushed policymaking. The hurried implementation of the new Youth Allowance program in 1998 and new contract arrangements for the Job Network in 2002 and 2004 were such examples. The introduction of the family tax payments in 2004 again exposed Centrelink to the press, though there was some recognition that most of the confusion was due to rushed policymaking on the eve of an election rather than to any failure of implementation.

Customer relationships

Australia has a highly tuned, targeted social welfare system. The Australian Government has sought to target specific groups of citizens in greatest need. One side effect is that a great deal of information about citizens must be stored in order to determine their entitlements. Each time Centrelink makes a payment to a customer, it must consider many other items of information about that person (and sometimes their partner) to ensure that the payment is correct, thereby protecting program outlays. With 6.5 million customers on file, each being paid approximately every fortnight, there is considerable data processing for each pay run. In total, Centrelink was performing about 3.4 billion transactions each year on its mainframe (Centrelink 2003e).

Centrelink regularly sought feedback from customers on service quality and employed several processes for this purpose. While Centrelink initiated customer surveys, other processes—for complaints, reviews and appeals—derived from customers. The ANAO undertook a series of audits of Centrelink's customer charter and the community consultation program, customer satisfaction surveys and systems for handling complaints, reviews and appeals (ANAO 2005a, 2005b, 2005c, 2005d). The ANAO's (2005a:22) overall conclusion was that Centrelink had 'a well developed, extensive and diverse range of customer feedback systems'. There were, however, also opportunities for improving 'the effectiveness, efficiency and economy of the systems and the data they produce. Such improvements would make the systems more accessible to customers, and provide more robust information to Centrelink for use in enhancing its service delivery and identifying cost savings.'

ENDNOTES

[1] The authors of the customer satisfaction surveys pointed out that the very positive attitude to Centrelink in the November 1997 survey, shortly after its launch, which was not matched before or until November 2000, was the result of a halo effect generated by a campaign that 'cultivated a positive impression of the new organisation, which transcended…Centrelink's ratings of service and process areas, as well as corporate image dimensions. In other words, it is possible that the high level of performance in November 1997 may have resulted from a positive halo effect generated by the promotional campaign' (CSS November 2001:23).

[2] There were 12 national customer satisfaction surveys (CSS) that focused on overall perceptions of Centrelink. The first two related to the DSS (November 1996 and May 1997), the next 10 to Centrelink. Until the end of 2000, they were undertaken every six months and then annually until November 2003. The consultants running them varied, as did the titles of the reports, hence the use of CSS and dates to identify each. Many questions also varied, either a lot or a little. Some questions disappeared after a while. Most surveys focused on customers who had had contact with Centrelink in the previous three or six months, but the later surveys expanded the coverage to include all customers, whether they had had contact or not. As a result, the figures should be used carefully to indicate trends and the extent of change rather than treated as directly comparable.

[3] The responses were so strong about the way staff felt unsupported that the written account was modified for fear of offending too many people.

[4] Note that the unemployed still had to be referred to the Job Network for job placement and other services, and that the states handled a range of services delivered to individuals.

[5] The details were: easier, 52 per cent; quicker, 38 per cent; convenient (that is, don't have to leave home or work), 27 per cent; and can be used at any time, 21 per cent).

[6] The three key tasks customers sought were, first, those requiring a transactional response—'just let me do it'; second, those requiring a problem be fixed—'help me'; and third, those requiring personal assistance from Centrelink staff who understood the context of the problem—'relate to me'. The first approach could usually be handled through technology—online or on-call; the second might need a person but not necessarily one face-to face, and could be handled most effectively by the call centres; the third was more likely to require personal, face-to-face interaction. Paper information supported all three channels.

[7] Respondents appreciated the greater convenience of the call centres, but only 29 per cent agreed that 'I have more trust that things will be done right if I ring up the call centre rather than go into the office' (DBM Consultants Pty Ltd 2003c:43).

[8] The significant variation between figures is a reminder of the need to look carefully at which group of customers is being surveyed and the basis of their selection. The national survey in 2003 was drawn from all Centrelink customers and sought primarily an overall view of Centrelink as an organisation, whereas the surveys of satisfaction by channel were drawn only from those who had made contact with Centrelink in the previous four months and sought opinions on their experience of their most recent contact.

6. Governance

Centrelink represents a departure from the APS departmental model because of the scope of its design and operations, in particular its complex and unusual governance arrangements. Its emergence coincided with the growth of corporate governance in the public sector.

Of the four primary stakeholder groups nominated by Centrelink—the portfolio ministers, client departments, internal customers (board of management and agency staff) and the people using Centrelink services—this chapter is concerned with the role of the minister and the board.[1] The central features of Centrelink's governance have been, first, the formal political and executive elements involving the minister, board, departmental secretary and chief executive, and second, their interactions and operations in practice. In other words, there have been three sets of primary relationships, each involving Centrelink and either its board, its minister or the key purchasing departments.[2]

Three perspectives inform the approach to Centrelink's governance. First, there is the corporate governance perspective, which looks at the formal elements of relationships and seeks to compare them and how they operate with good governance principles. The board features here as the key and most interesting element of corporate governance, particularly in consideration of what difference it makes. Second, there is the political management perspective. Here, centrality is given to the minister, who is operating in terms of one of the organisational imperatives, the political, outlined in the introductory chapter. Third, there is the perspective of the agency in its dealings with the other stakeholders. This reflects a second organisational imperative, the entrepreneurial, which requires advocacy and building and mobilising support for activities.

Given such distinctive roles and relationships, how do the actors work through these imperatives and what is the impact on other stakeholders? This chapter explores the governance operations of Centrelink, in particular, the political management of an agency that is outside the formal and normal departmental loop, and the relationship between a board dominated by businesspeople and those concerned with Centrelink's social policy focus.

New governance arrangements

Minister Ruddock (1996:7624) made it clear that Centrelink was to be a statutory agency with full public service responsibilities as

> a core part of government operations. All the mainstream legislation for the operation of Commonwealth departments and agencies will apply to this agency. It will be subject to the *Audit Act*, finance regulations and finance directions…these scrutiny and accountability arrangements are

central to the management structures for the agency given that it will be responsible for the day-to-day administration of large sums of public moneys.

Minister Newman (1997) regarded Centrelink as significant because it would not operate solely within one department or portfolio. This feature had implications for governance.

Governance covers the overall management of the affairs of organisations and is 'generally understood to encompass authority, accountability, stewardship, leadership, direction and control' (ANAO 1997a:1). Elements of good governance include corporate planning, business plans, audit committees, performance information and standards, client service focus and planned and professional development. The main questions of good governance concern appointments to the board and its composition, the role of the board and the relationships between the board, the minister and Centrelink and, finally, the board's impact.

Centrelink, as a statutory agency, operated under the *Financial Management and Accountability (FMA) Act 1997*, which required a high level of accountability. The chairman of its board of management was regarded as the chief executive for the purpose of the *FMA Act* and was given specific powers in the legislation establishing Centrelink, which included direct accountability to the portfolio minister. The accountability and reporting mechanisms were quite complex. Not only did the CEO, who was appointed by the board, report to the board, the CEO reported directly to the minister (or ministers) of client departments and was responsible for the delivery of programs for which these departmental secretaries were funded and accountable. The *Review of Corporate Governance* (Uhrig 2003) commented that Centrelink, while under the *FMA Act*,

> unusually, is also governed by a board. Apparently, given the need to strengthen the governance power of the Centrelink board, the [FMA] Regulations 1997 establish the chairman of the board as the chief executive for *FMA Act* accountability purposes. However, the actual chief executive officer is the agency head for [*Public Service*] Act purposes. This situation creates an anomaly of having two chief executives for accountability and governance purposes.

Centrelink provides the case of an organisation that combines some formal autonomy through corporate governance arrangements (an independently appointed CEO and board) and operations (involving relationships with several departments), with informal features that facilitate conformity with government policy and preferences in politically sensitive fields.

Located within the core public service and a statutory agency, Centrelink is subject to the requirements of a department of state. How its position and relationships operate depends on its statutory basis and practice as it has evolved.

Where functions derive from a department of state and remain in the core, some features will endure. As the organisation's functions have been separated out from those of a department, it is also expected to display non-department-like features, such as being entrepreneurial and business like.

The standard departmental model consists of a direct relationship between a minister and a departmental secretary, who, under the *Public Service Act 1999*, has clear responsibilities in relation to the minister. In contrast, until 2004, Centrelink reported to the minister through the board on administrative issues relating to the portfolio. The client departments are the purchasers of services detailed in negotiated agreements with the agency, which requires effective working relationships to ensure policy is implemented to the standards and quantities agreed.

Centrelink board

Centrelink's complex and unusual governance derived from several features. The agency lay within the Family and Community Services portfolio and was responsible to the Minister for Community Services through an appointed board of management. It was, however, a separate entity to DFaCS and had its own accounting and reporting requirements.

The board was selected by the government and appointed by the Minister for Family and Community Services and consisted of a chairman, the CEO of Centrelink and at least four other members, of whom at least two were not to be principal officers of Commonwealth authorities. Moreover, any principal officer of a Commonwealth authority appointed to the board was not accorded voting rights. While not a requirement of the act, it was the practice until 2002 that the secretaries of the two principal purchasing agencies, DFaCS and the Department of Employment, Workplace Relations and Small Business (DEWRSB), were appointed to the board as non-voting members.

Phases

There have been two principal phases in the development of the board. In the formative period—with a new organisation, the CEO and board chair—considerable time was spent establishing roles and relationships. After about 12 months, the rivalry between Centrelink and its client departments and the clash of personalities between the CEO and the chair created a dysfunctional situation and eventually the chair resigned. He was replaced by John Pascoe, whose style was less confrontational and was more about persuading people to work together (in contrast with his predecessor, who tried 'to bang heads').

In the evolution of the relationship between a new board and a new agency, Centrelink had to 'work out what did the new people control—what did

[Centrelink] control, and what did the board control? And it took us a while to build up a board agenda.' It was necessary, a senior Centrelink official continued,

> to report somehow to the board on how we were going. And then we started to write what we had been doing, and then the board said, 'We want to make the strategic decisions for the organisation.' So we sent up some strategic decisions for them to make...they weren't the sorts of decisions that would make or break the organisation.

In the Pascoe era, the board's role 'evolved towards supporting the management team at Centrelink...Under John's leadership, the current board will stand their ground and support the Centrelink management' (Board member). This period was also important in moving towards better relationships with client departments because there was

> a lot of tension to explode. The chairman let us run for a while, then he slapped the table hard and he said, 'This is intolerable.' We as an organisation can't progress until we and our client departments have a better understanding about what we're on about, and form an alliance. (Senior Centrelink official)

Pascoe introduced the concept of an alliance and insisted that it become the basis of key relationships. The result was 'unquestionably a strong partnership that has grown up between Centrelink and FaCS. As a result of the deliberate relationship between us, we have become very tightly interlinked' (Senior Centrelink official).

Board's role

The board of management set the overall objectives, gave strategic direction and set broad business rules for the organisation (CSDA 1997a).[3] The board was responsible for Centrelink's goals, practices and priorities and focused initially on balancing the need for accountability, risk management and auditing with the demands to achieve best practice in service delivery and reduced costs (Blunn 2000) in order to meet the government's efficiency expectations and to remain competitive in what might become a more commercial environment.

The board's conception of its roles covered a high level of strategic input across a broad canvas (IT, future directions, and so on), ensuring the right financial controls were in place, delivering on budgeted outcomes and management support. What was outstanding was the view that the board's key role was assisting Centrelink's management in setting strategic direction. Another role, according to a Centrelink board member, was

> overseeing Centrelink's financial management and the way in which Centrelink achieves its service targets...And a lot of our time...is spent around the future, where is Centrelink going? What are the challenges

that the agency is going to face? What should we be doing, for example in the area of IT…And generally supporting the CEO, in particular, and management generally, in the carrying out of their roles.

Two equally important roles for the board were to assist the 'day-to-day management team with their strategic view [and] to provide support for the organisation in dealing with issues with the government of the day—because the four of us are outsiders' (Centrelink board member).

Two examples of the board's behaviour indicated how it operated in handling financial and performance aspects. The balanced scorecard became the board's main means of monitoring performance, the 'primary tool used to inform the board on the organisation's performance' (Centrelink 2001c). Significant intervention followed a recommendation from the CEO, when the board commissioned a report by BCG because it 'wanted a better understanding of Centrelink's cost efficiency performance, partly in response to questions raised about Centrelink's costs by its client agencies and other stakeholders' (BCG 2002:9).

Mediating the relationship with client departments emerged as another role. It was felt that there was a need

> to encourage almost a seamless boundary between FaCS and Centrelink so that FaCS can feel totally confident that it knows what's happening at Centrelink, and that there is input into the way in which their services are delivered by Centrelink. But…to some extent, the responsibilities of the secretary of FaCS are tied up with what Centrelink does. So, there's always going to be some creative tension in that relationship. (Centrelink board member)

The board's roles of strategic direction, mediation with the minister, consensus development and legitimisation reflected smart practices in designing and operating steering processes (Bardach 1998:210).

Committees

The board established several committees to help it do its job:

- an Audit and Risk Committee, which was required under the *FMA Act* to ensure that Centrelink 'operated with appropriate financial management and internal controls and in accordance with statutory requirements' (Centrelink 2003b: attachment 4.3)
- an Information and Technology Committee, which advised 'the Board on current performance of the I & T environment as well as on strategic issues and future directions' (Centrelink 2003b: attachment 4.3)
- a Quality Committee, which assisted 'the Board with its responsibilities for ensuring that Centrelink's functions are properly, efficiently and effectively

performed' (Centrelink 2003b: attachment 4.3). The committee also assisted with developing the strategic alignment with customer issues.

Private sector members each chaired one of the committees. One member of the board with a very strong financial background chaired the Audit Committee (initially John Thame, then Elizabeth Montano). Another board member with a strong IT background chaired the Information and Technology Committee (Christina Gillies). A third board member (Don Fraser, who resigned in December 2004), who had spent a lifetime in retail, chaired the Quality Committee and was described by another board member as having 'an enormous understanding for drivers around customer satisfaction'.

The board saw committees as important because of the opportunities provided

> for more informal contact between management and board members, and if you have the right board members, and…a very good mix of skills, the experience of the board members can be put to very good use by Centrelink management for adding value to the things we are trying to do. (Board member)

Relations between the board chairman and Centrelink's CEO

For the chairman, the relationship with the CEO was very important because the

> chairman should be there as a sounding board…that can be particularly important in government organisations, where the CEO…can benefit from being able to talk to someone who is not part of the political process…if there are complementary skills, that's another way of adding value. (Board member)

Much of the chair's role is 'around promoting harmony and making sure that the board is working together all the time' (Board member). Because the relationship between the CEO, the chairman and the board is crucial, it is 'very important that everybody feels totally confident with one another. And that the CEO understands that he or she is supported by his or her colleagues on the board, and…everybody operates in an environment of openness, and complete honesty' (Board member). The chair sought to encourage 'full and open communication between the senior management of Centrelink, and the client departments' (Board member).

The board members

Over the years, the board experienced a changing membership but the preference for 'strong commercial credentials' (Board member) was maintained. Of the seven members of the board, four were usually private industry representatives who brought with them a wide experience of commercial business practices. For example, Pascoe (chairman and non-executive member, 2000–04) came from retailing and was CEO of George Weston Foods; Gillies (non-executive member) came from management positions in banks; Fraser's background was in retailing, supermarkets and customer relations; and Thame came from banking. Their expertise in the retail industry gave them 'bone deep understanding of customer service [and] customer satisfaction' (Board member). Of the other appointments, Susan Rapley was a businesswoman and the last chair, Montano, was a lawyer and consultant with private sector and government experience. In addition, there were initially two departmental secretaries from the main client departments as non-voting members (after 2002, only one, the secretary of DFaCS) and the CEO of Centrelink, Sue Vardon.[4]

The core of the board's skills and expertise, therefore, was based on business sector knowledge and experience and service delivery/network experience. Business thinking lent itself to an organisation aspiring to be entrepreneurial and cutting edge. The 'huge challenge facing Centrelink is around information technology…Centrelink has got to be world's best practice, in the IT area, and my feeling is that we're already at the cutting edge' (Board member). The connection with a private sector-oriented government also meant 'ministers knowing that they have some private enterprise people guiding this organisation [who] will help them' (Board member).

The support of the board was relevant to the evolution of the customer service model because it helped drive the building of a customer-centred culture. The business perspectives of private sector board members helped guide the organisation to a competitive and commercial footing. In a commercial and contestable environment, they helped refine the strategic edge needed to offer improved services at reduced costs and to beat potential competition, particularly in the call centre area.

The philosophy during Pascoe's time as chairman illuminated how businesspeople could relate to a social policy organisation. It was hard nosed but sympathetic:

> Centrelink is not just a cheque payer, it really is a place of contact for many people who are disadvantaged, or alienated, and it can play a very positive role in how those people relate to government and get on with their lives. And…the board can also play a role, working with the executives to make sure that the agency delivers cost-effective service and…makes that contribution back to government by keeping its costs down, by keeping itself at the cutting edge, and by providing a very high level of service to the people who interact with Centrelink. (Board member)

Composition of board and departmental secretaries

While not a requirement of the act, the practice until 2002 was for the secretaries of the two principal purchasing agencies, DFaCS and DEWRSB, to be appointed as non-voting members of the board. The DEWRSB secretary's membership was discontinued in 2002 due to perceptions of a conflict of interest.

There was widespread criticism of the practice of appointing board members from the purchasing agencies. The position essentially was that you could not be on the board if you were also representing a purchasing agency requiring an independent, arm's-length relationship. 'At the moment the Centrelink board is not a separate commercially oriented board, it's a public service board' (Senior DoFA official). A senior Centrelink official appreciated the secretaries' roles during the transition period for the new agency when there needed 'to be an assurance in both resource management and a program deliverer and therefore a political sense that this major structural change wasn't going to just blow up in the government's face. So you can see an element of security…in having the secretaries represented.'

By the early 2000s, it was thought that Centrelink had reached a stage at which it was appropriate to question continuing this practice. One of the arguments was that having the secretaries as board members limited what Centrelink could say to the board because, for some purposes, there was seen to be a conflict of interest in having the purchaser on the provider's board. At the same time, departmental secretaries were regarded as playing distinctive and valuable roles because they

> bring their own insights to Centrelink; it gives us an opportunity…to resolve issues within the board structure and within a collegiate structure…it gives the departmental secretaries an opportunity to understand…in depth the issues that Centrelink faces, and for the board of Centrelink and our management, although they deal with it outside of the board, to understand the drivers for the secretaries of the departments. (Board member)

Centrelink's major job was 'to educate our client departments on what are the major drivers in customer satisfaction. That is, what the customers are saying, as opposed to what the other departments perceive. Now to do that without the two secretaries on the board would be that much more difficult' (Board member).

There was also a mediation role, according to the DFaCS secretary, until 2002:

> These disputes can surface as issues for the board. The secretary has used the board processes to express dissatisfaction, at a fundamental level, with Centrelink's performance vis-à-vis financial reporting. The board shared the concern. Similarly, Centrelink has expressed dissatisfaction with FaCS' interference with management responsibility.

Debate on the board can be helpful in resolving these disputes and therefore helping to ensure effective policy delivery. Because the board sees FaCS as a key partner, and not a predatory monopsonist, it is able to steer a middle path and to mediate between a purchaser and its own agency. (Rosalky 2002:11)

There was a dilemma in acting in Centrelink's interests across departments compared with the special interests of DFaCS.

Challenging the government on IT

In one prominent case, the board's advice challenged the government's official position. The government had a policy of outsourcing IT services. The board members agreed that the proposed approach was a serious threat to the security of Centrelink's operations and therefore to social security program delivery. According to a board member, '[T]he IT outsourcing issue is a pretty good example of where the board empathised, and agreed where Centrelink was coming from...John Pascoe in particular put in a case very strongly with the support of all of us'. 'Eventually, and close to the denouement, the government began to listen to the voices of the external directors—the public officials were not trusted to act in other than their own interests—and the Humphry inquiry was set up' (Rosalky 2002:4).[5] '[We] wouldn't let go of [the] board for all the tea in China, because they came to the fore when, over IT outsourcing...they took a stand when the public service people couldn't' (Senior Centrelink official).

The Humphry report (2000) concluded that, while it was the 'prerogative of the government to set overall direction, the introduction of the FMA and CAC [*Commonwealth Authorities and Companies*] Acts places responsibility for implementation of policies with chief executives and boards. Accordingly future responsibility for implementing the Initiative should be fully devolved to agency chief executives or boards.' The government agreed (Halligan 2001). On Centrelink, the report (Humphry 2000) concluded: 'The outsourcing process for Centrelink should not proceed until the Centrelink board is satisfied that the transition and implementation risks can be effectively managed.' Again, the government agreed, which, in effect, was a face-saving way of allowing Centrelink to proceed by outsourcing only what its board wished to outsource.

The great value of the external representation on the board to the governance systems was most apparent during this outsourcing debate.

There is absolutely no doubt [that] Centrelink would not have been able to influence the direction of government policy to the extent that we were able to...the potential role of the board in carrying on that role in a much broader context...is an extremely potentially powerful force, something that [we need to] retain at any cost. (Senior Centrelink official)

Reciprocity in the relationship with the minister

The primary relationship for the board and Centrelink must be with the minister. The minister and the government more generally play a determining role in strategic directions in accordance with policy preferences and management objectives. Almost all governments modified and amended social welfare and employment policies during their lifetime, so a degree of policy change was anticipated—but not the radical changes that occurred soon after Centrelink's inception. The government undertook a wholesale review of social welfare and the policy decisions taken in 2001 flowing on from that review substantially changed how Centrelink operated and significantly extended its core business.

There was a perceived problem with DFaCS when it initiated policy without discussing delivery with Centrelink (Board member). A Centrelink view was that 'it would like a place at the policy table'. A board member advanced the view that

> we can ensure that our views are heard by working with the secretaries of our client departments, and trying to ensure that they understand completely what Centrelink's views are, and where we are coming from. And that can be reinforced by the contact which the Centrelink board, and Centrelink management [have] with the relevant ministers. [There has] been a very good working relationship between the board of Centrelink and the management of Centrelink, and the ministers, Jocelyn Newman, Larry Anthony and Amanda Vanstone.

As chairman of the board, Pascoe had a close relationship with the government.

The chair had financial responsibilities under the act. He would report to the minister on board proceedings after each meeting and periodically meet with the minister to discuss Centrelink issues. It was initially more regular and routine, but as they got to know each other, it became on the basis of need. The board, according to Rosalky (2002:8), was concerned largely with 'navigating the course that it interprets government has ordained for it'.

It was also understood that the CEO would keep the minister well informed. 'We're all working together as a board in making sure that the minister is properly informed, and [are] really very happy for Sue to keep the minister up to date' (Board member).

The CEO reported to the minister once a week about what was happening and, as a consequence, was depicted as being 'much more intimately connected to the decisions of Centrelink' than the board (Senior Centrelink official).

The agency is subject to the legislative requirement that it performs any function directed by the ministers in writing to the chairman of the board (with details to be provided in the annual report for the agency for that year), and providing it has consulted with the board before issuing directions (CSDA 1997a: s. 8–9). The minister's directions to the board can cover the 'performance of its functions, the exercise of its powers or the conduct of its meetings, or in relation to the terms and conditions of appointment of the chief executive officer' (CSDA 1997a: s. 13).

While ministers have the power under Centrelink's legislation to intervene directly in Centrelink's affairs, such occurrences have been rare. Two examples come to mind. The first was in July 2000, when the minister notified the board of the government's policy in relation to IT outsourcing. The second was in January 2001, when there was a change in approach and the minister notified the board of their power to make decisions to outsource IT infrastructure in accordance with the government's new policy approach (Centrelink 2001a:25).

The secretary of DFaCS for much of Centrelink's existence provided insights into a different relationship: the relationship between the minister and the department responsible for purchasing services from Centrelink. Several types of ministerial intervention were indicated: 'Cost-reducing management strategies...have been overruled by the minister as a potential political threat...The minister required close oversighting [sic] by the portfolio secretary of politically sensitive decisions within the prerogative of the Centrelink management' (Rosalky 2002:10).

There is evidence from the original design and subsequent practice that ministerial accountability could continue to operate as under the former DSS. Ministers routinely accepted public responsibility for Centrelink's activities: the agency's performance was defended and new services announced by the minister. Ministerial correspondence in relation to Centrelink was handled as if staff were dealing with a department. Less politically attractive decisions, however, such as retrenchments, were matters for Centrelink management (Mulgan 2002:52–4). Mulgan's (2002:54–5) overall conclusion about ministerial responsibility was that there were

> slight changes of emphasis but no major breaks with convention. Ministers still take responsibility for administrative decisions, particularly in Parliament. Except for issues of staffing and employment conditions, there has been no public attempt to delineate separate spheres of public responsibility and accountability for ministers and the Centrelink managers as implied by the Act.

The significance of 'oversight mechanisms', political and executive, in supporting large-scale change is well established (Nutt 2004). An important role of the Centrelink board was to contribute to the steering function and to act as a buffer and an intermediary between the public service agency and politicians. With the life-events case (see Chapter 5), it was about affirming the extension of a service delivery role that had major policy implications. The secretaries of the two main client departments were members of the board at that time and could be expected to be supportive of life events within that arena. Securing the support of the board was tantamount to tying in key departments as well as the government's business sector appointees who had access to the minister.

On the political side, there was a close symbiotic relationship between the ministers and Centrelink and, in particular, the CEO. There was a need to be highly responsive to new political requirements, particularly those with public implications, and to reflect more generally government priorities. In these respects, Centrelink was poised to respond like a department of state and this could be problematic when it was confronting the primary department within the same portfolio. More significant was the role in which the purchaser and the provider were involved. The close relationship between Centrelink and the minister did mean, in the view of a former secretary of DFaCS, that the department at times was seemingly either marginalised or at least out manoeuvred: 'The minister intervened directly with Centrelink regularly in a direct one-to-one link with the CEO, overriding the roles of the secretary and the board' (Rosalky 2002:10).

Given that Centrelink had responsibilities for one of the largest components of the budget, with programs that could be highly sensitive, this forging of a direct relationship with its minister was not unexpected. Ministers accepted responsibility for Centrelink. There are also expectations and pressures to respond to government agendas and public crises with regular use made of Centrelink's capacity to deliver assistance to people (for example, support for those affected by drought, economic structural reforms and the Bali bombings). A difficulty arises, however, in relation to other imperatives that also drive Centrelink. Since Centrelink was part of the Family and Community Services portfolio, the responsible ministers regarded it as a department of state rather than a separate service delivery agency that was operating at arm's length.

> When the minister wants a call centre to be set up quickly to do something, he just calls on Centrelink to do it. And they just do it, and no one actually worries about what the charge will be, and who's going to negotiate the contract—that comes afterwards. (Central agency official)

Reconciling general and specific agendas was also problematic. Major cutbacks in staff (mandated by government expectations of efficiencies) coincided with the demands of major policy change. According to the former secretary of DFaCS, ministerial priorities produced frequent changes in outputs that could not be captured in the purchaser–provider relationship and 'undermined the terms of business agreements between the two organisations' (Rosalky 2002:10). The department's attempts at oversight were frustrated by such departures.

The situation, as represented by a senior Centrelink official, was more complex:

> The truth is, it was the politicians who hadn't let go of the board, they hadn't let go of their power for the board. And to this day it remains the biggest government issue. Because the politicians think they run Centrelink. But the board thinks they run Centrelink. The secretaries think they run Centrelink. Centrelink is not satisfactory unless they're totally happy. And so we've got this very subtle power shift.

The fate of governance

The relationships between the key players—ministers, the board and Centrelink—have evolved with time. Various modes of operation were reached regarding the nexus of relationships and how to handle political dimensions.

There was much that was commendable in how these arrangements were worked through. If there were unconventional governance elements they were made to work in practice by the key participants. The practical realities of the conduct of governance, however, mattered less for steering the system. The government's *Review of Corporate Governance* (Uhrig 2003:45) was insensitive to the subtleties of corporate governance practice in this case. It observed that under the *FMA* and *Public Service Acts*, the chairman of the board and the CEO had responsibilities and this created the anomaly of two chief executives for accountability and governance. The review 'identified the need for a consistent approach to structuring agencies and establishing effective governance frameworks, including where to use boards and the application of the FMA and CAC Acts' (Uhrig 2003:46).

Several tensions and issues in governance were apparent, including the internal contradictions in the model. These questions touched on the impact on departmental secretaries and were related to the move towards a more mature partnership with client departments. In the end, Centrelink emerged during its formative years much like a department of state, in part because of pressures to fit the core public service culture. This was simply confirmed when new corporate governance arrangements were introduced.

ENDNOTES

[1] Other papers cover the relationship with client departments, customers and other stakeholders: secondary clients, the Public Service and community.

[2] In addition to the portfolio minister, a junior minister could have Centrelink responsibilities.

[3] The act states 'to decide the agency's goals, priorities, policies and strategies; and to ensure that the agency's arrangements are properly, efficiently and effectively performed' (CSDA 1997a: s.12).

[4] Two later non-executive appointments were David de Carvalho, CEO of the National Catholic Education Commission, and David Deans, CEO of the National Seniors Association.

[5] The government announced an independent review into the 'Whole of Government IT Outsourcing Initiative' on 7 November 2000, to be conducted by Richard Humphry (2000).

7. Relationships with client departments

Relationships with other agencies are significant to public organisations. These relationships are especially important for a delivery agency that is defined in terms of the services that it provides for policy departments. This is even more the case when this relationship is formalised through purchaser–provider arrangements.

By far the most important relationship for Centrelink in its formative years was that with DFaCS. This accounted for most of its services. Centrelink also provided services to a range of other Commonwealth departments although the total proportion was relatively insignificant. They included DEWR, DEST, the Department of Health and Ageing (DoHA) and the Department of Agriculture, Fisheries and Forestry Australia (DAFFA). The most relevant central agency was the Department of Finance and Administration (DoFA) because of its role in overseeing financial management in the APS.

As Chapter 1 indicated, Centrelink was the product of an unusual opportunity in the mid-1990s, which dictated some of the features of the organisation in terms of key principles (such as purchaser–provider functions) and the need for streamlining to achieve savings. The original concept envisaged a policy/delivery split that would produce a large agency with several small policy departments. The delineation of the interface between policy and delivery ended up adding a middle area representing program management or operational policy. The department retained product design of delivery and program control and the policy department and agency competed in the middle ground.

There has been some confusion about the nature of the core relationship, how it should be conceptualised and depicted and the extent to which it has evolved with time. The relationship has come out of two impulses: one to separate policy and execution; the second to define the relationship in terms of purchaser–provider relationships. Neither required the other, and each was the subject of variation in practice.

Bases of relationships

Part of each role in a newly formed purchaser–provider relationship is to become skilled in contract management. This is complicated when each side includes former colleagues doing substantially the same job as before. The tension between the insistence on viewing the relationship as a partnership—as much management rhetoric has demanded—and a type of contract is an additional factor in the development of 'smart buying' skills. A further factor is the contrast between the concept of a one-stop shop, with its overtones of monopoly, and the conventional purchaser–provider model, with implications of competition among providers.

On the other hand, as noted in a study of social security delivery mechanisms (Mabbett and Bolderson 1998:9), one of the rewards of studying devolved administrative systems is that institutional separation brings out into the open issues that are repressed internally in a centralised system. In the case of the Centrelink arrangements, there were 'repressed tensions' as a legacy of the old DSS and new ones embedded in the very structural arrangements that Centrelink represented (Rowlands 2003).

From the point of view of the departments using Centrelink, a key question was whether or not they could become 'smart purchasers' of the 'products' of Centrelink as a delivery agency (Kettl 1993). The most obvious problem was maintaining sufficient understanding of program delivery to inform policy development and to enable it to specify policy 'products' to purchase from Centrelink. As one APS departmental secretary noted: 'A lot of the policy comes out of administration and policy that is developed without fully understanding the way it's going to be managed, almost always goes wrong' (Halligan et al. 1996:15).

Central relationships

The new agency's relationships with its client departments were to be through purchaser–provider arrangements, governed by a contractual agreement with each. These agreements evolved from service agreements into more comprehensive documents entitled Business Partnership Agreements (BPAs). As discussed earlier, BPAs established the scope and provided the detail for a formal purchaser–provider relationship between two organisations, and were used to manage and review the operating and performance relationships between them.

Centrelink's revenue came overwhelmingly from client departments, with a small percentage coming as direct appropriation from the government (Table 7.1). Each client (usually a policy department) negotiated a purchase price for specified services that Centrelink agreed to undertake. The BPAs detailed the services, the funding arrangements, agreed performance outcomes and related reporting mechanisms. The majority (92.4 per cent in 2003–04) of Centrelink's business was undertaken for DFaCS, with DEWR a distant second (5.3 per cent). The other 14 Commonwealth purchasers (10 departments and four agencies), plus the states and territories, accounted for 2.3 per cent of Centrelink's revenue.

The relationships with other agencies are summarised briefly here before turning to the main cases. As Table 7.1 indicates, these other contractual arrangements can be less stable with time: they involve purchasing services that can decline or fluctuate (for example, with DoHA) or even stop once the task has been completed (for example, with DAFFA).

Table 7.1 Centrelink relationships by revenue, 2003–04 to 2006–07

	2003–04	2004–05	2005–06	2006–07
Department	$'000	$'000	$'000	$'000
Family and Community Services	1 951 091	2 005 272	2 017 321	2 016 456
Employment and Workplace Relations	111 800	106 000	106 000	106,000
Education, Science and Training	13 543	13 579	13 732	13 908
Health and Ageing	8 229	6 351	6 059	5 386
Agriculture, Fisheries and Forestry	8 887	1 993	326	426
Subtotal (service delivery)	2 093 550	2 133 195	2 143 438	2 142 409
Revenue from other sources*	18 681	15 592	14 168	14 233
Total	**2 112 231**	**2 148 787**	**2 157 606**	**2 156 409**

*Includes directly appropriated amounts and anticipated revenue from new business outside existing partnerships and other agreements with client agencies.
Source: DFaCS 2003:263.

For example, Centrelink was responsible for the day-to-day administration of the Tasmanian Freight Equalisation Scheme and the Bass Strait Passenger Vehicle Equalisation Scheme. It made all payments of financial assistance under those schemes, while the Department of Transport and Regional Services (DoTRS) retained all responsibility for policy matters. The Minister for Transport and Regional Services, John Anderson, wrote to Minister Anthony as input to the Centrelink Review saying that DoTRS and Centrelink were generally in day-to-day contact on a range of administrative and policy issues. DoTRS received monthly performance reports from Centrelink. Although, at that time, the service arrangement had been in 'full operation' for only a short period, DoTRS was 'very pleased with the performance of Centrelink'.

Department of Family and Community Services

The DSS/DFaCS purchased most Centrelink services and only this department could buy these same services. In fact, most of the services DFaCS purchased or funded were bought from Centrelink. While there was nothing in the legislation requiring Centrelink to undertake work for the DSS/DFaCS, there was a clear expectation that it would continue to do so and there was a provision in the legislation that allowed the minister to instruct it to do so.

Formal agreements under the *CSDA Act* needed to be put in place to authorise Centrelink to undertake work for the DSS. The first agreement between the DSS and Centrelink, the Strategic Partnership Agreement (SPA), was drafted quickly by a small team. The document, a 10-page 'core agreement' with some 84 pages of various 'protocols' and 'memoranda', largely set out what the DSS formally required and what Centrelink would deliver during 1997–98. The SPA also provided for committees at operational and senior management levels to facilitate the two organisations in conducting their business. The document was succinct compared with later such agreements.

At the end of the first year, a new agreement was signed with the name Business Partnership Agreement 1998–2001, reflecting the view of the relationship of the new departmental secretary, Dr David Rosalky. This was intended as a three-year agreement, with an expectation that some modification would be undertaken if necessary at the end of each year. The level of specification, however, had now expanded substantially and the agreements grew accordingly (for details, see Rowlands 2003).

A major point to bear in mind when analysing the DSS/DFaCS–Centrelink relationship was the near monopoly–monopsony arrangement. Equally important was that even though there was an influx of staff to Centrelink initially from other organisations and an attempt by Centrelink to define itself as 'not the DSS', the two organisations were once one. That had a strong practical effect on continuing relationships at a personal level between officers who formerly worked together and at an aggregate level between organisational units and the organisations as a whole. The main dimensions are examined later in this chapter.

Department of Employment and Workplace Relations[1]

Centrelink's second most important purchaser–provider relationship was with DEWR, later renamed the Department of Employment, Workplace Relations and Small Business (DEWRSB). The department took a different stance to DFaCS in its relationship with Centrelink, especially on Centrelink's performance. DEWRSB's key objective in 1999 was building an effective partnership between purchaser and provider. Centrelink was acknowledged as being committed to this approach but it was difficult to achieve with the provider having a monopoly over most services delivered and when issues existed over the pricing of these services.

The position of DEWR was argued to have been different to that of DFaCS because about $1 billion worth of services were bought in the market based on service delivery arrangements that were almost entirely outsourced. Employment services were being delivered through 200 providers in the Job Network and services were also bought from a network of community work coordinators and providers for the delivery of Work for the Dole projects, the Return to Work Program and community sport programs.

In each case, these arrangements were a product of a competitive tender that was mostly price competitive. There was therefore a competitive market, in which the price of services was known and contracts allowed people and organisations to lose or gain business according to their performance against standards. The contrast with the Centrelink situation was that the department was negotiating with a government monopoly without generally having an alternative (Senior departmental official).

From DEWRSB's point of view, the main obstacle to a viable relationship with Centrelink was differences about the costs of services being purchased. The department regarded Centrelink's role as crucial to the implementation of the government's mutual obligation policy for the unemployed. In 1999, at the time of an official but private review of Centrelink, there was concern about how policy might founder on the quality of the management. The DEWRSB position appeared to question Centrelink's commitment and effectiveness in implementing its services.

Centrelink's interaction with the unemployed had been (as with the DSS before it) more demanding than that with other recipients of income support. Recipients in the pensioner and family payment categories tended to interact only at the time they lodged a claim for a payment and at various review points, perhaps a year or so apart. In contrast, the number of personal interactions with job seekers was much higher. As well, the prominence of the mutual obligation policy in public debate helped increase the relative importance of the services being purchased by DEWRSB in comparison with those purchased by DFaCS.

DEWRSB's experience with the Job Network and purchaser–provider arrangements through managing labour market programs led it to require strong, explicit contestability for specific components of service delivery, and to moving the Centrelink operation towards a contestable environment. It was apparent to DEWRSB, however, that Centrelink did not fully appreciate the implications of a purchaser-provider approach in terms of being responsive to the purchaser and consistent in service delivery (Rowlands 2002). This produced frustration when the department had contractual obligations with its Job Network service providers.

One difficulty in this relationship, which was also common to that between the DSS and DEETYA, was uncertainty about who was the client. For the DSS, the unemployed person was the client, while DEETYA related to industry. This problem had been identified by Moran (1996:19) in vocational education and training: 'An emphasis on competition within vocation[al] education and training has meant that the definition of "the client" has been a difficult and controversial point to resolve…at least as far as governments are concerned, the principal client is industry.' The DEWRSB view was influenced partly by the perspective of the private organisations it served. Its more robust view than DFaCS', assuming DEWRSB to be a successor to DEETYA, could also reflect an organisation that had lost a regional network and an operational arm (ie CES) (Rowlands 2002).

DEWRSB was, however, able to cite performance information to substantiate its views. DEWRSB had retained its own computing systems—unlike DFaCS, whose main IT facilities went to the new Centrelink—and was therefore less dependent on Centrelink for management information. In addition, DEWRSB had developed experience in working in a genuinely contestable environment—specifically with the Job Network—and was enthusiastic about seeking the competitive supply of Centrelink services. It had consciously removed work—the Community Support Program—from Centrelink and outsourced it to private providers (DEWRSB 2001). It had also arranged independent customer surveys of Centrelink performance, something DFaCS had never done. It seems likely that the more businesslike and formal approach DEWRSB took to managing its relationship with Centrelink helped the ANAO form a more positive view of the arrangements between the two organisations. The ANAO attributed this to more formal consultation between the organisations at various levels and better performance reporting and analysis (ANAO 1999b:85).

DEWR then took a more aggressive role than DFaCS in dealing with Centrelink and was suspicious of its potential monopoly position. According to Rosalky (2002:8–9), DEWR worked with central agencies, such as the Department of Prime Minister and Cabinet and DoFA to limit Centrelink's independence.

From Centrelink's point of view, much of the problem was that DFaCS and DEWR provided different instructions in relation to the unemployed (differences that were echoed at the ministerial level). According to Vardon (Interview), 'They played football with my head as the ball' because they could not reconcile the different policy positions.

Central agency: Department of Finance and Administration

DoFA did not have a direct relationship with Centrelink as it had with policy departments because Centrelink's funding was appropriated overwhelmingly to departments which then purchased services from it. Nevertheless, DoFA's view of Centrelink was important because as an agency it reflected and influenced the views of key ministers and therefore had a major influence on government agendas. One example of this power was its role in the annual budget process. It provided advice to ministers in cabinet's Expenditure Review Committee on the proposals brought to it by individual ministers.

Second, DoFA had a strong role in public sector reform for many years. DoFA's support for the creation of Centrelink was attracted by casting the arrangements in the purchaser–provider form as well as by providing an opportunity for savings in operating costs. The secretary of DoFA viewed the split as comprising 'the effective re-engineering of DEETYA and DSS to become essentially policy departments purchasing services from other suppliers (either in the public sector or elsewhere)' (Sedgwick 1996). There was, however, an unfinished agenda from DoFA's point of view in terms of the full implementation of the model. Under the devolved financial management and accountability arrangements, DoFA was charged with ensuring that the government was obtaining value for money when purchasing services from Centrelink and it retained strong views about the agency and the nature of the institutional arrangements.

DoFA's position was that there was a need for reform in two areas to enable Centrelink to deliver a more efficient and higher-quality service. Both of these areas were seen as significant purchase issues: the appropriateness of Centrelink's governance arrangements and corporate form; and the financial arrangements that underpinned these structures. It was clear that DoFA did not see the 1997 arrangements as final. In particular, it was not convinced that representation of purchasers on the board of Centrelink conformed to best-practice governance arrangements. DoFA continued to see Centrelink as a business enterprise. It viewed Centrelink as an 'income support business' and part of an 'income support industry'. Government ownership of Centrelink was seen as comparable with that of Employment National and Telstra and there was preference for a private sector model for delivery.

DoFA supported the position that a contestable environment and genuine purchasing of services produced improvements in quality and price reductions. Its view, however, was that Centrelink did not have genuine competitors. Departments had to use Centrelink to deliver income support services and Centrelink was legislatively required to deliver these services. The purchaser–provider model had not worked with DFaCS because it was not sufficiently at arm's length.

From DoFA's perspective, the crucial issue in setting a course for Centrelink's development was how the government ultimately wanted income support to be delivered. Two broad options were envisaged. The first model was income support operations that were fully integrated into the core business of government, and represented the old DSS, the model the Howard Government had moved away from. The second was income support operations separate from government. If there was no middle position, the obvious conclusion was that stability would be achieved only by either moving back or completing the move away from government. What DoFA apparently could not accept was a hybrid. What it seemed to find particularly frustrating was that, while Centrelink was a separate agency, with a CEO appointed by a board in turn appointed by the government, it was not sufficiently distant from the government. The issue turned on the trade-off between control and efficiency. Locating operations at arm's length was meant to facilitate improvements in efficiency and service quality through exposure to the market and best business practice at the expense of direct ministerial control.

Relational issues

Several types of issues have been salient, deriving from the nature of the split, the debates about funding and the costs of the arrangement.

Roles in the DFaCS–Centrelink relationship

The consultant firm Rush Social Research Agency undertook the first independent analysis of the relationship between Centrelink and its major client in early 1998. The purpose of this review was to examine the working relationship between the two organisations, particularly by focusing on the original service agreement between them, the SPA. It was based on interviews with 'key managers' in Centrelink and what was then still the DSS.

The consultants concluded that there was a 'positive attitude' attributable partly to many of those involved having formerly worked together. They reported, however, a 'lack of clarity around the boundaries between policy and delivery'. An idea of 'partnership' also flowed from the two organisations having one minister and the 'sink or swim together' situation of the two. This needed to be taken into account along with the formal purchaser–provider arrangement. The collaboration between the two organisations was, however, failing: 'more emphasis needs to be placed on the importance of co-organisational planning and strategic mechanisms for collaboration at executive and managerial levels' (Rush Social Research 1998:8).

The consultants reported a host of seemingly equal and opposite complaints about communication and perceptions of roles. From Centrelink's perspective, the DSS was not able to 'let go' of delivery matters that the former saw as its domain. Similarly, the DSS perceived Centrelink as 'butting in' on policy matters that were the domain of the DSS. While the DSS complained of slowness and the unreliability of data provided to it by Centrelink (especially management information on programs as well as on Centrelink performance in delivery), Centrelink complained of a lack of clarity in these requests and insufficient funding to meet them (Rush Social Research 1998:7–10).

The report summarised the perceived threats and fears (Table 7.2). Some of the concerns seemed to flow directly from the rhetoric of prospective contestability. This was apparent, for example, where the DSS expressed concern about the prospect of Centrelink using its DSS-supplied resources to reduce prices for other client departments. Similarly, Centrelink was concerned that if the DSS found other service delivery agents, this will be used to press Centrelink to reduce its prices. In practice, neither of these outcomes eventuated in any substantial way. DFaCS did not engage any other major service delivery agents and so much of Centrelink's funding still came from that source that DFaCS could not be losing substantially through cross-subsidisation of other departments' work. Both agreed that there was a need for more transparency and trust between the two organisations.

Table 7.2 The DSS and Centrelink: mutual perceptions

The DSS thinks...	Centrelink thinks...
Centrelink will use DSS resources to facilitate discounting their services to other clients.	To some extent, the agreements with other departments are better elucidated than the agreement with the DSS.
They are seen as 'tied in' to Centrelink because currently there is a lack of other suitable service providers: 'Centrelink think they have us over a barrel.'	The DSS can look elsewhere for service delivery agents and use this as 'leverage' against Centrelink.
The DSS feels it is losing control over delivery, which has an impact on the way it achieves its ministerial requirements.	The DSS does not credit Centrelink with the expertise to develop more efficient ways of delivery and won't allow entrepreneurial activity in this.
The DSS feels that Centrelink keeps it in the dark by not providing good data, and this is because it fears being 'judged'.	The DSS makes unreasonable requests for information/data that are over and above those agreed in the SPA and does not provide further funding to help allocate resources to answer its needs.
Centrelink is performing well (no disasters) but needs good data to realise the DSS's role as a monitor of performance.	Centrelink feels the DSS performance indicators are inadequate, too process oriented and need to be explicit about outcomes.
Micro-policy dealing with delivery mechanisms stays with the DSS as part of its policy role.	DSS interference in delivery modes stretches resources to the limit.
	The DSS needs to include Centrelink in discussions on new micro and other policies to ensure it does not request deliverables that are NOT deliverable.
Some areas (micro-policy) cannot be too rigidly specified: these 'fuzzy' areas are where partnership will be cemented.	Some areas (micro-policy) cannot be too rigidly specified: these are areas where partnership is necessary.

Source: Rush Social Research 1998:10–11. Adapted from Rowlands 2003.

There are several possible interpretations of the results (Rowlands 2003). First, they can be seen as a predictable set of attitudes emerging between the members of two organisations that have been separated in this way. Second, they can be seen as evidence of the sort referred to by Mabbett and Bolderson (1998:9) of repressed issues being brought out into the open by institutional separation. Even a rather self-congratulatory review of the DSS–Centrelink split drafted some six months after the formal separation acknowledged the following lesson: 'frustrations and performance problems that were once contained within the original unitary organisation are exposed, gain greater visibility and can rapidly lead to inter-organisational conflict in the new environment' (Worthington 1999:23).

During the development of the 1998–2001 BPA, the ANAO conducted an audit of the performance assessment framework specified in the agreements between the principal purchasers and Centrelink. The audit examined whether this framework provided an adequate assessment of performance. It covered the monitoring and reporting of performance; the process of developing the 1998–99 agreements; the performance information contained in the agreements, including the accuracy and reliability of the data for performance measurement; the cost of providing performance information; and the progress made by the organisations in defining and costing outputs and outcomes (ANAO 1999b). The audit was in progress as the 1998–99 agreements were being negotiated between Centrelink and the departments, which meant that the ANAO's expectations had some influence on the new DSS–Centrelink agreement.

The ANAO was positive about the new BPA, but found that performance reports provided by Centrelink to DFaCS contained little analysis of significant variations in performance. Therefore, when the data provided were examined, the reason for under/over-performance was not given. This made it difficult for the responsible party to take action to address performance problems. The ANAO (1999b:2.15) also reported that DFaCS staff were generally satisfied with the content of the performance reports, but were dissatisfied with the level of analysis of the performance variations.

The relationship between DFaCS and Centrelink had still not yet matured (but see the next chapter). An internal audit by DFaCS of the management of the relationship reported that its staff members were unclear about what they should be regularly doing to manage the relationship. Staff primarily regarded the relationship with Centrelink as a partnership, but this view seemed to flow from the lack of discipline and sanctions comparable with those in place for other relevant purchaser–provider arrangements. A contributing factor was the lack of information available on the resources being applied to provide each service delivered by Centrelink (DFaCS 1999). At the same time, DFaCS managers were concerned with the frequency with which Centrelink counterparts responded to a request by saying that it was unfunded.

A further internal audit by DFaCS in 2001 on the BPA as the basis of the relationship found that it was too complex. Those who worked with it might not be able to grasp the elements of the agreement relevant to their responsibilities (Rowlands 2003). There were also unresolved problems for DFaCS in acquiring management information from Centrelink about programs and performance information on costs and quality.

The ANAO also audited DFaCS' oversight of Centrelink's performance focusing on its assessment of new age pension claims. It found that DFaCS was unable to monitor and evaluate Centrelink's performance effectively. This was attributed to the lack of availability of accurate data from Centrelink (ANAO 2001a).

The ANAO audited not only Centrelink's delivery of programs and payments; it audited DFaCS' oversight of Centrelink's performance. In its performance audit of DFaCS' oversight of Centrelink's assessment of new age pension claims, it examined the 1999–2000 and 2000–01 BPAs as central elements of the business framework. It found that DFaCS was unable to monitor and evaluate Centrelink's performance effectively—a substantial deficiency in a purchaser–provider relationship. It attributed this to the lack of availability of accurate data from Centrelink (ANAO 2001a).

The *Centrelink Annual Report 2000–2001* records one of its major organisational challenges as being able to add value to client services through 'feedback on policy implementation and contributing ideas for future policy consideration' (Centrelink 2001a:53).

Interface

The interface—the intermediate zone between policy formation and service delivery, covering program management or operational policy—has been a source of debate and at times acute disagreement. A particular concern from the Centrelink side was how to handle micro-policy and implementation, which tended to overlap.

When dividing the parts of the DSS into the two new organisations, was the optimum line of separation selected? The relationship that subsequently developed between DFaCS and Centrelink was influenced by the dividing line chosen, which, in turn, was probably affected by the restructure that took place within the DSS before Centrelink's creation.

There is a sense in which the structure of the national office of the old DSS could be viewed as moving in increments from strategic policy through to the most practical matters of day-to-day administration. The then Social Policy Division was responsible for developing new policy at a strategic and a budget level. Moreover, it developed and controlled all advice on policy change that resulted in an item appearing in the portfolio budget. Several 'benefits administration' divisions 'owned' the administration of particular programs/payments. They took responsibility after any budget announcement for translating a policy into action, teasing out the detailed micro-policy and providing detailed instructions for legislative drafters and systems developers, providing guidance to the staff in the regional office network as to the correct policy detail on the inevitable queries that arose.

They dealt with issues that arose in the continuing administration too, such as precedents set by appeals tribunals and the like, which might need new guidance to the network or a micro-policy amendment. The Systems Division translated the detailed policy instructions into a practical, working computer system that would be the basis for regional office staff doing their daily work of assessing claims for payment and so on. Indeed, almost all regional office work was—and had been for some years—integrated into the computer system.

These divisional structures were not rigidly separate. The Social Policy Division generally tested policy options with the benefit divisions and Systems Division for 'implementability' and, often, for comment on the policy itself. Policy options—especially when there were minor inconsistencies or desirable small changes particularly apparent at the implementation level—would be fed in from outside the Social Policy Division. Note that the benefits divisions straddled policy, detailed administration and associated systems work.[2]

The DSS was reorganised in the early 1990s to incorporate the Social Policy Division and the benefits divisions into three program-oriented divisions (focusing on family policy and programs, the labour market and retirement programs). Thus, when the time came to divide the DSS into the new DSS and Centrelink, the Systems Division, being almost wholly concerned with providing the daily working tools to the regional office network, went to Centrelink. The new program divisions, which all had new policy responsibilities, formed the core of the new DSS.

The question that arises is, had the split occurred before that earlier reorganisation, would the division between the DSS and Centrelink have been made so that the Social Policy Division provided the basis of a much smaller DSS than eventuated? The benefits divisions were as much concerned with day-to-day administration as with policy matters and could easily have been seen as belonging in the Centrelink environment. It is arguable that the 'customer segment teams' developed within Centrelink's National Support Office are little more than a mirror image of those portions of the former benefits divisions that dealt with the Systems Division and the regional network.

Had the Social Policy Division formed the basis of the new and yet smaller DSS it would have been left ill equipped to purchase services from a Centrelink comprising most of the rest of the former department. There would have been very little practical, operational administrative experience and insight available to it except through consultation with Centrelink. It would have been much more subject to Centrelink's views in preparing its policy advice (and hence, at some risk of provider capture). At a minimum, it would have been, in Kettl's (1993) terms, not a very 'smart buyer' and would have had little capacity to become one. In other words, to have made a cut in a different place could have incurred fewer transaction costs but the relationship could not have been that of purchaser–provider. It might have been closer to that between the Treasury and the Australian Taxation Office, in which the former sets policy but in no sense purchases delivery services from the latter.

Because of the way the division was made between the two organisations, DFaCS had a capacity to be, and made some attempt to be, an active purchaser. It has been, at some cost, a more active superintendent of its provider because it has that capacity and expectations of future contestability in its service delivery options (albeit derived from rhetoric). The supplier's response is (at further cost) to have structures in place to deal with that superintending and to complain about micromanagement by its purchaser.

The Centrelink position was that departments continued to micromanage what it did.

> DSS should have been a true policy department, mirroring the policy departments that are overseas…Most of what they do is micro policy, or another way of saying it is micromanagement…that's been a constant problem in the relationship ever since, because FaCS can never decide where that boundary is. (Senior Centrelink official)

A purchaser view was that there was a need to have Centrelink involvement in providing advice on the implementation challenges involved in specific policy, but it opposed a more prominent role in policy development.

Centrelink's annual report (2001a:53) records one of its major organisational challenges as being able to add value to client services through 'feedback on policy implementation and contributing ideas for future policy consideration'. This issue is picked up again in the section on transaction costs.

Understanding the business transacted across the organisational boundary between the DSS and Centrelink, and its costs, raises the question of how the two were divided in the first place. This issue, often discussed by DSS/DFaCS management after the split, was articulated internally with the question 'Did the "knife" fall in the right place?' In other words, did the choice as to where to make the cut give rise to the high transaction costs of each organisation in dealing with the other? The crucial point was not where the cut was made but what was to be the nature of the relationship between the two organisations once it had occurred.

Funding and the price of services[3]

A rationale of purchaser–provider relationships was to produce clarity about what was being produced at what cost. In practice, the notion of 'output prices' for Centrelink services consumed considerable effort over a number of years.

Each BPA contained a 'price' to be paid by the DSS, later DFaCS, for the outputs or services to be provided by Centrelink. Despite the increasing amount of detail set out in these agreements, however, they did not include a substantial breakdown of the elements making up this overall price: for example, identifiable prices or average costs for delivering specific benefits. Apart from a few minor exceptions, there was only one global price. Considerable effort, however, was expended over the years to achieve price clarity. Centrelink's 1997–98 annual report indicated that work was proceeding in this direction and that a program had been established to determine the cost of services provided to client departments.

> A services costing model has been developed as a baseline for introducing Activity Based Costing to the organisation. The Activity Based Costing will build on the services costing model data and framework to provide service level cost information for managers by December 1998…[and] will help attribute full service costs to activities and enable pricing of similar services to be estimated for new or enhanced business. (Centrelink 1998a:75–7)

The ANAO reported that various measures of administrative costs were not forthcoming as per client agreements (ANAO 1999b; Rowlands 2003). In late

1999, the ANAO audited Centrelink's 'planning and monitoring for cost effective service delivery'. That audit was hampered by difficulties Centrelink had in providing various data sets for analysis (ANAO 2000:12). It concluded that, although it had managed successfully to that point, this had drawn extensively on experienced managers' knowledge. In future, it would need 'ready access to more robust management information, particularly on cost, to support its managers to implement and evaluate major business initiatives and to set prices with its purchasers' (ANAO 2000:13–14).

A 'Cost Optimisation Project' was established to enhance Centrelink's approach to strategic cost management including the use of 'activity-based costing'. Work was also undertaken to develop a new funding model because the existing 'arrangements were out of date, complex, different for each client, create instability, encourage accountability for inputs not outputs and do not capture changes in cost drivers across all payment types' (Centrelink 2000a:95, 96). A new funding model was expected for the 2000/01 budget and in the next round of BPAs. The 2000–01 annual report noted the beginning of the 'development of a new funding model and an output pricing review. These two projects will…ensure greater transparency of results', and the model was expected to be agreed with the government for the 2002/03 budget (Centrelink 2001a:171–2).

Debate about costs, however, continued to be a pervasive feature of the relationships. The Employment Minister, Tony Abbott, joined the debate about options in conjunction with DoFA, arguing for a 'pure' fee-for-service model for Centrelink. Three departments (DFaCS, DETYA and Abbott's DEWRSB) together with Centrelink were reported as arguing for a two-pronged model that included core funding (*Canberra Sunday Times*, 25 February 2001:25). Secretary Rosalky (2002:10) observed that DFaCS had 'viewed the state of knowledge of Centrelink's cost structures as quite unsatisfactory, making it impossible to price outputs and therefore to make allocative decisions across outputs as priorities emerge'. According to DoFA, there was no transparency in pricing, so it was difficult to price services.

Another element absent from BPA documents was the provision of sanctions for non-performance. A great deal of effort was made with each BPA to specify the expectations of Centrelink's performance more satisfactorily, but they included no sanctions for under-performance or non-performance. One of the consequences of there being no breakdown of Centrelink prices was that it became difficult to construct appropriate sanctions for, as an example, the failure to deliver a specific service. There was a capacity to relate funding to performance in the 2001–04 BPA but this was taken up in only a few cases.

Transaction costs of managing the relationship[4]

The management of a complex 'contractual' relationship has direct financial costs for both parties. Substantial resources are required for the tasks of negotiating agreements, monitoring compliance and generally managing the relationship from the purchasing and providing sides.

The DFaCS *Portfolio Budget Statement* (2002: Appendix 6.3) provides a general indication of the DFaCS resources required for managing the relationship with service providers, including Centrelink. The figures under the heading of 'Purchasing, funding and relationship management' cover DFaCS' costs for the purchase of Centrelink services (plus management of services provided by other providers of childcare and disability services). Rowlands (2003:178) estimated the total cost for 2002–03 was more than $107 million.

> [A] reasonable estimate on the basis of staff numbers is that each of these functions accounts for half these costs. This implies that FaCS' transaction costs in dealing with Centrelink are around $50 million a year. It is reasonable to presume that there is a counterpart cost on Centrelink's side of the relationship. (Rowlands 2003:178)

If this calculation is accepted, Rowlands (2003) asks why the transaction costs between the two organisations are so high? In seeking an answer, he focuses on the concept of asset specificity as a significant influence on transaction costs. DFaCS and Centrelink have large and complex apparatus for either producing specifications for products for purchase or delivering those products.

To underscore the demands, it is useful to characterise briefly the management of social security work. The budget will include portfolio measures that will be subject to implementation processes that require significant and complementary inputs from both organisations (Rowlands 2003:181):

> FaCS takes responsibility for legislative change...micro-policy development, and the preparation of detailed guidance on its interpretation. Centrelink takes responsibility for systems development, training, publicity and other final implementation tasks. Extensive consultation is required...in every implementation simply by virtue of the complexity of each change.

The consequence is that with a major implementation, daily interactions are usual between DFaCS programs and Centrelink customer segment teams. 'The project nature...means that contingencies frequently arise requiring action...This also limits the capacity of the purchaser to specify in advance the work required and the provider to cost it accurately' (Rowlands 2003). Ministerial priorities can also lead to regular changes in agency outputs that cannot be readily handled within a purchaser–provider type of relationship and which have implications for the contents of business agreements between organisations.

In the end, the question of transactions across the organisational boundaries raises the issue of the original split between the DSS and Centrelink. Rowlands (2003) concludes that it is difficult to discern a point on the continuum between policy and administration where the split could have occurred without a high level of activity across that boundary. This has implications for the boundary and the issue of choosing between the use of hierarchy or agencies as a basis for delivery of services.

Changing client relationships: purchaser–provider to alliance

Centrelink's relationships with its main client departments have been through purchaser–provider arrangements, governed by a form of contractual agreement with each agency. These agreements evolved from service agreements into more comprehensive documents, the BPAs, which established the scope and provided the detail of a formal purchaser–provider relationship between two organisations. The details cover the services, funding arrangements, agreed performance outcomes and related reporting mechanisms. BPAs are used to manage and review the operating and performance relationships between the partners.[5]

For several years, these relationships were the subject of wrangling and debate. DoFA's central agency position was that Centrelink was monopolist and did not have genuine competitors. In its view, the purchaser–provider model had not worked with DFaCS because they were not sufficiently at arm's length. There was a lack of transparency in Centrelink pricing, so it was difficult for DFaCS to understand the pricing of particular services being charged by Centrelink. 'The budget just flows through FaCS, more or less as a lump sum grant, to Centrelink' (Senior DoFA official). The interface between policy formation and service delivery covering program management or operational policy continued to be a source of disagreement.

As previously mentioned, Centrelink believed that departments micromanaged its activities. As one senior Centrelink official observed, '[T]here's a fine line between micro-policy and implementation. So there's a nice grey area there where we need to sort it out together.' In contrast with the policy department in other systems that concentrated on macro-policy, the client department focused mainly on micro-policy or, in practice, micromanagement. Because DFaCS could not locate the boundary, micro-policy led it into micromanagement.

Looking across the life of Centrelink, the tensions in the relationships were significant in its formative years. The rhetoric from an early stage was couched in terms of partnership, but the basis was defined and operated in formal purchaser–provider terms. There were, however, continuing problems arising from the competition for the middle ground and the mutual concern that both organisations were either insufficiently engaged in each other's primary responsibilities or too involved in their respective roles. This tension could be 'tolerable and creative', but was 'destructive' in the late 1990s. 'The model shifted then, from pure purchaser–provider, to partnership underpinned by the elements of purchaser–provider' (Senior departmental official).

This was not the case with the other key relationship (with DEWR), in which there had been some movement in the direction of 'a more mature partnership, but…we're not there, and it's basically because of this endless argument about funding for the delivery of services, which constantly undermines that partnership arrangement' (Senior departmental official).

The official public view about the DFaCS relationship was expressed in the BPA between DFaCS and Centrelink, which stated that the relationship had evolved over four years into 'a dynamic, mutually beneficial association. FaCS and Centrelink are committed to the continued mutual development of the partnership…a unique arrangement, which blends elements of purchaser–provider responsibilities with elements of partnership and alliance' (DFaCS 2001a). Even then, however, the relationship did not mature until the development of a more systematically worked through 'alliance'.[6]

'Alliance 2004' emerged from a complex project that involved inter-agency teams working at different levels on specific elements for 12 months.

These elements addressed weaknesses in the previous relationship between Centrelink and DFaCS and focused on a set of frameworks designed to 'reshape the relationship from one that largely focused on inputs and processes to one that more clearly focused on achieving Government outcomes' (DFaCS/Centrelink 2004:3). This included the Outcomes and Outputs Framework, a joint version of the standard public service requirement, but one that made explicit each organisation's contribution to achieving outcomes (a DFaCS responsibility); the Business Assurance Framework, providing a framework for risk-management strategies and controls; and the Centrelink Funding Model, providing a pricing structure for services, and information protocol, covering responsibilities for reporting. A new BPA incorporated these business tools and was replaced with a *Business Alliance Agreement 2004–2008* (DFaCS/Centrelink 2004).

Interpretation

The redefinition of inter-agency relationships was strongly influenced by principal-agent principles. There was eventually consensus among the purchasers and the provider about the limitations of this approach. The commercial approach underlying the purchaser–provider model required an arm's-length relationship between the two with regard to financial results. Because of Centrelink's character and the shortage of financial data, however, the model was seen to be 'artificial and inimical to the primary portfolio purpose. The government's fiscal interests are tied more closely to effective joint management of program funds than to a competitive model aimed at reducing administrative costs' (Rosalky 2002:14).

The changing stance of central coordinating agencies was also apparent. Not so long before, DoFA perceived the relationship in formal terms and took issue with Centrelink's location within the Family and Community Services portfolio as to whether it was a separate service agency model or a traditional departmental model. The minister was seen to appreciate the 'big mushy-looking bucket of money...but it's not a purchaser–provider relationship' (Senior DoFA official). It is now generally accepted that this type of relationship is problematic if the two parties are located within the same portfolio. This position had been endorsed by the Uhrig *Review of Corporate Governance* (2003:47), which failed to 'identify a net benefit' and favoured direct ministerial accountability.

The organisation's smart practices produced more effective relations based on the value-chain conception of responsibilities and a more integrated alliance approach to the most important relationship, that between DFaCS and Centrelink. A group that included clients and the key central agency, DoFA, subsequently produced a new funding model. Broader issues about the substantial transaction costs arising from the original structure (that is, those of purchaser and provider in managing a complex contractual relationship) are not explicitly factored in because the separation remains a given, but there are efficiencies from reducing micromanagement, duplication and the competitive aspects of adversarial behaviour.

The conflicts between models outlined earlier derived partly from the limitations of purchaser–provider principles and their application to a purchaser and provider within the same portfolio. Once an adversarial dimension cloaked in partnership was succeeded by real collaboration, there were opportunities to confront other questions.

Purchaser–provider

Initially, the secretary of the DSS depicted its relationship with Centrelink as a partnership. Blunn contrasted 'partnering' with a purchaser–provider relationship and argued that the relationship was based on the mutual understanding of their respective roles and responsibilities, which were defined in the SPA, the 'contract' between the two organisations (Blunn 1997a:4; Rowlands 2003). A partnership was chosen rather than the purchaser–provider approach for the following reasons:

- a legalistic, contractual relationship on the adversarial model was negative, based on the absence of trust between the partner organisations and would not work out in the longer term...
- no contract between Commonwealth agencies could be litigated...so why pretend a legal or quasi-legal arrangement existed?

- there is very low political tolerance…for income support services to be disrupted for any substantial period or for Commonwealth agencies to enter into public conflict over delivery of government policy. We therefore needed a contractual framework oriented to solving problems, not assigning blame; and
- the basis of an effective relationship between the two organisations was the relationship between managers and those who had to work together across the organisational boundaries…Therefore the development of a complementary corporate culture in both partner organisations was seen as essential to the success of a functional partnership approach. (Blunn 1997a:4)

According to Rowlands (2003), these reasons appear 'to repudiate explicitly the purchaser–provider model at least by contrasting it to the notion of partnership. Indeed, it focuses on…reasons [why] purchaser–provider might be inappropriate in a social security environment.' Another interpretation is that the language of purchaser–provider was de rigueur in the mid-1990s, although its full implications in a formal sense were seen to be of questionable value. The competition between the agencies, however, and concerns about control precluded the earlier emergence of mature partnerships.

According to the *Review of Corporate Governance* (Uhrig 2003), purchaser–provider arrangements were regarded as 'a means to provide leverage to the portfolio department to ensure the services being delivered are in line with their requirements'. Uhrig concluded, however, that purchasers had 'minimal leverage' in the procuring services because of:

- The annual cost of the services is established and paid for in advance of the services being delivered.
- There are no alternative providers for the majority of services.
- The service providers are, as yet, not able to identify accurately the transaction costs for the services being delivered. This reduces the purchasing department's ability to link the price paid to the volume delivered and to develop benchmarks. (Uhrig 2003:46)

Furthermore:

- The incentives for the major purchasing agencies to be good purchasers are diminished by the fact that they do not benefit from any price reduction.
- Any attempt by the purchasers to withhold money based on under-delivery of services will result in greater risk to the purchasing department in services not being delivered adequately, undermining the achievement of the outcomes for which the purchasing department is responsible…
- There are considerable resources being consumed in managing the purchasing agreement with very little or no benefit. As the large majority of services being delivered by a service delivery authority is within the purchasing

department's portfolio, greater leverage over price and quality of services being delivered could be achieved through direct accountability of the authority to the Minister. (Uhrig 2003:47)

The review found it was unable 'to identify a net benefit in the use of purchaser/provider arrangements for services being delivered within a portfolio due to the lack of purchasing power of the portfolio department' (Uhrig 2003:47).

Conclusion

The DSS and Centrelink understood the challenges of new relationships at the outset, yet despite the recognition of the need for partnerships and work on cultivating the relationship, weaknesses surfaced and dominated for some time. They derived mainly from the purchaser–provider and financial arrangements.

The debates about the roles of the purchasing department and the provider agency derived from the combinations of models that could be discerned in Centrelink's organisational imperatives. In particular, there were the different interpretations about the relative importance of managerial dimensions as expressed through purchaser–provider principles and partnerships.

The central relationship between Centrelink and DFaCS

has been perpetually hampered by an uncertainty as to its nature. There is a tension between the collegiate partnership sought by managers and the formalism of purchaser–provider. The former posits mutual objectives and enjoins trust and co-operation; the latter encourages formalism and caution as to the other's motives. This tension has flowed through to relationships at all levels in the two organisations. (Rowlands 2003)

The formal legislative framework produced detailed specification of DFaCS' requirements that increased with time, leading to claims of micromanagement by Centrelink. In this environment, it can be difficult to handle contingencies that require resources to be moved between tasks in the short term unless effective relationships exist between managers (Rowlands 2003).

At the same time, purchaser–provider relationships remained unrealised through the appropriate performance information including output prices. There were also difficulties in other portfolios with purchasing agreements at this time, a notable example being the Department of Immigration and Multicultural Affairs (Tucker 2008).

The models differentiated earlier continued to contribute to the ambiguity in Centrelink's environment. There were attempts to mitigate the environmental ambiguity through relegation of two of them and some reworking of the features of others. The emphasis on partnerships facilitated more productive relationships, but the structural features of the original design of Centrelink meant that tensions remained and that much energy had to be channelled into working though the creative options.

ENDNOTES

[1] The section draws on Rowlands (2003).

[2] Brown and Rowlands (1995) discuss program implementation under these arrangements.

[3] The historical aspects draw on Rowlands' (2003) more detailed survey.

[4] This section relies on David Rowlands' treatment (2003:177–82). For a description of the implementation process, see Brown and Rowlands (1995).

[5] BPAs take the form of a memorandum of understanding because the Commonwealth cannot enter into a contract with itself in which the purchaser and the provider are its agencies.

[6] This was not the case with the other key relationship, that with DEWR, in which there had been some movement in the direction of 'a more mature partnership', but this progress continued to be retarded because of 'endless argument about funding for the delivery of services, which constantly undermines that partnership arrangement' (Senior departmental official).

8. Entrepreneurship and challenging boundaries

The concept of an entrepreneurial public organisation has been commonplace for some time, but it is unusual for a major public service agency to be perceived as operating in the market to secure existing core work as well as to seek new business. Centrelink was concerned with market share and with competition in the public and voluntary sectors, and even with extending operations to the private marketplace. This imperative derived from the government injunction to operate more like the private sector and reflected the in-vogue dictums of the 1990s about new public management and entrepreneurial government (Halligan 2003).

This chapter provides the perspective of the agency in its dealings with the other main stakeholders, reflecting an organisational imperative: the entrepreneurial model. Entrepreneurial advocacy includes building legitimacy for initiatives, shaping mandates for action, mobilising support and investing them with political support (Moore 1995). The dimensions covered here are: extending policy roles, expanding business horizontally, positioning within the Public Service and expanding out from the formal structure through governance processes to the community.

Constraints on and opportunities for positioning the agency

Centrelink originally emerged from a combination of agendas and opportunities after the election of a new government committed to rationalisation and cutbacks. In the process of formulating options that would be accepted by the government and given organisational form, those proposing its creation were constrained by the new government's philosophical and political expectations and the interests of existing departments. The concept was then shaped by a compromise with long-term consequences for operations and relationships between client departments and Centrelink (Halligan 2004).

The continuing constraints and parameters for this new public organisation, as outlined earlier, covered changing reform agendas and expectations and contradictory imperatives. These imposed different types of discipline on Centrelink. The new government that created Centrelink was otherwise pursuing the most intense neo-liberal policies since the reform era began as it sought to address the budget deficit and to review the management and financial activities of government, including what efficiencies might be achieved. Reform was characterised by marketisation and outsourcing that included an intensification of cutbacks and promotion of the private sector over the public sector. This agenda was supplanted in the early 2000s as its limitations were exposed and refinements became necessary (Halligan and Adams 2004).

At the same time, the policy framework took a dramatic new direction midway through this period as mutual obligation was mainstreamed by the government and welfare reform produced significant changes with 'Australians Working Together' (AWT) designed to establish a new balance between incentives, obligations and welfare assistance.

There were also constraints resulting from the ambiguity underlying the Centrelink concept and potential conflicts among the different imperatives. The combination of models that could be discerned in these organisational imperatives allowed for different interpretations, in particular, about the relative importance of managerial dimensions as expressed through purchaser–provider principles and partnerships. (Halligan 2004).

These differences were also established by the bureaucratic politics attendant on the entrance of an interloper. In contrast with Britain and New Zealand, where 'agencification'—the separation of policy and delivery—was implemented across the civil service, in Australia, Centrelink was the exception.[1] As a delivery agency, it dealt with a wide range of departments but was excluded from their club, although performing work that several of them had recently undertaken.

Centrelink was, however, an innovation of a government that conformed to the premises of the time. The ambiguity and conflicting imperatives also provided scope for initiative. Through advocacy and smart practices, opportunities could be turned to advantage providing organisational longevity could be ensured.

The original mandate was as a one-stop delivery agency providing services to purchasing departments in social security and unemployment, but Centrelink's unconventional character also provided a platform from which to position itself within the APS. The positions advocated, in addition to the one-stop shop, were the 'provider of choice' for the Commonwealth, 'inclusive service delivery' covering those who were marginalised and disadvantaged (Vardon 2000c), the gateway for electronic communications and the 'premier broker' (Tannahill 2000).

In the following discussion, Centrelink's positioning is examined through cases in different operational spheres and different types of inter-agency interaction: one is about competing for policy and contributions to the process; a second considers positioning within the Public Service; the third examines the process of employing entrepreneurial and advocacy skills to consolidate and expand the agency's role while evolving a distinctive service delivery focus; and the final case is about the elaboration of a community relationship.

Policy innovation by an executive agency

Centrelink's role as a policy advocate needs to be located within ideas about the decoupling of policy formulation (ministry or department) and implementation (executive agency) and the associated experiments with separate delivery agencies (Rowlands 2003).

The original concept was for a separation of policy and delivery to produce a large agency and convert two large departments into two smaller policy departments.[2] One of Centrelink's founders, Tony Blunn, had second thoughts about reducing his large DSS to a small policy bureau, which led to the reformulation of the interface between the agency and the department, which added a middle area covering program management and operational policy between policy formation and delivery. Under this revised concept, the department and the agency were to compete in the middle ground and achieve effective working relations at the interface. These choices laid the basis for the later debates about the relative responsibilities of the provider agency and its purchasing departments and the interface remained a significant source of disagreement.

The weakness with the separation model is that it is difficult to maintain in practice. Two different problems are that the separation goes too far or that it is insufficiently applied. Schick (1996) reports that 'decoupling may be counterproductive', citing the case of the New Zealand Ministry of Defence, where increased overhead and transaction costs resulted and the organisational linkages had to be re-established to provide policy feedback. 'Policy and operations are not necessarily separated by decoupling because of the tendency of service delivery units to "grow" their own policy capacity' (Schick 1996:31).

At the same time, there is an argument in favour of policy activity. An observer of different public management systems comments that the explicit separation of policy from implementation has been significant in only a few countries (New Zealand and the United Kingdom), because elsewhere delivery agencies can retain a role in policy monitoring and development. Nordic countries, particularly Sweden, have not only had long experience with agencies, they can be active in policy advice and evaluation in addition to providing service delivery (Shand 1996:6, 8).

There is a need therefore to balance the advantages of separate organisations for policy and operations while ensuring that there are effective communication mechanisms and dialogue between them on policy directions and implementation. As with other debates about separation of levels of government (for example, the federal system), is it necessarily optimal or realistic to strive for separational purity? The department may continue to intervene in implementation. The blurring of responsibilities between departments and agencies in the United Kingdom was revealed by an early review of the 'Next Steps' (Trosa 1994).

A core issue for Centrelink was the role that it might play in policy development and how it was perceived by other key players to be shaping the policy agenda. The main instance was a proposal for significantly developing the service delivery model and Centrelink's policy advocacy of it.

As discussed in Chapter 2, an official welfare review occurred in 1999 and 2000. A comparison of Centrelink's submission to the initial inquiry on welfare reform by the McClure reference group with the recommendations indicates substantial congruence.[3] The submission had an important impact on the inquiry's work and recommendations, and indicated that this non-policy agency correctly anticipated the policy direction of the inquiry. The recommendations of the McClure report (2000) reinforced a new service delivery model that was already under conceptual development in Centrelink and provided a basis for the government's *Australians Working Together—Helping people to move forward* (DFaCS 2001).

The main purchasing departments, DFaCS and DEWR, accepted a role for Centrelink in providing advice on the delivery aspects of specific policy proposals. This was regarded as a secondary role and one the agency had in the development of AWT. There was, however, strong opposition to leading on policy agenda. Centrelink 'should be consulted and should argue very forcibly in terms of the implementation of the policy agenda. And that may even mean that the policy agenda gets...amended...But I don't think they should be taking the initiative in terms of driving policy' (Senior departmental official).

The contrary position was that all policy could not be left to the clients:

> [Y]ou've got to have opinions about how the whole thing fits together. You can't just say, 'I deliver it and everything is passed onto me and I just deliver it'...you've got to provide advice about the facts that this will not work or this will affect x thousand customers. (Senior Centrelink official)

Minister Newman had often said that the best ideas came from the front line and she would listen to them. It was this capacity that was believed to be lost because DFaCS did not want Centrelink to send it ideas.

Centrelink's proposal for a new approach to delivering services needed to be seen in this light. Senior Centrelink officials had taken a new concept to their agency's board that contained several principles, including the fundamental aspect that customers

> should only have to tell their story once, they shouldn't have to repeat their story if they are eligible for more than one benefit or...entitlement...Up until then, there had been...an ethos that the customer was expected to know what they were coming to Centrelink to ask for...The idea was that as long as the customer was prepared to

come to us and tell us the truth, and tell us what they were experiencing in their own lives, it was…Centrelink's responsibility to tailor that service package to the individual. (Senior Centrelink official)

The life-events approach, as it was called (see Chapter 5), was a new approach for delivering services that was developed within Centrelink and was 'based on the experiences of people in the community, rather than the payments, services or programs devised by government departments' (Bashford 2000:12; Vardon 2003c).

The development of this approach by the delivery agency rather than the policy department confounded senior departmental officials. One secretary had not fully comprehended that introducing this

> delivery mechanism actually has a reflection back on the policy, and therefore, it's very important for them to accept that they have to really consult with, and…be led by the policy departments. Often, in the past, Centrelink had developed these strategies, and…consulted the policy departments, almost after the event, about what they think about these new delivery mechanisms. I was outraged at how far Centrelink had gone along the track of…the life events model, and the one main contact…before there were meaningful consultations with the department.

The resolution of the policy-implementation conundrum occurred, at least for the main relationship, once an alliance had been forged between Centrelink and DFaCS (see Figure 8.1 and Appendix 7). The evolution of the relationship to a closer partnership arrangement was eventually defined on the basis of a value chain of interaction. This chain specified the roles and responsibilities and value-added process interlinked along a continuum and acknowledged the mutuality of involvement in all processes, although either DFaCS or Centrelink was dominant in all but one. Accordingly, three processes were identified as belonging mostly to DFaCS (policy development, legislation and policy guidelines), three as mostly to Centrelink (service development, service integration and implementation, and program management) and one as a joint function (evaluation of policy and service delivery) (DFaCS/Centrelink 2003).

In terms of furthering the mutual but complementary objectives, a strategy was articulated for achieving the goal of accountability to government and client agencies as supporting the policy development process. This involved supporting policies with analysis of trends in customers and service delivery and providing feedback on service gaps, issues, needs and information program impacts (Centrelink 2004b).

Figure 8.1 Client to Customer Value Chain

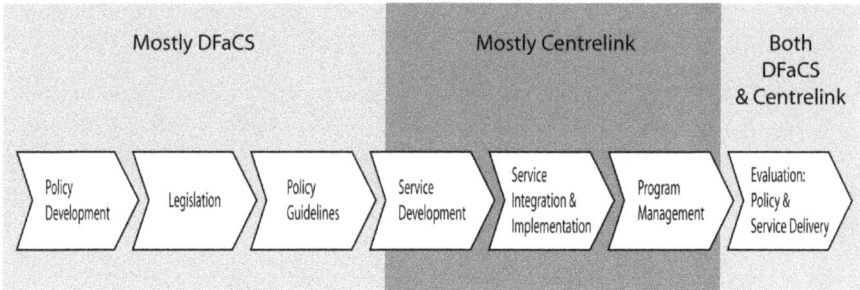

Positioning within the Public Service

In positioning itself, Centrelink sought to be entrepreneurial within the terms of its original mandate to become a one-stop shop. At various times, the question arose as to whether Centrelink was *the* Commonwealth delivery agency and should have comprehensive responsibilities for multiple delivery arrangements. The competition for business is discussed in the next section.

Establishing limits on the one-stop shop

Centrelink advocacy has been centred on being the 'provider of choice' and the electronic gateway. Its mandate was to improve service delivery and customer service. The agency consistently represented itself as being established by the government to improve customer service by providing a one-stop shop. It aspired to be the 'provider of choice' for government services (Rowlands 2003:143).[4]

The government, however, did not always choose to support these aspirations. The first case of this involved a major revision of the Australian tax system in mid-2000. The design of the new system combined numerous family assistance payments to produce two enhanced family benefits. Centrelink delivered the majority of the existing types of family assistance, but the Australian Taxation Office and the Health Insurance Commission, which also had shopfront offices, delievered the other benefits. The government opted for delivery of the payments by a 'virtual' organisation, the FAO, which would have outlets in each of these three agencies. The following of precedent was one factor. Another was whether an agency concerned primarily with delivery of welfare payments should deliver assistance of this sort. Family assistance was seen to involve 'horizontal equity' between families in contrast with 'welfare' payments (Rowlands 2003:144). As a result, Centrelink did not become the sole provider of choice in delivering family benefits.

The second case was about becoming the Federal Government's electronic gateway; the development of Internet portals represented an area where

Centrelink's advocacy of its role as a one-stop shop was not officially endorsed. Centrelink had made electronic communication with customers a priority (for example, Vardon 1999a). An aim of its business plan was for Centrelink's portal to be established by 2004 as the important gateway between citizens and the Federal Government and eventually state governments. In particular, 'Access Australia' would be deployed as the 'principal individual-to-Government portal' (Rowlands 2003) by the end of 2004. This portal was intended to provide direct links to all levels of government; however, the Federal Government's National Office for the Information Economy supported development of a range of Internet portals to provide a single electronic point of access to available online information and for transacting services. Responsibility for each portal was assigned to 'lead agencies' rather than assigning a primary role to Centrelink for developing and supporting the portals (Rowlands 2003:144–7).

Gateway to the welfare system

The Reference Group on Welfare Reform report (McClure 2000) identified a new role: the need for a gateway to the new welfare system. Minister Anthony (2000) referred to Centrelink as the gateway, which was reaffirmed by the Minister for Family and Community Services, Senator Newman (2000), after the government's response to the report in December 2000: 'Centrelink will remain the main gateway to the participation support system.' This became clearer in May 2001, when the government announced AWT, substantially changing the social support system for working-aged people, with Centrelink to be responsible for implementation. In their joint press release announcing the initiative in May 2001, the Ministers for Social Security and Employment declared that 'Centrelink will be the gateway to the new system'. The ministerial statement (Vanstone and Abbott 2001a) observed that 'a vital element in a better, more balanced system is offering personalised assistance and support. Accordingly, improving Centrelink services will be the key to making *Australians Working Together* a success.'

Competing for business

The two strands to this question are being in a contestable position for core business and competing for business.

The contestability of Centrelink's core business

The government's National Commission of Audit (NCA 1996:2.3) proclaimed the principle of contestability in terms of mechanisms 'to ensure competitive or contestable program delivery', defining the concept as 'the threat of competition in areas where traditionally the market cannot accommodate a number of suppliers'.[5]

The notion of the competitive environment was a view promoted by government ministers and officials from Centrelink and other departments. In particular, the possible applications of contestability impacted on the agency's conception of roles and strategies. This depiction reflected the official rhetoric during Centrelink's formative years, which accorded centrality to contestability and competition. The Labor opposition had argued during the original legislative process that the use of an agency was a step towards removing public delivery of services. The NCA (1996) regarded income support services as an option for contracting out (Rowlands 2003).

Centrelink CEO, Sue Vardon, reflected this environment in recognising that while the government had positioned Centrelink 'within the public sector, there are many potential competitors. Overseas experience identifies these competitors. To retain our competitive edge we must deliver on cost and quality and excellent customer service will prove to be that competitive edge' (quoted in Rowlands 2003:152).

This position was premised on the existence of several organisations in the private, public enterprise and voluntary sectors that had possible delivery system capacity to take on responsibilities. The question of contestability needs to be viewed within the climate in which operating like the private sector was a foremost principle. In Centrelink's case, its operations were akin to a monopoly in relation to its major client.

One of the key players in the development of Centrelink observed that there was awareness that

> Australia Post had been playing around with idea that they could provide social security services through the Australia Post network…Or look at the health insurance people…because they've got a fairly extensive network and a good reputation in terms of the customer. So we'll give you three of four years to establish but if you are not performing then you've got no guarantee that we won't look [for] other ways. (Former departmental secretary)

There were also concerns about customer loyalty—that customers might go to another supplier if it were able to provide payments currently delivered by Centrelink. The customer satisfaction survey for November 1998 indicated that 68 per cent of respondents said they either definitely or probably would use another organisation if given the opportunity. Later percentages were much lower (34 per cent for November 1999, 27 per cent for November 2002, but 36 per cent for November 2003) but were still sufficiently high to cause concern.

A commonly expressed view was that Centrelink had three years (and a maximum of five) before facing competition for core business from the private sector, thereby creating the expectation that Centrelink might lose service delivery.

That it could face future competition was expressed in annual reports at this time. In addition, many senior staff in the main client department, Family and Community Services, believed in the inevitability of competition in delivering income support (Rowlands 2003:152–3). The fate of the CES, which had been converted into the Job Network dominated by non-public sector actors, was a reminder of another scenario.

These themes were carried into the organisation's midlife: 'Integral to the concept of Centrelink as a multi-purpose service provider [was] the notion of policy departments as purchasers of services in a contestable market environment' (Vardon 2000b:2). By 2000, however, the tone of senior managers was becoming more qualified, with the government reported to be unwilling to introduce contestability for the time being and providing Centrelink with scope to explore its potential before further competition came into play (Bashford 2000; Tannahill 2000; Rowlands 2003).

The McClure report provided an opportunity for the government to clarify its position, with the Minister for Community Services declaring that the report was not concerned with the privatisation of Centrelink, but with the need for a central gateway for delivering the best service. The new welfare system therefore provided opportunities for Centrelink as the gateway (Anthony 2000).

Extending the client base

There are two different modes of business to Centrelink's role as 'preferred provider'. Given Centrelink's national reach, the role of 'convenient supplier' is important in areas such as delivery of emergency relief. Regular use has been made of Centrelink's capacity to deliver assistance to people (for example, drought relief and support for people affected by economic structural reforms). The second is that of 'competitive supplier', which involves 'bidding for business on a competitive neutral basis' (Vardon 2002a).

Centrelink began with two main clients (the DSS and DEETYA) and attracted numerous others, with 20 or more receiving services in several years. Each client (usually a policy department) negotiated a purchase price for specified services that Centrelink agreed to undertake.

The government has made use of Centrelink as a convenient supplier and emergency provider and many of these short-term arrangements have turned into longer-term contracts. For example, an arrangement with DAFFA involving a number of different one-off relief packages—drought, farm inheritance and so on—resulted in a continuous stream of work for Centrelink and created a longer-term relationship.

Community engagement

The final area in which Centrelink extended its role was at the community level—a new venture for a nationally based federal agency.[6] This fitted a series of diffuse policy agendas about partnership, consultation and governance in the sense of linking more systematically with actors at different levels of government and particularly beyond government. It could be seen to serve the mutual interests of policy feedback to departments and policy inputs from community-level actors. The specific impetus came from the participation agenda in the sense of people assuming responsibility within an active welfare approach, but also from the need to improve policy and implementation communication on participation in the sense of consultation and engagement (Centrelink 2003a, 2004a).

Centrelink confronted the issue of what was its core business and had

> the big debates about what income support and what…tools we used to be able to enable people to participate. [So]…then the message started to change a lot…to change the understandings of how we did engage with particularly the community sector, because it was wider than who we traditionally engaged with. (Senior Centrelink official)

The catalyst was that Centrelink had 'won the gateway role because we were large, we were everywhere, but that was no good if we weren't linked in to where we needed to be as well, to move that next step' (Senior Centrelink official).

This involved redefining the approach to community organisations:

> We've had relationships with some of these organisations before, ACOSS [the Australian Council of Social Service] and welfare rights and Job Network but it's been very much around more antagonistic ones. When things go wrong that's when we meet, or we meet because for example with the Job Network, DEWR says we have to meet with them and work things out. It's actually been a reactive role not a proactive and not a relationship one. (Senior Centrelink official)

It also reflected being 'part of the same service delivery network…we are the broker of being able to send people in the right direction no matter who it is in terms of, it's just not the employed' (Senior Centrelink official).

The community did not regard the departments (DFaCS and DEWR, and still earlier the DSS and DEETYA) as operating on a proper consultative basis. Their modus operandi was to collect information but then to produce something that reflected their own agenda and ignored community issues and views. With policy feedback, Centrelink could report that something was not working on the ground and DFaCS and DEWR could react as they saw fit, but when there was a common voice coming through from many peak organisations as well as

Centrelink, it added substantially to the cogency of the feedback. In addition, there was the facilitation of consultation for small organisations: 'there's [sic] tens of thousands of these guys on the ground, and they don't get access to that policy process. They're too small; they don't have the resources' (Senior Centrelink official). Centrelink could be a means for getting 'the right messages across about…what's happening versus what's not…it's actually about getting that wider view of what's actually not working as well, and feeding that back to government' (Senior Centrelink official).

Centrelink's direct role in communities involved a range of activities at different levels of engagement, which it depicted in a pyramidal form (Centrelink 2003d). These could be represented as stages that moved from developing relationships and cooperation and collaboration through to community development. At the base is the foundation of communication, which entails establishing relationships with community actors and organisations. This is followed by cooperation through making services more accessible and includes sharing Centrelink resources. At a higher level is collaboration, which extends to changing services in response to community issues (Winkworth 2005).

The activity that involves the most significant extension of Centrelink's role is creating new opportunities. Community development involves partnerships with other organisations to support capacity building. An example is support provided to Multicultural Settlement in the Goulburn Valley in Victoria, involving resettlement of more than 2500 Arabic-speaking people.

Conclusion

These cases cover four different types of extension of Centrelink's role. They involve horizontal extensions into delivery for other agencies, broader public service roles and activities beyond the Public Service, particularly in conjunction with the community. The remaining area vertically extended Centrelink's influence in the policy process. Much of this was envisaged in the original ideas about the one-stop shop, but it still depended on the organisation's capacity to craft new roles for itself in practice.

These cases raise questions about modes of inter-agency interaction, process design, innovation and smart practices. There are several elements of positioning and legitimising the agency and defining entrepreneurial and service delivery roles; and about evolving more collaborative inter-agency relationships, as well as functioning as an agency that reflects integration by internalising otherwise separated responsibilities.

The advocacy of Centrelink's position was important for defining its roles and registering its place. Several themes were consistently promoted: the holistic conception of the individual and how the service delivery agency should respond; intra-agency integration of responsibilities; dealing with numerous clients simultaneously; competing for work (and the alternatives available); pushing policy agendas although a delivery agency; and provision of choice through channel management.

Centrelink was able to define a role within the APS that had hitherto been centred primarily on policy departments. In seeking to position and legitimise the agency, the core aspects were: evolving the service delivery system; consolidating, protecting and enhancing the concept of the one-stop shop and the delivery system; and expanding business through agreements with new clients. Much depended on the capacity of the organisation to define a vision and long-term objectives and then move towards realising them (Vardon 2003c).

ENDNOTES

[1] A few other cases existed, such as the Australian Taxation Office, but it was not a product of the move towards new-style executive agencies, but simply a conventional pragmatic solution to implementation.

[2] The concept was a product of discussions between Blunn, secretary of the then DSS, and Hollway, secretary of the then DEETYA.

[3] A review group produced a Green Paper known as the McClure report (2000) after its chair, which became the basis for the government's AWT.

[4] Rowland's (2003) dissertation examines the official documents of this period.

[5] The government defined the scope of the public sector in three ways: by the 'Yellow Pages' test (if there was more than one supplier listed in the telephone book supplement, the public sector role should be questioned), the emphasis on choice and contestability. The provision of policy advice by departments was also contestable.

[6] Business was later added in.

9. Lessons from Centrelink's formative years

This chapter reviews lessons from the Centrelink experience, which together span a significant range of questions about public management. Three themes permeate the discussion.

At one level, there are questions about designing the delivery of services that might best relate to particular types of agency. There are issues about Centrelink's organisational form and, as a solution to design questions, about how responsibilities are assigned and relationships between organisations determined.

Second, there are durable questions of public administration concerning governance, relationships among agencies, external relationships with society and the organisation of policy and implementation. The questions about delivery systems, organisational change and performance have been redefined in terms of customer focus and relationships and the role and significance of entrepreneurship and leadership in the external positioning of the organisation and the internal implementation of change.

Third, the role of the management and policy environments interacting with and influencing organisational change is identified because of the need to constantly respond to various agendas. The question of organisational positioning is conceived in terms of relations with the main stakeholders—client departments, the government and customers—and with regard to actively seeking an identity as a service delivery agency. In this, the role of entrepreneurial advocacy is important in an ambiguous environment with conflicting expectations for building support and legitimacy (Moore 1995).

Centrelink concept of delivery agency and government design

Centrelink as a horizontally constituted delivery agency operating through distinctive relationships with departments is interesting in Australian terms and internationally because it brings to the fore departures from conventional bureaucracy, the value of the agency model and the organisational distinctiveness of Centrelink.

How is it valued by government?

Romancing the agency concept: how design decisions were made

Centrelink was a product of the mid-1990s and a combination of personalities, agendas and opportunities associated with the election of a new government committed to reform and savings. Existing policy options were cemented as a solution was sought for the problem of departments confronting a reformist government. The essence of the problem was summarised by Rowlands (2003:203–4) as being about rationalisation and cost:

> [The] CES was seen by senior managers as moribund, a new government needed APS staff savings and the Department of Finance had long sought to have the two regional networks amalgamated: the alignment of these three factors alone meant that the change was inevitable...Achieving amalgamation of the CES with the DSS network was a major prize for Finance.

The relevant secretaries, Blunn and Hollway, engaged in pre-emptive action to meet the new government's expectations for staff savings in the Public Service for which the integration of two regional networks provided a solution.

The end was more obvious than the means. The second question was how to achieve these objectives in terms acceptable to the key bureaucratic actors, and again Rowlands (2003:205) captures the situation succinctly:

> [N]either DSS nor DEETYA would be 'taken over' by the other and both would have a seat at the Centrelink board. Finance could readily recognise and support the purchaser–provider model. [The] strategy yielded savings for the new government in a way that accorded with Finance views about how government should be organised.

Further, the scheme could be seen as 'a new step in APS reform' that also had a 'positive aspect rather than risk being seen primarily in terms of staff savings' (Rowlands 2003:205).

Out of the convergence came first an organisation that was different from the standard international experiments with new-style executive agencies: a delivery model with organisational distinctiveness and agency features. The legacy of this convergence of mutual interests and the basis for the continuing debates about the responsibilities of purchasing departments and their delivery agency were a result of combining several models in Centrelink's modus operandi (Halligan 2004). The resultant issues appear at different points in this chapter.

It is worth noting the culture of the environment into which Centrelink emerged. The enterprise had to confront a range of potentially unrealistic expectations in a sympathetic but also potentially inhospitable environment. There was strong political support from Jocelyn Newman while she was the minister. At the bureaucratic level, DoFA was sold on the concept of one delivery system rather than two and the incorporation of purchaser–provider principles echoing the neo-liberal ideas then in circulation. Client departments, however, were still operating within the old school that had yet to come to terms with the agency concept, and the small policy department was anathema and difficult to comprehend for those socialised in the art of running a traditional ministerial department. These factors provided the impetus for the bureaucratic politics that followed the entrance of an interloper. In other countries—Britain and New Zealand—the distinction between policy ministries and delivery agencies was generally applied, whereas Centrelink was the Australian exception. Despite the scale of its operation, which was based on work previously undertaken by departments, it was not accepted as a member of the departmental club.

As the remainder of the chapter indicates, however, the Centrelink concept of an agency has not only survived for 11 years, it has provided a range of insights about operating a large public organisation.

Agency positioning for innovation and opportunities

The environment reflected a government reform agenda that was neo-liberal in character and market and private-sector focused, which, with specific policy agendas, imposed multiple disciplines on Centrelink. There were also constraints resulting from the ambiguity underlying the Centrelink concept and the potential conflicts among the different imperatives and stakeholders, discussed later. Such obstacles need not prevent the generation of opportunities if an agency can take advantage of its other attributes. Opportunities could be turned to advantage through advocacy and smart practices.

The new entrant had to define a role within the APS that had hitherto been centred primarily on ministerial departments, often with their own delivery capacity. As a large agency with the capacity to take policy initiatives, Centrelink was a challenge to policy-focused departments, which had experienced a contraction of their responsibilities. In terms of the positioning and legitimising of the agency, the core agenda was evolving the service delivery system, consolidating, protecting and enhancing the concept of the one-stop shop and expanding business through agreements with new clients.

In positioning itself, Centrelink sought to be entrepreneurial within the terms of its original mandate to become a one-stop shop. There are two strands to this question: being in a contestable position for core business and competing for business. A related issue was whether Centrelink was *the* Commonwealth delivery agency and should have comprehensive responsibilities for multiple delivery arrangements.

The original mandate was to provide services to purchasing departments in the areas of social security and unemployment, but Centrelink's character provided other bases on which to position itself within the Public Service. The positions advocated covered the one-stop shop, provider of choice and premier broker for the Commonwealth, the gateway for electronic communications and inclusive service delivery.

The advocacy of Centrelink's position was important for defining roles and registering its place. Several themes consistently promoted were: the holistic conception of the individual and how the service delivery agency should respond; intra-agency integration of responsibilities and the one-stop shop concept; dealing with numerous clients simultaneously; competing for work; pushing relevant policy agendas as a delivery agency; and provision of choice through channel management. Much depended on Centrelink's capacity to define long-term objectives and to move towards achieving them (Vardon 2003c).

Positioning is ultimately about the question of organisational survival, growth and adaptation. Centrelink managed to reflect the tenor of the time: reading and adapting to the general government agendas and projecting its relevance to the contemporary philosophy. In Centrelink's early years, the mantra of competition and choice reigned supreme for the government, and Centrelink's stance reflected this. For a time, there was a fixation on growing and performing because alternative public and private delivery options were perceived to exist as potential competitors for Centrelink's core business, and this had obvious implications for the agency's survival.

There was something of a turning point about the turn of the century when limits to fulfilling a comprehensive vision emerged from decision making within the executive branch. As the fashion moved from markets towards partnering, governance and whole of government, Centrelink, as a horizontally constituted agency, was again seeking new relations (for example, with communities) and to lead on associated agendas. There was a sense of evolution with time beyond advocacy of a distinctive position towards a significant role in setting policy agendas. Centrelink's relationships with agencies evolved towards a reciprocal collaboration of the type of capacity envisaged by Bardach (1998). At the same time, Centrelink's smart practices were in step with the broader reform agenda: policy competition in a period of marketplace analogies, cooperative alliances in a period of whole of government in the 2000s.

Environmental change and the impact of integrated governance

Centrelink was able to adapt its approach to reflect policy directives and trends as they applied to delivery and at the inter-agency level, but it was not in a position to handle the changing broader reform agenda and the overall functioning of the public sector as new public management was subsumed and supplanted by integrated governance (Halligan 2006a).

Four dimensions were emerging in Australia's public administration in 2003, each embodying a relationship and designed to draw together fundamental aspects of governance: resurrection of the central agency as a major actor with more direct influence over departments; whole of government as the new expression of a range of forms of horizontal coordination; central monitoring of agency implementation and delivery; and departmentalisation through absorbing statutory authorities and rationalising the non-departmental sector. In combination, these dimensions provided the basis for integrated governance and addressing performance improvement (Halligan 2006a).[1]

The integrating-governance model has parallels in other anglophone systems that were once exemplars of new public management, with broadly similar movements reflecting a desire to review and tighten oversight through restructuring and rationalising public bodies. There were parallels in Britain, where the themes of coordination and integration were apparent under Tony Blair and 're-aggregation' was prevalent by the mid-2000s as the reversal of agencification reached an advanced stage (Bogdanor 2005; Talbot and Johnson 2007).[2]

The Australian trends shifted the focus to some extent from vertical to horizontal by emphasising cross-agency programs and collaborative relationships, but vertical relationships also received reinforcement. The whole-of-government agenda had a centralising element in so far as central agencies, particularly the Department of the Prime Minister and Cabinet, were driving policy directions systemically and across the Public Service. The result was the tempering of devolution through strategic steering and management from the centre and a rebalancing of the positions of central and line agencies. Underlying the model was political control through strategic coordination under cabinet, control of major policy agendas, organisational integration and monitoring implementation of government policy down to the delivery level. The overall result was greater policy and program control and integration using the conventional machinery of prime minister and cabinet, central agencies and departments.

The agenda for resurrecting the comprehensive ministerial department was given formal recognition through the Uhrig review into the corporate governance of statutory authorities and office holders. The focus was on nominated agencies with relationships with and impacts on business, particularly in regulation and taxation, but also including the delivery agencies of the Health Insurance Commission and Centrelink. The Uhrig report (2003) was grounded in private sector experience and offered two alternatives: a board template with full powers delegated by the government and an executive management template. Many public bodies did not readily fit either (Halligan 2006a; Halligan and Horrigan 2006).

The post-Uhrig agenda has been for ministerial departments to have tighter and more direct control over public agencies. This in part was a move against the 'dangers imposed by bureaucratic proliferation' (Shergold 2004) with most public servants working for agencies, many with statutory independence, whereas departments of state employed only 22 per cent of the APS. The head of the

Public Service registered concern about opaque governance. 'If implementation is to be driven hard it is important that there be clarity of purpose, powers and relationships between Ministers, public servants and boards. Good governance depends upon transparency of authority, accountability and disclosure. There should be no doubts, no ambiguities' (Shergold 2004).

Departmentalisation, then, was encouraged as an option for absorbing statutory authorities and reclaiming control of agencies with hybrid boards that did not accord with corporate governance prescriptions. The most significant was the creation of a Department of Human Services as a small agency for strategically directing, coordinating and brokering improvements to the delivery of services and incorporating six agencies, including Centrelink, under its umbrella. Centrelink was then subsumed within a new parent department and portfolio in late 2004, before which CEO Vardon departed for a state government position. The aftermath is discussed in the concluding chapter.

The effect of integrated governance on Centrelink was substantial because all dimensions had an impact: the relationship to ministerial direction, stronger ministerial departments in relation to policy leadership and control over public bodies, enhanced central agency capacity for monitoring service delivery and implementation and the clarification of what constituted appropriate corporate governance (thereby striking out Centrelink's executive board). The whole-of-government agenda meant that Centrelink was no longer the distinguished innovator in horizontal initiatives because all agencies were now expected to participate actively in collaboration.

Two agendas, then, were operating: one addressed agency governance and ministerial accountability and the need to rebalance the Public Service by tempering the high levels of devolution, including the number of non-departmental organisations (Halligan and Adams 2004). There were also Centrelink-specific matters that addressed issues arising from conflicts identified earlier, such as the operation of a purchaser–provider relationship within the same portfolio, governance by board and minister and inter-departmental tensions.

Core relationships

Redefining client relationships

The inter-agency relationships centred on Centrelink suggest lessons about modes of interaction, process design and innovation and smart practices, and about evolving more collaborative inter-agency relationships and functioning as an agency that reflects integration by internalising otherwise separated responsibilities.

The consequences for inter-agency relationships of the influence of principal-agent principles included inter-agency conflict, micromanagement, differences over policy roles and high transaction costs. The purchasers and the provider eventually came to understand the limitations of this approach. There were tensions also in ministerial roles: 'Ministers as purchasers want low output prices and efficient, effective operation. As owners they would want to maximise revenue, invest in future capacity and set strategic directions' (Rowlands 2003:211). In the end, the question of transactions across organisational boundaries raises the issue of the original split between the DSS and Centrelink. Rowlands (2003) concluded that it was difficult to discern a point on the continuum between policy and administration at which the split could occur without a high level of activity across that boundary. This had implications for boundary spanning and choosing between either a conventional hierarchy or agencies to deliver services.

There was also the changing position of the key central coordinating agency, DoFA, which came to perceive the relationship in more formal terms and took issue with Centrelink's location and identity within the Family and Community Services portfolio as a separate service agency model or a traditional departmental model. That this type of relationship was problematic—the two parties were located within the same portfolio—was endorsed by the Uhrig review of corporate governance and was eventually resolved in the machinery of government shakeout in November 2004 by incorporating Centrelink within the finance portfolio.

Conflicts between models derived in part from the limitation of applying purchaser–provider principles when the purchaser and the provider were located within one portfolio. The 'hard rationalist' variant of new public management being prone to micromanagement processes (Gregory 2003) dominated much of the dealings between Centrelink and its main clients. Once a 'partnership' that was substantially adversarial was replaced with serious collaboration, the opportunities for confronting other questions expanded. The parameters and scope for entrepreneurial action were clarified in practice and the political realities of the operating environment—of being a key agency for the government—were explicit. The customer focus received prominence through the reformulation of the delivery model and refining relationships.

The organisation's smart practices produced more effective relations based on the value-chain conception of responsibilities and a more integrated alliance approach to the most important relationship, that between DFaCS and Centrelink.

Customer-led service delivery

The main rationale for establishing Centrelink was improving the quality of service for those on income support and/or unemployed. A specialist service delivery agency would operate horizontally to integrate services as a one-stop shop. The bottom line for such an agency was how it performed on service delivery.

Centrelink was able to produce a reformation in thinking about and delivering service through addressing two questions about customers. The first was the change from supplying diverse but individual government programs to a more holistic and integrated customer service. The second was to take the customer's point of view and to conceive of the relationship systematically. This required fresh thinking about a range of matters extending from the physical layout of offices and delivery systems to staff engagement and culture.

A third question of interest to stakeholders such as the government and departments was how to balance cost efficiency and quality of service for the customer. Were services and benefits to which customers were eligible an entitlement or something that they had to discover? The outcome could have important implications for how the customers were handled and the mode of delivery of services. Was the objective to emphasise cost-efficient channels or customer-effective ones? Innovative improvements in technology to support these services became imperative.

Governance models

Centrelink's formal governance was depicted as idiosyncratic, unusual and ambiguous. The limitations of the model can be traced to the original decisions about the roles of minister and board, chair of the board and chief executive and the relationship between department and agency. In practice, however, Centrelink was able to work through the arrangements formally and informally. The Centrelink board contributed to the steering function and provided a buffer and an intermediary between the agency and the ministers. There was a close working relationship between ministers and Centrelink's chief executive, Sue Vardon. Given Centrelink's responsibilities for a major component of the budget, a direct relationship with its minister was to be expected, and there were regular policy changes and demands on Centrelink's capacity to deliver special assistance to people in need. There was also a general need to be highly responsive to government priorities. In these respects, Centrelink was responding like a department of state. This close and direct relationship also meant that the portfolio department was out-manoeuvred or bypassed on some matters.

These arrangements continued to work until a broader concern with corporate governance in the Commonwealth public sector surfaced. Then there was closer scrutiny of features that might be seen as anomalous to purist conceptions. The Uhrig review (2003) thought it was unusual for Centrelink to be under the *FMA Act* and be governed by a board. The report claimed that in order to strengthen the board's governance power under the original arrangements, the chairman was deemed the chief executive for accountability purposes under the *FMA Act*. At the same time, Centrelink's CEO was the responsible head under the *Public Service Act*. This position of having two chief executives for accountability and governance purposes was seen to be anomalous (Uhrig 2003:45).

The composition of the board was also depicted as 'an idiosyncratic governance model', which derived from the original settlement that satisfied the key departments. 'Neither DSS nor DEETYA would be "taken over" by the other and both would have a seat at the Centrelink Board' (Rowlands 2003). This practice had positive and negative aspects. While allowing a greater sense of partnership and cooperation between the board and its client departments, the presence of the heads of two major clients on Centrelink's board was at odds with the concept and role of Centrelink as an organisation required to operate competitively and produce an annual efficiency dividend on its operations for the government. Furthermore, the parties accepted these arrangements as appropriate for developing strong partnerships between Centrelink and its core clients and improving the effectiveness of policy development, process design and service delivery.

Centrelink (along with the then Health Insurance Commission) was funded through purchaser–provider arrangements based on agreements with purchasing agencies to provide services for them. Uhrig (2003:46) observed:

> While a funding arrangement does not in itself represent a mechanism of governance, there are issues of governance associated with these arrangements. The main issue for governance is the extent to which these arrangements affect the way those responsible for governing the organisation work towards ensuring its success.

The purchaser–provider model was intended to provide the portfolio department with leverage over agencies to ensure appropriate delivery of services, but that could not be ensured (Uhrig 2003). Ministerial priorities produced frequent changes in outputs that could not be captured by the purchaser–provider relationship and undermined the basis of the business agreements (Rosalky 2002).

The Uhrig review concluded that the cost of managing the purchasing agreement could not be justified. Most services delivered by Centrelink were within the departmental portfolio of its main purchaser and the desired leverage over price and service quality could be achieved by making Centrelink accountable directly to the minister (Uhrig 2003). With the new orthodoxy emphasising clarity and governance enforced by the imposition of one of two templates, the executive management template (rather than the board template) was seen as the inevitable option for Centrelink.

Overall lessons and significance

Responding to tensions and conflicts in models

A complex organisation with multiple stakeholders presents challenges to reconciling priorities and values. Each of the models identified in Chapter 1 for analysing different organisational imperatives offers a distinctive lens for examining conflicts between them. One model conceives of Centrelink as a customer-driven organisation responsive to recipients of its services and driven by customer relationships and satisfaction based on surveying and benchmarking. A second focuses on Centrelink's relationship with client departments as an agent and provider operating under purchaser–provider principles and expected to behave in specified quasi-contractual ways. The political management model derives from the political environment of an organisation that although subject to special governance arrangements is still directly or indirectly subject to political direction. Finally, there is the concept of an entrepreneurial organisation competing in the market to secure existing core work and seeking new business.

Reference was also made to Centrelink as a statutory authority that was subject to public service legislation and in many respects not much different from a department of state because of the centrality of public service principles. A large agency with extensive public interactions invariably attracts close scrutiny from external organisations, such as the Auditor-General, the Ombudsman and parliament.

The tensions between the client and customer imperatives were clear and expressed through the question of the cost of services (high quality or sensitive to the scarcity of resources) and the handling of customers—the strong customer focus of Centrelink versus the concern of the parent department, according to Rosalky, with 'accuracy, compliance, and assurance' (Husock and Scott 1999b).

A fundamental question for Centrelink, then, was how to respond to these multiple demands, particularly when they were in direct conflict. The incorporation of conflicting models in complex institutional design produces complications (Aucoin 1990). In the case of Centrelink, several models had to be reconciled, while other tensions remained as structural elements to be worked through. The models continued to have relevance and contributed to the ambiguity in Centrelink's environment. There were attempts to mitigate the environmental ambiguity through the reworking of several features.

The emphasis on partnerships facilitated more productive relationships, but the structural features of the original design meant that tensions remained and that energy had to be channelled into working though the resolution of issues as they arose. There were different interpretations about the relative importance of political and managerial dimensions as expressed through purchaser–provider principles, partnerships and political direction.

Purchasers and the provider came to agree about the limitations of the models related to the purchaser–provider arrangements. Centrelink's nature and financial information meant that it did not work from the point of view of the purchasing department. Centrelink had an issue with regard to its location within the Family and Community Services portfolio as to whether it was operating under a separate service agency or a traditional departmental model. The eventual judgment was that it was not a proper purchaser–provider relationship. Ministerial priorities changed frequently and could not be readily captured through a purchaser–provider relationship.

Centrelink's location and the requirements of public policy continued to constrain its potential to be entrepreneurial as an organisation. Despite different depictions of practice based on ministerial behaviour, Centrelink's self-image was not simply that of a department of state.

The resolution of several conflicts came through the Uhrig process (2003–04), which provided the opportunity for the government to strengthen the role of the minister in direction, oversight and implementation. Centrelink became even more explicitly an arm of government. The role of the department as policy leader and the place of Centrelink as an agent of purchasers were made unequivocal. Moreover, the oversight of the agency and its new parent department was expanded through its location under DoFA. This meant that the opportunities for entrepreneurial activity became muted and that the customer responsiveness agenda was increasingly subject to this nexus of expectations.

Centrelink passed through several stages after its formation as the CSDA in 1996. One can track the agency's movement through the stages as it pursued a developmental pathway while seeking to respond to its environment and most particularly government policy and directions. Finally, there was a period of consolidation. Centrelink, of course, was not a free agent when it came to responding to environmental challenges.

The role of transformational leadership

Leadership is critical in organisational change involving major processes. Transformational change also requires the attributes of transformational leadership that must be worked through interactions with the external environment and building management capacity through internal management systems. In Centrelink's case, Vardon had a set of principles derived from Kotter (1996) as a basis for action and was able to create a sense of vision, communicate it to staff and seek alignments between the different elements.

The ability to combine high capacity and high responsiveness, depicted as key attributes of change, were apparent in Centrelink's case. There was external advocacy from a base set of values and imperatives about mission and purpose and centred on improved delivery of customer service. The board and the CEO established clear strategic direction. These were built into an explicit plan of development for Centrelink (Vardon 2003c). Effective use was made of internal capacity—a product of scale of operation, the allocation of resources and strategic decisions about agenda setting—to produce and advance policy and service delivery ideas and innovations in public management.

The nature of and limits to transformation in a complex organisation are important questions for the study of public administration and the Centrelink case provides a range of lessons after its formative years of operation.

There are also specific lessons from the perspective of the chief executive about the timing of initiatives, the emphasis given to specific agendas and design questions (see Appendix 5; Vardon 2003c). These essentially cover models, roles and relationships and the handling of information.

Centrelink's significance

Centrelink has operated now for 11 years. Counterpart organisations in other countries (for example, New Zealand and the United Kingdom), although not constituted quite like Centrelink, have been merged and reorganised. While Centrelink's genesis was influenced to some extent by international agencification, there had been other agencies with special features as part of Australia's long and creative tradition of creating different forms of statutory authorities and corporations (Wettenhall 2003, 2007).

The Australian variant was similar to the British executive agencies as a specialised delivery agency but otherwise different because it served multiple departments.

The politicians of the time recorded their intention to produce a historic innovation and the original design has now been demonstrated to offer durable features that could be reworked and finetuned to serve the government of the day.

As an example of integrated service delivery, Centrelink has received international recognition for its handling of responsibilities of numerous departments and across levels of government. Recently, Centrelink was joined by Service Canada as an agency relying on a similar model for delivering comparable services nationally.[3] Centrelink continues to see itself as a primary model of integrated service delivery.

Centrelink can claim to have realised the original objectives specified by the government. These were essentially to make services more accessible to citizens and to improve the efficiency of service delivery.

As a multi-purpose delivery agency available to take on work on behalf of other departments and agencies, Centrelink has been highly successful. It has expanded from the several initial departments to 25 or more clients, including client agencies in the states and territories. Correspondingly, and also in response to new tasks required by the government, the range of products and services has more than doubled—from about 60 in 1997–98 to about 140 in 2000–01 (Hickey 2002).

Centrelink has been subject to a range of efficiency dividends imposed by the government as a condition of its operation as a statutory agency and as a consequence of its establishment as a merged body of several agencies. These funds are removed from the agency's budget allocation on the presumption that the operational efficiencies will be achieved in the coming year. This dividend increased progressively since the agency was established and was capped at a continuing rate of 10 per cent per annum of an agreed budget base. This cut was in addition to the continuing, standard efficiency dividend of 1 per cent per annum that was applied to all budget agencies.

Centrelink has also been subject to continuing IT outsourcing savings amounting to $14.5 million in running costs and $10.9 million in capital costs. All of these reductions have been applied to Centrelink's forward estimates of receipts. Centrelink reduced the cost of service delivery by approximately $211 million from 1999–2000, rising to $270 million by 2003–04, returned as efficiency dividends to the government. This resulted in cumulative savings to the budget of $1.352 billion for the period 1997–98 to 2003–04 (DFaCS 2000:228).

Structural reforms of government organisation involving functional boundaries can leave public officials with the problem of how to bridge vertical separation and horizontal divisions. In Centrelink's case, the embedding of several models in its organisational imperatives led to debates about the division of responsibilities between the provider of services and the purchasing departments. The tensions between models also provided opportunities for advocacy of a distinctive agenda and employing smart practices in pursuit of public management innovation and inter-agency collaboration. Centrelink developed a new service delivery model and reformulated external relationships despite obstacles and the need to balance the several imperatives of customers, clients, competitors and politicians. Importantly, Centrelink was able to transcend relying on its own capacity within a competitive environment to develop inter-agency collaborative capacity with claims to thereby enhance public value.

Under Vardon's leadership, a major new entity was created out of existing delivery networks. The organisation evolved through a series of developmental stages and Centrelink's capacity was extended greatly as a multipurpose service provider.

ENDNOTES

[1] The reasons for the shift from new public management are complex and involve internal (for example, shortcomings of reform initiatives) and external (for example, environmental threat from terrorism) factors (Halligan 2007a).

[2] New Zealand displays similar dimensions to Australia, including rationalising governance of non-departmental organisations (Boston and Eichbaum 2007).

[3] Service Canada was announced in 2005 and is being developed into an integrated network over three years (Tan 2007).

Epilogue: Back to the future[1]

The resurrection of the traditional machinery of bureaucracy—central agencies and departments of state—impacted significantly on the governance and internal structural arrangements of Centrelink after 2004. The departure of the inaugural CEO, Sue Vardon, on 10 December 2004, heralded the demise of an eight-year period of innovative administration during which Centrelink spontaneously adapted to ever-changing market forces and government agendas.

It was replaced by a return to a traditional model of public administration based on two theoretical foundations: first, the bureaucratic model of administration, and second, the particular conventions of accountability and responsibility derived from the Westminster system (Hughes 1998). There was, however, an added complexity, in that governance and reporting arrangements had to accord with the new integrated governance model of bureaucracy established by the Human Services Legislation Amendment Bill, which passed through the Senate on 5 September 2005.

The period 2005–06 was marked by two phases within Centrelink: October 2004 to October 2005 was a period of intense strategic direction setting and internal restructuring in preparation for its transition to a clearer status as a statutory agency; and October 2005 to December 2006 saw Centrelink strive to achieve its new service delivery priorities as set out by the then Minister for Human Services, Joe Hockey, under the new administrative arrangements.

This concluding chapter looks at the governance and strategic changes and new administrative arrangements that took place in the organisation during those two phases and compares and contrasts the new order with the Vardon years. In many ways, it was an exercise in 'back to the future'—a return to the traditional model of departmental governance and administrative arrangements to deliver on a revised model of social welfare reform, 'Welfare to Work'.

Centrelink in transition

With the announcement of Prime Minister Howard's new ministry on 22 October 2004 came the creation of a new Department of Human Services (DHS) within the finance portfolio, with Hockey as minister. Centrelink was to be one of six agencies under the new department, together with the Health Insurance Commission, the Child Support Agency, Health Services, Commonwealth Rehabilitation Services and Australian Hearing.

The Prime Minister (Howard 2004) outlined the key drivers for the creation of the new department as:

- greater recognition of the importance of service delivery
- a sense that good policy was being undermined by poor delivery

- a need to address public perceptions about agency performance
- a need to improve client-agency relationships
- Uhrig's focus on increased ministerial responsibility and the role of portfolio secretaries.

He then went on to express his view, and that of many Centrelink executives, that '[w]e tend to look at service delivery as an afterthought rather than a policy priority…I will expect…to see…efficient, timely and sympathetic service delivery as a policy goal in itself'. At the same time, he also acknowledged that 'service delivery policy for all agencies has been buried too far down the policy formulation process'.

Centrelink executives had long bemoaned the fact that they were left out of policy formulation discussions that had a direct impact on the way they delivered services, often impeding their effectiveness, so they were positive about this aspect of the new arrangements. On the other hand, it would be reasonable to suggest that they were more cautious about the implications for Centrelink's operations of being integrated with other agencies under the umbrella of the DHS.

To appease that uncertainty and to explore opportunities for Centrelink within the new governance arrangements, the secretary of the newly forming DHS, Patricia Scott (2004), outlined the immediate priorities for her new department. These were to:

- improve accountability
- consider service delivery issues upfront when policy was being developed
- improve the flow of clients from Centrelink to the Job Network
- increase the speed of referrals for assessment or intervention and rehabilitation support
- further develop a client-focused participation network across government agencies.

In summary, the focus of the DHS was to 'improve the delivery of services to Australians by re-invigorating public administration and ensuring strong ministerial control with clear lines of responsibility through the Secretary [Scott]' (Vardon 2004).

As a gesture of commitment to the integration, relevant staffers from Centrelink were seconded to the DHS to help establish the new department in its early weeks. Some of these staff members stayed on in the DHS while others returned to Centrelink when their job was completed. This engagement of staff had the benefit of a free exchange of information and advice between the agencies and it fostered a feeling of unity and a 'joined-up' government approach.

Having been at the head of Centrelink for almost eight years, Vardon chose this as an appropriate time to take up a position as CEO of the Department of Families and Communities in South Australia, and she left Centrelink on 10 December 2004.

Vardon's departure ushered in a new era for Centrelink and a new CEO, Jeff Whalan. For Centrelink to integrate with the other agencies under the DHS, it became necessary for the organisation to undergo a transition to bring it into line with a more traditional model of public administration. Whalan immediately began the task of reshaping the organisation and he consulted widely on the proposed changes, ensuring that all staff understood the new arrangements while conducting 'business as usual'.

In his first television broadcast to all staff in March 2005, Whalan (2005:1) gave the business reasons for the shift in governance arrangements:

- the shift in government focus signalled by bringing a range of service delivery providers from across the APS together under the new DHS
- the change in Centrelink's major clients with DFaCS remaining a key player but with DEWR becoming a major client and DEST also taking a greater role
- advice from the secretaries of purchasing departments that some non-core Centrelink business was likely to be open to competition
- feedback from customers, client departments and staff.

He continued the wide consultation process with all staff, including the executives, in the early months of his tenure, as they set about redefining Centrelink's purpose, its core values, core business processes and strategic priorities in keeping with government and client expectations. Some of the more significant changes that took place during that period are documented below.

Corporate governance

As mentioned previously in this book, on a political level, the creation of Centrelink was hailed as 'a unique model of public administration in human services' (CSDA 1997c), which called for non-traditional governance arrangements. In keeping with the prevailing structural reform agenda in the APS, Centrelink's enabling legislation provided for an executive board of management that reported to the Minister for Social Security (Chapter 6). The CEO reported to the minister through the board. As Centrelink subsumed the service delivery role of the former DSS, the CEO reported to the senior minister in the Family and Community Services portfolio.

This situation, however, changed after 2004. In early 2004, Vardon had alerted members of the guiding coalition to the possible outcomes and potential consequences for Centrelink of the Uhrig report. The most obvious concern was the likely abolition of its board of management and associated repercussions, which eventually came with an announcement by Minister Hockey (2005:18) during an address to the National Press Club:

> An obvious first step in improving accountability is to address the governance structures of the organisations [in my portfolio].

> The existing Boards had an important governance role when Agencies were part of a sectoral portfolio such as Health and Ageing or Family and Community Services. However, with the new Administrative Arrangements, the Government is keen to have a more direct ministerial role in the running of these Agencies.

> I can announce today that I will be introducing legislation…to make the necessary changes to bring the Health Insurance Commission and Centrelink closer to Government by recreating them as statutory Agencies.

> Under this structure the heads of these Agencies will now report directly to me through the Secretary of the Department of Human Services. They will no longer be accountable to Boards.

> The existing boards of the Health Insurance Commission and Centrelink will be dissolved.

The Human Services Legislation Amendment Bill passed on 5 September 2005, abolishing Centrelink's board and amending Centrelink's enabling legislation, the *Commonwealth Services Delivery (CSDA) Act*. By 1 October, regulatory changes brought the *FMA Act* in line with the *CSDA Act* as amended.

Another important change was the shift in portfolios. As an agency within the DHS, Centrelink now came within the Finance and Administration portfolio, instead of the Family and Community Services portfolio. This was presumably for increased management and business accountability, a view supported by the description of the new CEO's role as 'Financial and Staff Management in accordance with the Financial Management and Accountability (FMA) Act' (Scott 2004).

The board continued to operate from December 2004 until 1 October 2005. During that period, Centrelink's corporate governance arrangements were split between the Centrelink board of management and the CEO. The CEO was accountable to the board and to the Minister for Human Services. To meet his accountabilities, the CEO delegated responsibilities to senior executives in Centrelink and held them accountable for the decisions and actions taken on his behalf. The CEO also convened an executive committee to assist with decision making. Accountability was further devolved through subcommittees chaired by those reporting directly to the CEO (Centrelink 2005b:24).

With the abolition of the board, its powers, functions and duties passed to the CEO of Centrelink, creating a return to the traditional model of governance. The CEO became responsible, under the minister, for deciding Centrelink's objectives, strategies, policies and priorities, its overall management and for ensuring that it performed its functions in a proper, efficient and effective manner. At that time, the CEO called on all staff members to assist him in fulfilling those obligations to the minister, the DHS, the purchasing agencies, customers and community and business stakeholders (Whalan 2005). At the same time, new internal governance arrangements and strategic frameworks were being developed.

Internal governance

While Centrelink's corporate governance arrangements might have appeared to be innovative during the Vardon period, its internal governance arrangements were equally unusual for the public sector. Given the scale and extent of change involved in setting up Centrelink, and in the interests of a flat structure of participative management, Vardon had followed Kotter's (1996) framework for leading change, including the concept of a guiding coalition. As already discussed, the guiding coalition was the peak internal management group consisting of all SES officers, and numbering approximately 90 in December 2004.

In setting the organisation's new strategic framework, Whalan used the guiding coalition as one of his sounding boards, along with other stakeholders such as the minister, the secretary of the DHS, secretaries and client departments, the chair of the Centrelink board, area managers and staff at all levels through 33 workshops. The guiding coalition took into account feedback from these key stakeholders, which indicated that although Centrelink had fundamentally improved the customer experience, its operations and service delivery costs lacked transparency, it was unresponsive to customers and clients, governance and accountability needed improvement and Centrelink's focus needed to be on delivery, not policy. Staff also wanted clearer direction as they felt there were too many goals, strategies and plans and a lack of clarity about for whom Centrelink was working—the customer or the government. From this feedback, the March 2005 guiding coalition meeting identified seven new strategic priorities to be the primary focus and to set Centrelink's direction for the next six to 12 months. These were to:

- Re-prioritise our work and resource allocation in terms of Strategic Direction
- Align accountability and responsibility with authority
- Provide costing for all services within 6 months
- Develop united leadership throughout Centrelink
- Develop and implement our service delivery model

- Communicate the Strategic Direction
- Deliver the 'work first' and 'pathways to work' agenda. (Centrelink 2005b:13)

Whalan's brief, set out in a statement of expectations from the minister (Hockey 2006) aimed to bring the organisation back to a traditional model of administration and, in so doing, to increase efficiencies and effectiveness through improved accountability and customer service. Whalan's *Letter of Intent* (<www.centrelink.gov.au>) in response to the minister demonstrated how he proposed to deliver on the expectations.

The guiding coalition initially advised Whalan on how to meet the expectations as the group continued to meet in early 2005. As part of the process of change, however, the term 'guiding coalition' was disbanded, even though SES executive roles were maintained. By mid-April, the 'guiding coalition mailing list' had been replaced by the 'Centrelink SES mailing list', under the new governance arrangements (Centrelink internal email, 15 April 2005). This was another step back to the future.

As the organisation 'moved forward' during the early months of 2005, Whalan communicated frequently with all staff about reviewing priorities, directions and structure using the Business Television network, through business briefings, 'question and answer' bulletins, emails and personal visits to teams. One of the most powerful communication channels was the 'business briefing', broadcast by Centrelink's Business Television network, entitled 'Moving Centrelink forward—the new Strategic Framework and changes to our structure'. The briefing suggested the primary reasons for change were twofold: a shift in focus on the part of the government by creating the new DHS, bringing a range of service delivery providers from across the APS under that department, and 'for Centrelink, this meant reviewing our direction and priorities to ensure we could deliver the Government's program' (Centrelink 2005b:2).

This wide consultation produced a new strategic framework, which had five core elements: its purpose, core values, core business processes, strategic themes and strategic priorities. In essence, it set out Centrelink's reason for being, what it aimed to achieve and how the organisation wanted to be seen. It was underpinned by a united leadership model that focused on the expectations of its leaders and cited the behaviours they were expected to use. The overall framework set the foundation for business transition.

The first noticeable change was in the purpose of the organisation. The new statement of purpose was given as 'Serving Australia by assisting people to become self-sufficient and supporting those in need' (Centrelink 2005c:2). There were no accompanying vision and mission statements and no goals, as the strategic themes set out what was to be achieved in the medium to long term and provided a high level of focus that integrated issues from the internal and external environment. The aim of the new model was simplicity, to provide a model that was more transparent and easily understood by staff and stakeholders than that which existed in the past, while building on the successful approaches used in the Vardon era.

The new strategic framework was simpler than the complex model called *Future Directions* developed during Vardon's tenure. *Future Directions* was reviewed annually to ensure the organisation was focused on the issues of greatest importance and to draw out the key future issues. In contrast with the strategic framework, *Future Directions* embodied Centrelink's mission, vision, values, risk-management framework and five goals that expressed the organisation's aims and key performance indicators, targets and strategies for accountability to the government and client agencies, business and the community, customers, Centrelink people and the efficiency and effectiveness of operations and processes. The strategies, however, did not stand alone. At the core of *Future Directions* were the balanced scorecard, the business improvement plans and personal performance plans. Underpinning these elements were four themes (see Chapter 3) given to the organisation by Senator Vanstone, the then Minister for Family and Community Services:

- Protecting the integrity of outlays;
- Supporting participation outcomes;
- Providing more flexible service for business, customers and Government; and
- Demonstrating that we provide value for money. (Centrelink 2004a:18)

The intertwining of these strategies and associated themes made for complexity in understanding, especially by those staff in 'the network' who were removed from its development and often received little explanation of what it meant and how it was to be implemented.

Through the transition to a simpler strategic framework, there were some elements that endured, including the core values. Vardon and Whalan saw the values as essential building blocks for the organisation and, more importantly, they had to remain as they had been included in the *Public Service Act 1999*—not as prescriptive rules of process or aspirational statements of intent, but as legislated principles. There was, however, one significant difference. Before 2005, the core values in Centrelink were given expression through the 'shared behaviours', discussed in Chapter 3, which were used as a foundation for how to behave in Centrelink (Centrelink 2001d). While these were part of the innovative administrative arrangements of pre-2005 Centrelink, great care had been taken to align them with the APS guidelines:

> Customers and the community observe the conduct of Centrelink employees. Employee's [sic] behaviour and conduct must be of the highest

standard and uphold the APS values and comply with the APS Code of Conduct. APS employees are required, under the APS Code of Conduct, to behave at all times in a way which upholds the APS Values. (Centrelink 2001d:1)

Another element of *Future Directions* that survived was the balanced scorecard, which needed to be adjusted to accommodate measurement of the strategic themes. Some new key performance indicators also needed to be developed. Other key performance indicators remained, as they were specific to Centrelink's continuing purchasing agencies' requirements. The Centrelink business plan and the local business plans were also retained but needed redeveloping for the new environment to ensure they aligned with the strategic directions.

Internal structure

At the same time as the new strategic framework was being developed, one of the then deputy CEOs, Graham Bashford, was heading a team to look at the internal structural arrangements and issues to support the new strategic directions. A transition plan was developed through April 2005 with a view to the new structure being in place by 1 July 2005. The plan was for the full transition to occur over 12 months in a number of phases. Accordingly, the new high-level management/governance structures for Centrelink were first to be announced, reflecting the priorities outlined in the strategic framework. Once again, simplicity was the key to its development, so that, 'as far as possible, everyone understands who is responsible for what and to maximise support to the front line' (Whalan 2005:1). As so often accompanies restructures, there was a cut in staff numbers, with two fewer deputy CEOs, two additional general manager positions and 10 fewer national manager positions. The reduction in national manager positions was the first step in reprioritising the deployment of resources following the key principle that the right resources must be in 'the network' and the right resources were supporting service delivery.

One noticeable feature of the new structure was the introduction of the traditional bureaucratic lines of authority and titles: deputy CEOs led groups, general managers led divisions, national managers led branches and business managers led sections. For example, the group level consisted of the CEO, two deputy CEOs, the chief information officer, the chief finance officer, the general manager of people and planning, the general manager of audit and risk and the general manager of communications.

The return to traditional administration was exemplified clearly in the case of Centrelink's Virtual College, which was established on Vardon's instigation in 2001 as another team within Centrelink, led by an SES officer. With the restructure that took place in early 2005, the Virtual College reverted to a branch and was given the conservative name, Organisation Learning and Development

Branch, still headed by an SES officer. The innovative college concept and name were apparently unfitted to the more traditional structure post 2004.

The traditional model was considered to be a more appropriate structure to support the new directions for Centrelink and was based on a number of principles in that it:

- promoted the effective delivery of Australian government services
- ensured clear accountability
- limited ambiguity and overlap
- recognised that executive leadership set direction and priorities
- provided capacity for whole-of-government and DHS approaches
- provided for equitable distribution of work
- enabled good governance and performance
- reflected Centrelink's core business processes
- produced a structure that was clear and meaningful to internal and external stakeholders
- supported the integration of service delivery to the government and customers
- attracted and retained capabilities.

During the first half of 2005, a new framework of strategic committees was developed to support the CEO in carrying out Centrelink's broader powers and functions. The six strategic committees were the first to be established under the traditional model of administration and they served a purpose by which: a joint committee was required (contributing decisions required by accountable people from different groups); the decision being taken had significant impact on cross-agency/group/division stakeholders; or it was important to have a clear record of decisions and accountability for a complex or cross-program matter. The chair of each committee was empowered to make decisions and delegate responsibility for actions that aligned with the accountability statement of their own position, but, unlike a board, the committees themselves did not have any separate power. Committee membership was determined according to each committee's scope of business, with terms of reference varying to provide for appropriate and continuing contributions.

Their role was to provide a forum for collaboration across Centrelink's divisions and to advise the Centrelink executive. At the time of the abolition of the Centrelink board of management, there were six new subcommittees under the framework: people and planning, investment and major projects, IT, service delivery performance, welfare to work and finance. A new audit committee was also formed to coincide with the start of the human services legislation.

The strategic committees were considered to be a key part of the 'governance committee framework'. A range of other meetings, however, relating to particular programs, steering committees that included non-Centrelink members and committees in support of group or division accountabilities continued to exist and were mapped to the governance committee framework in subsequent months. On the other hand, there were several meetings that occurred between senior executives that were not part of that structure. These included forums (National Support Office SES meetings held each Monday) and executive catch-ups (CEO and direct reports each Monday). These meetings had no formal agendas, minutes or actions arising and were primarily information-sharing meetings.

It is reasonable to suggest that these subcommittees with their underlying emphasis on accountability were established in response to the need for better definition and transparency of Centrelink's costing structure, a focus emphasised by Prime Minister Howard in announcing the creation of the DHS and by Minister Hockey (2005) in his address Making life easier—the role of human services in improving Commonwealth service delivery.

This structure replaced the one built on teams, which dominated the Vardon period. Before 2005, the executive team consisted of the CEO, two deputy CEOs and the chief information officer. Customer segment teams representing life events dominated 'the network' and functional teams, such as people management, formed the structure of the National Support Office. Each team was led by an SES officer, all of whom were conceived to be of equal rank. The rationale behind this team approach was that a flatter structure enabled a more participative management and decision-making style of administration.

The Area Network Review was another extensive change-management project within Centrelink after 2004. One of the first decisions under this review was to keep the existing 15 area offices, with a view to possible boundary changes in 18 months, when the Welfare to Work initiative would be well on the way to being implemented. Perhaps the most significant change in this field, however, was the adoption of a business-lines model of operation in all areas, with some areas having already gone down this path. Business lines are divisions of work much like the customer segments of the early days of Centrelink. The difference after 2004 was that Centrelink defined customer groups within business lines and staff training and delivery systems for customers were similarly arranged. The reason for this change was that it was seen to create new opportunities to further develop the consistency with which Centrelink delivered service. Initially, three business lines were planned: Welfare to Work, seniors, carers and rural, and families.

One of the real drivers for a move to business lines was the further development of the government's Welfare to Work agenda, which held 'Work First' as its primary platform.The conceptual basis for theWelfare to Work program was the notion of mutual obligations. Within this model, government, business, communities, non-governmental organisations and individuals were seen as having social obligations to society at large. It provided a framework from within which people with the capacity and availability would be expected to undertake some form of economic participation with the goal of returning to work. Others, such as those with permanent incapacities, would not be required to participate economically but their social participation would be seen as discharging their mutual obligation. The ultimate goal was a return to work so individuals could be released from dependence on benefits.

To deliver on these initiatives, Centrelink needed to position itself so that purchasing agencies, support staff and staff with service delivery roles had a clear focus on service to Australian citizens that was thoroughly consistent with the government's agenda. One particular advantage of the move to business lines was the potential to link the stakeholder group with the service delivery group around process, practice and performance and the opportunity it would provide to give national stakeholder teams access to quick, unified and expert advice on product impact and potential issues with products on the ground.

Another outcome of the Area Network Review was the analysis and streamlining of support functions performed in the 15 areas to free up resources that could be moved to front-line service delivery.

2006 and beyond

In retrospect, 2006 and beyond could best be described as the congruence of continuity, capability and contestability for Centrelink. Continuity was a fundamental element for the organisation as staff was called on to maintain day-to-day business expectations; capability was tested as the organisation contributed to the development of major new initiatives and reacted decisively in times of community crisis; and contestability became more obvious as demand was made for an increased emphasis on accountability and better customer service. These elements were pitched against a background of fundamental change for Centrelink as it experienced its first full year of operation reporting to the Minister for Human Services.

The transition from the board of management to the new Centrelink governance arrangements was completed and consolidated during 2006, marking a significant step towards implementing the recommendations of the Uhrig report. The resultant shift towards 'joined-up government' made for 'more efficient and effective linkages between the DHS agencies' (Centrelink 2006:2) and improved service levels—one of the minister's highest expectations. One notable example of improved service from a new partnership arrangement was Centrelink's partnership with Medicare Australia, whereby the availability of family assistance services was extended to Medicare offices. According to the *Centrelink Annual Report 2005–2006* (2006:3): 'this has provided the Australian public with more choice about how and where they can access family assistance payments and services. With the extra 190 Medicare outlets, and the rest implemented by December 2006, over 100,000 Australians have already exercised this choice.'

Another demonstration of Centrelink's capability was its impressive response to several crisis situations in Australia and overseas in 2006. Centrelink staff 'value added' to the organisation's community responsibilities by assisting at times of natural disasters such as Cyclone Larry in Queensland, the Beaconsfield mine disaster in Tasmania and medical evacuations from Timor Leste. The importance of Centrelink's role in responding to national emergencies has been recognised by the Federal Government providing funding for the establishment of a National Emergency Call Centre (NECC). Centrelink's leading role in this and other initiatives suggests that it is still the dominant player in the DHS configuration, with additional capabilities from smaller agencies when required.

From a continuity perspective, many of the initiatives begun during the Vardon period and presented as priorities by Minister Hockey (2005) were advanced still further with the same long-term goal of lifting workforce participation and reducing welfare dependency. For example, self-service options for customers via the Internet and automated telephone services and SMS messaging as alternatives to letters increased during the period. Better management of major projects, especially in the area of IT, increased accountability.

All these initiatives were designed to pave the way for future fundamental shifts in ministerial expectations. Further challenges that lay ahead for Centrelink, post 2006, as indicated in the minister's statement of expectations for the period 1 December 2006 to 30 June 2007 (Hockey 2006:1–2), were to:

1. support and contribute to the government's development and implementation of the Health and Social Services Access Card
2. continue to make improvements in assisting customers into sustainable employment through the Pathways and Welfare to Work programs
3. make further improvements in the areas of compliance and reducing fraud, errors, debts and overpayments to customers
4. make it easier for the Australian public to access services through such initiatives as improvements to forms and letters, online capability and reduced queue waiting times
5. continue to foster collaboration with human services agencies, with particular emphasis on achieving procurement synergies and co-location benefits where appropriate
6. demonstrate that it is delivering its day-to-day services as required by the government and policy departments and as detailed in service delivery agreements
7. continue building organisational and workforce capabilities to meet current and future demands and expectations

8.   deliver the government's commitments according to agreed implementation schedules
9.   continue to build confidence in the way it conducts its business
10. be in a position to complete the Letter of Compliance as required by DoFA.

It can be concluded therefore that the new administrative arrangements put in place with the establishment of the DHS enhanced Centrelink's potential capability and contestability as seen by the way in which the organisation coped with massive organisational change while delivering on the minister's expectations throughout 2005 and 2006.

ENDNOTES

[1] Margaret Hamilton drafted this chapter.

Appendix 1. The study

Original questions and objectives

A set of research questions provided the starting point for this study:

- Where did this organisation come from and why did it emerge? What were the specific circumstances under which Centrelink emerged and how can this be interpreted in terms of organisational creations?
- What is Centrelink? Given its multi-faceted character, how can it be characterised in organisational and management terms?
- How does this organisation operate? What is the extent of its internal and external relationships?
- What provides the organisational dynamic? What factors account for its capacity to evolve and change rapidly?
- What is its future? How does it ensure that it is a sustainable enterprise in the public sector?
- What can we learn from this management experiment? Given its uniqueness, what international comparisons and benchmarking are possible? What lessons are there for Australian and international public and private organisations?

Interviews, 2001–04

Bartos, Stephen, Deputy Secretary, Department of Finance and Administration

Bashford, Graham, Deputy Chief Executive Officer, Business, Centrelink

Blunn, Tony, Former Secretary, Department of Social Security

Conn, Paul, General Manager, Business Planning, Centrelink

Fraser, Don, Member of Board of Management, Centrelink

Gillies, Christina, Member of Board of Management, Centrelink

Hickey, Paul, Deputy Chief Executive Officer, Business Capability, Centrelink

Pascoe, John, Chair of Board of Management, Centrelink

Rogers, Vic, Chief Auditor, Centrelink

Rosalky, David, Secretary, Department of Families and Community Services

Ross, Sheila, Chief Customer Experience Manager, Centrelink

Shergold, Peter, Secretary, Department of the Prime Minister and Cabinet

Silkstone, Brian, National Manager, Centrelink

Tannahill, Leslie, National Manager, Strategic Services, Centrelink

Thame, John, Member of Board of Management, Centrelink

Treadwell, Jane, Deputy Chief Executive Officer, Digital Business/Chief Information Officer

Vardon, Sue, Chief Executive Officer, Centrelink

Wadeson, John, General Manager, Major Projects, Centrelink

Walker, Norman, General Manager, Centrelink

Williams, Marcia, Senior Executive, Centrelink

Zanetti, Carmen, National Manager Strategy, Centrelink

Appendix 2. Social welfare developments

Since the creation of Centrelink in 1996, there have been considerable changes to existing income support and welfare programs. For the first few years, these were fairly limited in scope but in 1999 a complete rethink of the welfare system was announced. The effect on Centrelink has been immeasurable.

Most changes focused on those receiving support who were of working age.

1997

Work for the Dole program

Legislation was introduced to parliament in March 1997. Pilot programs began in September 1997. This program involved local communities in activities of value to them that provided work experience for the unemployed for a period of six months as a step towards possible paid employment. Selected job seekers between the age of 18 and 34 could be asked to participate in or could volunteer for Work for the Dole projects to meet their mutual obligation requirements (see below).

1998

Youth Allowance

Youth Allowance was introduced from July 1998 and featured the rationalisation of income support arrangements for the young unemployed and students. The pre-existing Austudy, Youth Training Allowance and Newstart Allowance programs for young people were rolled into the one Youth Allowance program. While many young people benefited, the new parental means test meant that more than 50 000 people lost payments or had them reduced because of their parents' income.

Job Network

The Job Network was introduced from May 1998 and completely changed the employment-placement assistance arrangements for the unemployed and replaced the arrangements that had been in existence under the previous government's 'Working Nation' arrangements.

Mutual obligation policies

Mutual obligation policies were based on the expectation that unemployed job seekers should contribute in some way to their community by:

* actively seeking work

- constantly striving to improve their competitiveness in the labour market
- giving something back to the community that supported them.

The long-term objective of mutual obligations was to encourage greater self-reliance and motivation in job seekers by encouraging them to take responsibility for, and to be more focused on, their job searches and preparing-for-work activities.

Selected job seekers aged between 18 and 34 were formally required to meet mutual obligation activity requirements from July 1998. This required them to undertake one of a range of accepted 'activities', such as part-time work or training, Work for the Dole programs, Community Development Employment Projects, voluntary work, literacy or numeracy training or career counselling.

1999–2000

Welfare review

On 29 September 1999, the Minister for Family and Community Services, Jocelyn Newman (1999), announced, at an address to the National Press Club, the government's intention to conduct a review. In announcing the review, the government outlined a set of welfare principles that should be the aim of reform:

- maintain equity, simplicity, transparency and sustainability
- establish better incentives for people receiving social security payments so that work, education and training are rewarded
- create greater opportunities for people to increase self-reliance and capacity building, rather than merely providing a passive safety net
- expect people on income support to help themselves and contribute to society through increased social and economic participation in a framework of mutual obligation
- provide choices and support for individuals and families with more tailored assistance that focuses on prevention and early intervention
- maintain the government's disciplined approach to fiscal policy.

A high-level Reference Group was established on 29 September 1999, chaired by Patrick McClure, CEO of Mission Australia. The group presented an interim findings report in early 2000 and a final Green Paper (the McClure report) to the minister on 17 August 2000. The Green Paper became the basis for comprehensive welfare reform. Unusually, members of the reference group were drawn from the community sector, business, academia and government to guide the development of a comprehensive report on welfare reform. After extensive consultations, and numerous submissions and workshops, the report was issued publicly in August 2000.

It reported that while the unemployment rate in Australia was falling, the proportion of working-aged people receiving some sort of benefits was increasing. Thirty years ago, one in 20 working-aged people were receiving payments. It was now one in five—more than 2.5 million people. About 60 per cent of these, under the current system, were not required to look for work or contribute to their communities in any way. The report called for fundamental change and suggested action in five major areas:

- individualised service delivery
- a simple and responsive income support structure
- incentives and financial assistance
- mutual obligations
- social partnerships.

2000

Family assistance changes

As part of the government's new tax system, reforms to family assistance were introduced from 1 July 2000. The new arrangements rationalised the low-income family assistance and tax transfers previously provided under the social security and tax systems. The government decided to deliver a 'new' family assistance package, family payments, family tax benefits and childcare benefits through Centrelink, the Australian Taxation Office and Medicare outlets.

Job Network second contract

Rural Transaction Centres

During this period, thousands of small communities throughout Australia suffered a decline in government and business servicing with an increasing number of young people leaving for the cities to work. A strong backlash against the perception of government withdrawal led to attempts to redress the decline. As a result, the Commonwealth Government developed services through community-based Rural Transaction Centres—administered by the Department of Transport and Regional Services—to rural and regional Australia. Centrelink was involved in the first centre and continued to find the centres a unique opportunity through which to establish a presence in remote and rural communities.

2001

Welfare reform implemented through Australians Working Together

In May 2001, the government responded to the welfare review report and announced *Australians Working Together—Helping people to move forward*, substantially changing the social support system for working-aged people.

A key aspect of this reform program was a determined effort by the government to move away from passive forms of welfare and 'dependency' to ones that emphasised the mutual obligation of welfare recipients to the community that supported them. To achieve this, the government instituted a range of measures designed to get people to become more active within their community by gaining employment, undertaking educational and vocational training or participating in voluntary community work.

AWT would strike a new balance between incentives, obligations and assistance in welfare.

> We will create about 850 new Centrelink Personal Advisers, in addition to existing Jobs, Education and Training Advisers, in order to ensure that people's needs are assessed better, so that they get the right assistance. Centrelink Personal Advisers will provide extra help to assist mature age workers, parents with school age children, Indigenous Australians and people with special needs to get a job or participate as fully as possible in their community
>
> Centrelink will form partnerships with non-government organisations, community groups, outside experts, and its customers, to provide the right help. Staff will get additional training to improve customer service. This will build on the successful Jobs, Education and Training model.
>
> Centrelink Personal Advisers will ensure that people are aware of the range of help available to people who want to take part in activities. (<http://www.together.gov.au/aboutThePackage/governmentStatement/personalSupportAndAdvice.asp>)

New assessment times for the long-term unemployed and independent, external assessment for disability assistance would be introduced.

2002

Australians Working Together implementation

Meanwhile, the AWT initiative was being implemented in stages. The budget announced changes and, by September 2002, the following initiatives had begun:

- Transition to Work

- Personal Support Program
- training credits for Work for the Dole and community work participants
- quality-assurance system for disability employment services
- enhanced Job Network arrangements
- job-search training and intensive support for mature-age and Indigenous job seekers as soon as they start receiving income support
- access to training accounts for mature-age and Indigenous job seekers to gain work-related skills
- community participation agreements starting to be developed with about 100 remote Indigenous communities
- voluntary participation interviews for people receiving Mature Age, Widow and Partner Allowances
- annual participation planning interviews for those on Parenting Payment whose youngest child is aged 12–15
- additional places in disability employment services
- better assessment and early intervention introduced for those on Disability Support Pension and Newstart Allowance/Youth Allowance (incapacitated)
- 12 new Centrelink service centres being set up in remote areas
- personal advisers begin work in Centrelink.

2003

Job Network third contract

The third contract covered 109 network providers with 1129 sites. The payment system was changed so that Job Network members were paid to monitor clients more closely with a series of scheduled Job Network interviews that matched the client's unemployment record. Clients were referred to the Job Network after registering with Centrelink for benefits. Network members were originally to be paid when clients attended an interview with the Job Network but the number of 'no shows' led to a cash-flow crisis for the agencies. From September 2003, they were paid for their work whether the client came to the meeting or not.

Australians Working Together

The AWT legislation was not passed by parliament until March 2003. Passage of the legislation then allowed the complete package of incentives, assistance and extra requirements to be introduced. In September 2003, the following initiatives began (O'Neill 2003; Yeend 2000a, 2000b):

- Working Credit
- Language, Literacy and Numeracy Supplement
- close access to Mature Age Allowance and Partner Allowance

- more flexible participation requirements for mature-age (50-plus) Newstart Allowance recipients
- new requirements for Parenting Payment customers with a youngest child aged 13 or older
- more personal advisers to begin work in Centrelink.

Appendix 3. Strategic directions

Appendix Table 3.1 Centrelink Strategic Directions, 2001–06

Goal	Details	Outcomes
Client partnerships To build partnerships with client agencies that deliver the required results and provide value for money	Retain current business by delivering agreed business outcomes Market Centrelink's capabilities Explore possibilities for new business Build partnerships and alliances for effective program development and service delivery Build effective and balanced communication mechanisms with client agencies Build and maintain optimum competitive advantage	Client agency satisfaction Business Partnership Agreement outcomes
Customer and community To increase customer and community involvement and satisfaction with services	Maintain customer and community focus Connect the citizens of Australia to community and government services Simplify and personalise service Effectively integrate and target service delivery channels Ensure equity of access for all customers to services that are culturally appropriate Promote Centrelink's image in the community	Customer satisfaction with overall service Customer satisfaction with service delivery channels
Centrelink people To provide Centrelink people with confidence, knowledge, skills and tools to meet the challenges of current and future business and their own career aspirations	Employ people who have the appropriate skills and experience needed to do their jobs effectively Continually provide Centrelink people and our agents with the skills and knowledge required to do their jobs Promote a culture in which people perform highly and accept responsibility for their actions Ensure Centrelink is an employer committed to providing first-class working conditions Strengthen leadership and succession planning at all levels	An environment that develops our people's skills and commitment to service
Cost efficiency To manage our business efficiently and return a dividend to the government	Enhance business management systems at all levels across Centrelink Adopt best practice in financial systems fundamentals to provide better decision support Enhance a business culture that reduces cost while maintaining satisfactory service levels Promote efficient, effective and ethical use of resources including alternative sourcing arrangements and service delivery channels	Return required efficiency dividends to the government Cost for service

The Centrelink Experiment

Goal	Details	Outcomes
Innovation To provide innovative and personalised solutions consistent with government policy	Exploit new and emerging technologies and methods to support our goals Explore and develop new markets, products and services Capitalise on Centrelink's intellectual property Actively support and promote innovation and creativity in Centrelink people Explore innovative business partnerships and strategic alliances with the federal, state and local governments, business and community-based organisations	Business improvement
Best practice To be first choice and benchmarked as the best practice in service delivery	Establish a systematic approach to benchmark Centrelink business and services Share and implement best practice throughout Centrelink Maximise learning through links with other organisations Ensure effective internal and external governance and accountability arrangements	Measured by the level of achievement of the other five goals

Appendix 4. Comparing strategic directions

Appendix Table 4.1 Comparing Centrelink's Strategic Directions, 1997–2001

Strategic issue	1997	2001
Goals	Build partnerships with client departments that deliver the required results and provide value for money	Same
		Same
	Increase customer and community involvement and satisfaction with services	Provide Centrelink people with the confidence, knowledge, skills and tools to meet the challenges of current and future business and their own career aspirations
	Create an environment in which people in Centrelink are proud of their contribution and are making a difference	Manage our business efficiently and return a dividend to the government
	Return an efficiency dividend to the government	Same
	Provide innovative and personalised solutions that are consistent with government policy	Same
	Be the first choice and benchmarked as the best practice in service delivery	
Purpose	Provide exceptional service to the community by linking Australian government services and achieving best practice in service delivery	Same
Vision	Make a difference to the Australian community through responsive, high-quality government services and opportunities and providing value for money	Make a positive difference to Australian individuals, families and communities particularly during transitional periods in their lives
Mission	Centrelink's mission identifies its business and the way the organisation will need to operate to build a stronger community by:	Centrelink will build a stronger community by:
	providing opportunities for individuals through transitional periods in their lives	simplifying access to government services by providing a single entry point
	delivering innovative, cost-effective and personalised services for individuals, their families and community groups	providing innovative and personalised services, opportunities and support that are culturally appropriate during 'life events'
	being an organisation committed to quality	maintaining a high level of customer service, while ensuring strong accountability to stakeholders
	making best use of available funds	building quality relationships with our stakeholders to continually improve the social wellbeing of the Australian society
	listening to the community's ideas for providing better service	
	building a quality relationship between customers and Centrelink	

Appendix 5. CEO lessons

If we were to start again, I would:

- audit service levels at the beginning
- build a strategic alliance, not a master–servant model
- develop mutual key performance indicators
- clarify the value chain early
- create a better funding model
- develop a way of contributing network information to policy
- place greater emphasis on technical training
- emphasise 'One business' more strongly and earlier
- recognise team leaders
- make clear from the start that service delivery has goals of its own
- better clarify management information. (Vardon 2003)

Appendix 6. Tables

Appendix Table 6.1 Centrelink Customer delivery details, 1998–2004

Year	Sites	Key client agencies	Customer base (million)	Payments ($ billion)
1997–98	417	8	6.2	43.4
1998–99	421	9	6.1	45.0+
1999–2000	1 000	15	6.4	43.5
2000–01	>1 000	20	6.3	51.7
2001–02	>1 000	25	6.4	53.4
2002–03	>1 000	25	6.3	55.3
2003–04	1 000	25	6.5	60.1

Source: Centrelink annual reports.

Appendix Table 6.2 Centrelink staff, 1998–2004

Year	Employees	SES (no.)	SES female (%)	SES female Bands 2 & 3 (%)	Indigenous (%)
1997–98	23 745	n.a.	n.a.	n.a.	n.a.
1998–99	22 641	62	45.6	16.6	3.9
1999–2000	22 178	59	40.7	25.0	3.6
2000–01	24 356	71	45.1	40.0	3.6
2001–02	24 641	82	46.3	55.6	3.6
2002–03	27 173	86	44.2	58.3	3.6
2003–04	25 448	103	43.7	64.3	3.6

n.a. not available
Source: Centrelink annual reports.

Appendix Table 6.3 Department of Family and Community Services portfolio expenditure estimates, 2002–03: departmental appropriations ($'000)

Output group	Policy advice	Purchasing, funding and relationship management	Research and evaluation	Total service delivery*	Total
1.1 Family Assistance	17 997	21 947	3950	377 549	421 443
1.2 Youth and Students Support	4 962	4 608	2 245	228 359	240 174
1.3 Child Support	83	28	126	223 640	223 877
1.4 Child Care Support	3 575	24 132	2 086	102 138	131 931
2.1 Housing Support	2 691	2 131	785	779	6 386
2.2 Community Support	13 335	17 040	6 668	12 677	49 720
3.1 Labour Market Assistance	11 058	5 924	2 766	639 806	659 554
3.2 Support for People with a Disability	6 055	27 424	2 136	353 494	389 109
3.3 Support for Carers	1 101	1 412	310	16 154	18 977
3.4 Support for Aged	5 952	2 764	1 913	210 097	220 726
Total	66 809	107 410	22 985	2 164 693	2 361 897

* Mainly Centrelink with the significant exception of child care and, to some extent, support for people with a disability.
Source: Modified from a compilation by Rowlands (2003) from *Portfolio Budget Statements 2002–03: Family and Community Services Portfolio.*

Appendix 7. Roles of DFaCS and Centrelink in Business Alliance Agreement 2004

Role	Leader	Contributor
Develop policy, including: • Develop and advise government on policy, program and service delivery options to achieve outcomes • Provide whole of government context as need • Manage new policy proposal and budget processes	DFaCS	Centrelink
Establish high-level implementation frameworks for approved policies and programs, including: • Develop and support passage of legislation • Develop and issue policy guidelines • Determine service delivery levels to be provided by Centrelink	DFaCS	Centrelink
Develop service delivery frameworks, including: • Determine service delivery channels, business processes and operational targets • Integrate services from various clients to help policy effectiveness and seamless customer experience • Foster service delivery innovation and efficiency • Build IT systems for service delivery	Centrelink	DFaCS
Develop payments and services to customers, including: • Implement service delivery framework • Target services/payments to designated customers • Meet service delivery levels • Capture transactional information	Centrelink	DFaCS
Monitor and assure performance of programs and services, including: • Assess achievement of operational targets • Analyse performance trends against expectations • Take action to rectify performance deficits • Provide agreed performance information and analyses to clients, with alerts about any unexpected trends in key measures such as outlays, customer take-up	Centrelink	DFaCS
Monitor and assure achievement of policy outcomes, including: • Assess performance against expected outcomes • Refine implementation frameworks to rectify under-performance (e.g. revise guidelines, service delivery levels)	DFaCS	Centrelink
Evaluate service delivery, including: • The efficiency, effectiveness and/or responsiveness of service delivery functions • Assess the value for money achieved through particular service delivery initiatives	Centrelink	DFaCS
Evaluate policy impact, including: • Analyse and advise government on achievement of service/program outputs and policy outcomes • Develop new policy options to meet emerging needs	DFaCS	Centrelink

Source: DFaCS/Centrelink 2004

Bibliography

Anthony, Larry 2000, Delivering welfare reform, Media release, 16 August.

Aucoin, Peter 1990, 'Administrative reform in public management: paradigms, principles, paradoxes and pendulums', *Governance*, vol. 3, no. 2, April, pp. 115–37.

Aucoin, Peter, Smith, Jennifer and Dinsdale, Geoff 2004, *Responsible Government: Clarifying essentials, dispelling myths and exploring change*, Canadian Centre for Management Development, Ottawa.

Australian National Audit Office (ANAO) 1997a, *Applying Principles and Practice of Corporate Governance in Budget Funded Agencies*.

Australian National Audit Office (ANAO) 1997b, *Management of the implementation of the Commonwealth services delivery arrangements*, Audit Report No. 18, 1997–98.

Australian National Audit Office (ANAO) 1999a, *Costing of operational activities and services follow-up audit*, Report No. 60.

Australian National Audit Office (ANAO) 1999b, *Use and operation of performance information in the service level agreements*, Audit Report No. 30, 1998–99, <http://www.anao.gov.au>

Australian National Audit Office (ANAO) 1999c, *Planning and monitoring for cost effective service delivery: Centrelink staffing and funding arrangements*, Audit No. 43, 1999–2000.

Australian National Audit Office (ANAO) 2000, *Planning and monitoring for cost effective service delivery—staffing and funding arrangements*, Audit Report No. 43, 1999–2000, <http://www.anao.gov.au>

Australian National Audit Office (ANAO) 2001a, *Family and Community Services' oversight of Centrelink's assessment of new claims for the age pension*, Audit Report No. 34, 2000–01, Australian National Audit Office, Canberra.

Australian National Audit Office (ANAO) 2001b, *Information and technology in Centrelink*, Report No. 39, Australian National Audit Office, Canberra.

Australian National Audit Office (ANAO) 2001c, *Learning for skills and knowledge—customer service officers*, Report No. 9, Australian National Audit Office, Canberra,

Australian National Audit Office (ANAO) 2001d, *Management of fraud and incorrect payment in Centrelink*, Report No. 26, Australian National Audit Office, Canberra.

Australian National Audit Office (ANAO) 2002a, *Centrelink's balanced scorecard*, Audit Report No. 9, 2002–03, Australian National Audit Office, Canberra.

Australian National Audit Office (ANAO) 2002b, *Age pension entitlements: Department of Family and Community Services/Centrelink*, Report No. 17, 2002–03.

Australian National Audit Office (ANAO) 2003a, *Review of the Parenting Payment Single Program*, Report No. 44, Australian National Audit Office, Canberra.

Australian National Audit Office (ANAO) 2003b, *Business continuity management and emergency management in Centrelink*, Report No. 9, Australian National Audit Office, Canberra.

Australian National Audit Office (ANAO) 2005a, *Centrelink's customer feedback systems—summary report*, Audit Report No. 31, 2004–05, Commonwealth of Australia, Canberra.

Australian National Audit Office (ANAO) 2005b, *Centrelink's customer charter and community consultation program*, Audit Report No. 32, 2004–05, Commonwealth of Australia, Canberra.

Australian National Audit Office (ANAO) 2005c, *Centrelink's customer satisfaction surveys*, Audit Report No. 33, 2004–05, Commonwealth of Australia, Canberra.

Australian National Audit Office (ANAO) 2005d, *Centrelink's value creation program*, Audit Report No. 36, 2004–05, Commonwealth of Australia, Canberra.

Bardach, Eugene 1998, *Getting Agencies to Work Together: The practice and theory of managerial craftsmanship*, Brookings Institution Press, Washington, DC.

Barzelay, Michael and Campbell, Colin 2003, *Preparing for the Future: Strategic planning in the US Air Force*, Brookings Institution Press, Washington, DC.

Bashford, Graham 2000, The new interface between government and the community on social welfare delivery: is it working as hoped?, Paper presented to the Conference on Public and Private Sector Governance in Australia: Exploring the Changing Boundaries, 7 April, Canberra.

Bellamy, C. 1998, Joining-up government—thoughts from the UK, Institute of Public Administration Australia National Conference, pp. 1–11, viewed 7 August 2002, <www.ipaa.org.auhttp://www.ipaa.org.au/>

Bennington, Lynne, Cummane, James and Conn, Paul 2000, 'Customer satisfaction and call centers: an Australian study', *International Journal of Service Industry Management*, vol. 11, no. 2, pp. 162–73.

Blunn, A. 1997a, Building a new department: DSS Australia, Paper presented at the Six Countries Meeting, August, Dublin, Republic of Ireland.

Blunn, A. 1997b, '1996 revisited', *Canberra Bulletin of Public Administration*, no. 83, February, pp. 34–7.

Blunn, T. 2000, The new interface between government and the community on social welfare delivery: Centrelink, is it working as hoped?, Paper presented to the Conference on Public and Private Sector Governance in Australia: Exploring the Changing Boundaries, 7 April, Canberra.

Bogdanor, V. (ed.) 2005, *Joined-Up Government*, Oxford University Press, Oxford.

Boston Consulting Group (BCG) 2002, *Cost Efficiency Review*, 8 October, Boston Consulting Group, Canberra.

Boston, Jonathan and Eichbaum, Chris 2007, 'State sector reform and renewal in New Zealand: lessons for governance', in Gerald E. Caiden and Tsai-Tsu Su (eds), *The Repositioning of Public Governance: Global experience and challenges*, Best-Wise Publishing, Taipei.

Briggs, Lynelle 1996, The $64 million question: how do you bring about substantial organisational change?, Paper presented to Conference on Challenges and Opportunities: The next phase of public sector reform, 3 September, Rydges Hotel.

Brown, P. and Rowlands, D. 1995, 'Implementation of policy: some perspectives from recent experience in the Department of Social Security', *Social Security Journal*, December, pp. 3–23.

Brunsson, Nils and Olsen, Johan P. 1993, *The Reforming Organization*, Fagbokforlaget, Bergen.

Bryson, J. M. 1995, *Strategic Planning for Public and Non-Profit Organizations*, Revised edition, Jossey-Bass, San Francisco.

Carlton, J. J. 1986, 'Privatisation and deregulation', *Canberra Bulletin of Public Administration*, vol. XIII, no. 3, pp. 199–204.

Centrelink 1997, *Centrelink Strategic Framework, 1997–2002*, Canberra.

Centrelink 1998a, *Centrelink Annual Report 1997–1998*, Commonwealth of Australia, Canberra.

Centrelink 1998b, *Our Business Our Future. Centrelink Strategic Framework, 1998–2003*, September 1998, Canberra.

Centrelink 1998c, Strategy in Centrelink, Speaking notes, Strategic Services Team, August 1998.

Centrelink 1999a, *Centrelink Annual Report 1998–1999*, Commonwealth of Australia, Canberra.

Centrelink 1999b, Submission to the Welfare Reform Review, December 1999.

Centrelink 2000a, *Centrelink Annual Report 1999–2000*, Commonwealth of Australia, Canberra.

Centrelink 2000b, Board talk 2000, Unpublished Centrelink internal document.

Centrelink 2001a, *Centrelink Annual Report 2000–2001*, Commonwealth of Australia, Canberra.

Centrelink 2001b, *Centrelink Strategic Framework, 2001–2006*, Canberra.

Centrelink 2001c, *Corporate Governance in Centrelink Handbook*, Canberra.

Centrelink 2001d, The APS values, code of conduct and Centrelink shared behaviours, Unpublished internal document.

Centrelink 2001e, Presentation on Centrelink scenario planning, Guiding Coalition meeting, April 2001, Brisbane.

Centrelink 2002a, *Centrelink Annual Report 2001–2002*, Commonwealth of Australia, Canberra.

Centrelink 2002b, *Centrelink Business Plan 2002–2005*.

Centrelink 2003a, *Centrelink Annual Report 2002–2003*, Commonwealth of Australia, Canberra.

Centrelink 2003b, *Centrelink Annual Review, 2002–03*.

Centrelink 2003c, *Future Directions 2003–2006*, Canberra.

Centrelink 2003d, *Governance in Centrelink: shared roles in the production of outputs. Parts I and II and attachments*, Centrelink internal document, Canberra.

Centrelink 2003e, *Project quadrants*, Guiding Coalition Meeting, March.

Centrelink 2004a, *Centrelink Annual Report 2003–04*, Commonwealth of Australia, Canberra.

Centrelink 2004b, *Centrelink: the journey forward*, Business Briefing Paper, February 2004.

Centrelink 2004c, *Future Directions 2004–2009*, Canberra.

Centrelink 2005a, *Centrelink Annual Report 2004–05*, Commonwealth of Australia, Canberra.

Centrelink 2005b, Business briefing, Unpublished internal document.

Centrelink 2005c, Strategic direction framework, Unpublished internal document.

Centrelink 2005d, Questions and answers, Unpublished internal document.

Centrelink 2006, *Centrelink Annual Report 2005–2006*, Commonwealth of Australia, Canberra.

Centrelink Customer Satisfaction Survey (CSS), November 1998.

Centrelink Customer Satisfaction Survey (CSS), May 2000.

Centrelink Customer Satisfaction Survey (CSS), November 2001.

Centrelink Customer Satisfaction Survey (CSS), November 2003.

Codd, M. 1996, 'Better government through redrawing of boundaries and functions', in P. Weller and G. Davis (eds), *New Ideas, Better Government*, Allen and Unwin, St Leonards, pp. 164–85.

Commonwealth of Australia 1997, *Investing for Growth: The Howard Government's plan for Australian industry*, Canberra.

Commonwealth Ombudsman 1997, *Annual Report 1996–97*, Canberra.

Commonwealth Ombudsman 2004, *Annual Report 2003–04*, Canberra.

Commonwealth Services Delivery Agency (CSDA) 1997a, *Commonwealth Services Delivery Agency Act 1997*, no. 31, 1997.

Commonwealth Services Delivery Agency (CSDA) 1997b, *Commonwealth Services Delivery Agency Staff Orientation Package*, April.

Commonwealth Services Delivery Agency (CSDA) 1997c, *Second Reading Speech, Commonwealth Services Delivery Agency Bill 1996*, February 1997.

DBM Consultants Pty Ltd 2001, *Research into the service-related expectations of Centrelink's customers*, Report to Centrelink, September.

DBM Consultants Pty Ltd 2003a, *Centrelink's customers' views on timeliness standards for new claims grants*, Report to Centrelink, June.

DBM Consultants Pty Ltd 2003b, *Evaluation of mistakes with Centrelink experienced by customers*, Report to Centrelink, June.

DBM Consultants Pty Ltd 2003c, *Service integration survey: a survey to investigate the impact of cross-cultural experience on global perceptions of Centrelink*, Report to Centrelink, June.

DBM Consultants Pty Ltd 2004, *Centrelink national survey: a survey to investigate Centrelink's corporate image, reputation and service delivery*, Final report, February 2004.

Department of Employment, Workplace Relations and Small Business (DEWRSB) 2001, *Senate Estimates*, 21 February 2001.

Department of Family and Community Services (DFaCS) 1999, *Portfolio Agency Budget Statement—Centrelink*, Department of Family and Community Services, Canberra.

Department of Family and Community Services (DFaCS) 2000, *Portfolio Budget Statement 2000–01*, Department of Family and Community Services, Canberra.

Department of Family and Community Services (DFaCS) 2001, *Australians Working Together—Helping people to move forward*, Department of Family and Community Services, Canberra.

Department of Family and Community Services (DFaCS) 2002, *Portfolio Budget Statement 2002–03*, Department of Family and Community Services, Canberra.

Department of Family and Community Services (DFaCS) 2003, *Portfolio Budget Statements 2003–04*, Department of Family and Community Services, Canberra.

Department of Family and Community Services (DFaCS)/Centrelink 2001, *Business Partnership Agreement 2001–2004*.

Department of Family and Community Services (DFaCS)/Centrelink 2003, *FaCS/Centrelink Relationships*, Canberra.

Department of Family and Community Services (DFaCS)/Centrelink 2004, *Business Alliance Agreement 2004–2008*.

Department of Finance 1995, *Clarifying the exchange: a review of purchaser/provider arrangements*, Discussion Paper No. 2, Resource Management Improvement Branch, Canberra.

Department of Industry, Science and Tourism 1997, *Putting Service First: Principles for developing a service charter*, Canberra.

Derthick, Martha 1979, *Policymaking for Social Security*, The Brookings Institution, Washington, DC.

Derthick, Martha 1990, *Agency Under Stress: The Social Security Administration in American government*, The Brookings Institution, Washington, DC.

Divett, Ross 1998, 'A new role for senior executives? The Centrelink experience', *Canberra Bulletin of Public Administration*, no. 88, May, pp. 54–9.

Divett, Ross 2002, 'Meetings down under', in John P. Kotter and Dan S. Cohen, *The Heart of Change: Real-life stories of how people change their organizations*, Harvard Business School Press, Boston, Mass., pp. 55–7.

Donald, O. 1996, 'Competitive tendering and contracting out', *Canberra Bulletin of Public Administration*, no. 81, October, pp. 24–7.

Erin Research Inc. 1998, *Citizens First*, Canadian Centre for Management Development, Ottawa.

Flynn, Norman 2007, *Public Sector Management*, Fifth edition, Sage, London.

Forster, J., Graham, P. and Wanna, J. 1996, 'The new public entrepreneurialism', in J. Wanna, J. Forster and P. Graham (eds), *Entrepreneurial Management in the Public Sector*, Macmillan Education, Australia.

Goleman, D. 1996, *Emotional Intelligence*, Bloomsbury Publishing, London.

Gregory, R. 2003, 'Accountability in modern government', in B. Guy Peters and Jon Pierre (eds), *Handbook of Public Administration*, Sage, London, pp. 557–68.

Halligan, John (ed.) 2003, *Civil Service Systems in Anglo-American Countries*, Civil Service Systems in Comparative Perspective Series, Edward Elgar, London.

Halligan, John 1987, 'Reorganising Australian government departments 1987', *Canberra Bulletin of Public Administration*, vol. 52, pp. 40–7.

Halligan, John 1997, 'New public sector models: reform in Australia and New Zealand', in Jan-Erik Lane (ed.), *Public Sector Reform: Rationale, trends and problems*, Sage, London, pp. 17–46.

Halligan, John 1998, 'Agencification: a review of the models, lessons and issues', *International Trends of Administration Reform and Towards the Realisation of Japan's Administration Reform*, Institute of Administrative Management, Tokyo, pp. 153–71.

Halligan, John 2001, 'The implications of the Humphry report', *Canberra Bulletin of Public Administration*, vol. 99, March, pp. 1–4.

Halligan, John 2004, 'The quasi-autonomous agency in an ambiguous environment: the Centrelink case', *Public Administration and Development*, pp. 147–56.

Halligan, John 2005, 'Public sector reform', in Chris Aulich and Roger Wettenhall (eds), *Howard's Second and Third Governments*, University of New South Wales Press, Sydney.

Halligan, John 2006a, 'The reassertion of the centre in a first generation NPM system', in Tom Christensen and Per Laegreid (eds), *Autonomy and Regulation: Coping with agencies in the modern state*, Edward Elgar, Cheltenham.

Halligan, John 2006b, 'Interagency management of service delivery in a complex environment: the case of Centrelink', in Colin Campbell (ed.), *Comparative Trends in Public Management: Smart practices toward blending policy and administration*, Governance Research Program, Canadian School of Public Service, Ottawa, pp. 86–105.

Halligan, John 2007a, 'Advocacy and innovation in inter-agency management: the case of Centrelink', *Governance*, vol. 20, no. 3, pp. 445–67.

Halligan, John 2007b, 'Politics–management relations in an agency context: the case of Centrelink', in Rainer Koch and John Dixon (eds), *Public Governance and Leadership*, Deutscher Universitäts-Verlag, Wiesbaden.

Halligan, John 2007c, 'Reform design and performance in Australia and New Zealand', in Tom Christensen and Per Laegreid (eds), *Transcending New Public Management*, Aldershot, Ashgate.

Halligan, John 2008, 'Australian Public Service: combining the search for balance and effectiveness with deviations on fundamentals', in Chris Aulich and Roger Wettenhall (eds), *Howard's Fourth Government*, University of New South Wales Press, Sydney.

Halligan, John and Adams, Jill 2004, 'Security, capacity and post-market reforms: public management change in 2003', *Australian Journal of Public Administration*, vol. 63, no. 1, pp. 85–93.

Halligan, John and Horrigan, Bryan 2006, *Reforming corporate governance in the Australian federal public sector—from Uhrig to implementation*, Issues Paper 2, Corporate Governance ARC Project, University of Canberra.

Halligan, John and Power, John 1992, *Political Management in the 1990s*, Oxford University Press, Melbourne.

Halligan, John, Watson, Hugh and Macintosh, Ian 1996, *Australian Public Service: The view from the top*, Coopers and Lybrand and University of Canberra, Canberra.

Hamburger, Peter 2007, 'Coordination and leadership at the centre of the Australian Public Service', in Rainer Koch (ed.), *Public Governance and Leadership*, Deutscher Universitäts-Verlag, Wiesbaden.

Hamilton, Margaret 2007, Everything old is new again: a contemporary history of the establishment of the Centrelink Virtual College, Doctorate of Philosophy thesis, The Australian National University, March.

Hanson, D., Dowling, P., Hitt, M., Ireland, R. D. and Hoskisson, R. 2004, *Strategic Management: Competitiveness and globalisation*, Nelson Publishing, Southbank.

Harvard Business Review 1990, 'Leaders', *Harvard Business Review*, May–June 1990.

Hewson, John and Fischer, Tim 1991a, *Fightback! It's your Australia*, Liberal and National Parties Manifesto, 21 November.

Hewson, John and Fischer, Tim 1991b, *Fightback! Taxation and expenditure reform for jobs and growth*, 21 November.

Hickey, Paul 2002, Australia: Centrelink—a model for horizontal and vertical integration of government services, Presentation to Improving Performance: The articulation between different levels of administration, French Ministry of Finance, Paris.

Hickey, Paul 2004, Centrelink service delivery, Paper presented to the Guiding Coalition, 12–13 May.

Higgs, M. and Dulewicz, V. 1999, *Making Sense of Emotional Intelligence*, NFER-Nelson, Windsor.

Hockey, Joe 2005, Making life easier—the role of human services in improving Commonwealth service delivery, Address to the National Press Club, Canberra, 20 April.

Hockey, Joe 2006, Statement of expectations for the chief executive officer of Centrelink for the period 1 December 2006 to 30 June 2007, Parliament House, Canberra, viewed 30 July 2007, <http://www.centrelink.gov.au>

House of Representatives Standing Committee on Employment, Education and Training (HR SCEET) 1988, *Getting to Work: Report of the Inquiry into Training or Return to the Workforce by Social Security Pensioners*, Canberra.

Howard, Cosmo 2001, 'Bureaucrats in the social policy process: administrative policy entrepreneurs and the case of Working Nation', *Australian Journal of Public Administration*, vol. 60, no. 3, pp. 56–65.

Howard, Cosmo 2003, Triage in Commonwealth welfare service delivery, Seminar delivered to Centre for Research in Public Sector Management, Report on unpublished PhD thesis, 12 November.

Howard, Cosmo 2006, 'The new governance of Australian welfare: street-level contingencies', in P. Henman and M. Fenger (eds), *Administering Welfare Reform: International transformations in welfare governance*, Policy Press, Bristol.

Howard, John 1997, Transcript of the Prime Minister, the Hon. John Howard MP, Address at the official launch of Centrelink (Commonwealth Services Delivery Agency), 24 September, The Great Hall, Parliament House.

Howard, John 1999, *House of Representatives Hansard*, 29 September, p. 10900.

Howard, John 2004, Fourth Howard ministry, Media release, 22 October 2004, Canberra, viewed 24 May 2007, <http://www.pm.gov.au/media/Release/2004/media_Release 1134.cfm>

Hubbard, G. 2000, *Strategic Management—Thinking, analysis and action*, Prentice Education, Frenchs Forest, New South Wales.

Hughes, O. E. 1998, *Australian Politics*, Third edition, Macmillan, Melbourne.

Hughes, O. E. 2003, *Public Management and Administration: An introduction*, Third edition, Palgrave Macmillan, Basingstoke.

Humphry, R. 2000, *Review of the Whole of Government Information Technology Outsourcing Initiative*, December, Commonwealth of Australia, Canberra.

Husock, Howard and Scott, Esther 1999a, *Centrelink: a service delivery agency in Australia*, Kennedy School of Government Case Study 1524.0, Cambridge, Mass.

Husock, Howard and Scott, Esther 1999b, *Centrelink: a service delivery agency in Australia—sequel*, Kennedy School of Government Case Study 1524.1, Cambridge, Mass.

Innisfail Advocate 2003, 'CTIP/Centrelink translates information products', *Innisfail Advocate*, 11 October 2003.

James, Oliver 2001, 'Business models and the transfer of businesslike central government agencies', *Governance*, vol. 14, no. 2, April, pp. 233–52.

James, Oliver 2003, *The Executive Agency Revolution in Whitehall: Public interest versus bureau-shaping perspectives*, Palgrave, Basingstoke.

James, Oliver 2004, 'The UK core executive's use of public service agreements as a tool of governance', *Public Administration*, vol. 82, no. 2, pp. 397–419.

Kaplan, R. and Norton, D. 1992, 'The balanced scorecard—measures that drive performance', *Harvard Business Review*, January–February, pp. 71–9.

Kaufman, Herbert 1985, *Time, Chance and Organizations: Natural selection in a perilous environment*, Chatham House, Chatham, NJ.

Kernaghan, Kenneth 2005, 'Moving toward the virtual state: integrating services and service channels for citizen-centred delivery', *International Review of Administrative Sciences*, vol. 71, no. 1, pp. 119–31.

Kettl, Donald F. 1993, *Sharing Power: Public governance and private markets*, Brookings Institution, Washington, DC.

Kingdon, John W. 1984, *Agendas, Alternatives, and Public Policies*, Little Brown and Co., Boston, Mass.

Kotter, John P. 1995, 'Leading change: why transformation efforts fail', *Harvard Business Review*, March–April, pp. 59–67.

Kotter, John P. 1996, *Leading Change*, Harvard Business School Press, Boston, Mass.

Liberal Party of Australia 1996, *Pathways to Real Jobs*, the Liberal and National Parties' Employment and Training Policy for the March 1996 Australian federal election, February.

Light, Paul C. 1998, *Sustaining Innovation: Creating nonprofit and government organizations that innovate naturally*, Jossey-Bass Publishers, San Francisco.

Mabbett, B. and Bolderson, H. 1998, 'Open and shut cases: contrasting systems of benefit delivery in five countries', *Benefits*, September–October.

McClure, Patrick 2000, *Participation support for a more equitable society*, Final Report of the Reference Group on Welfare Reform, Department of Family and Community Services.

McNulty, Terry and Ferlie, Ewan 2003, *Reengineering Health Care: The complexities of organizational transformation*, Oxford University Press, Oxford.

March, James G. and Olsen, Johan P. 1989, *Rediscovering Institutions: The organizational basis of politics*, Free Press, New York.

Metcalfe, Andrew 2007, Opening address, Corporate Governance in the Public Sector 2007 Conference, 13 March.

Millward Brown 2000, *National Customer Satisfaction Survey: Wave 9*, Final report, November 2000.

Mintzberg, H. 1994, *The Rise and Fall of Strategic Planning*, Prentice Hall, New York.

Moore, Mark H. 1995, *Creating Public Value: Strategic management in government*, Harvard University Press, Cambridge, Mass., and London.

Moore, Trevor and Flynn, Paula 2004, 'The changing role of multi-channel service delivery', in Australian Government Information Management Office and Institute of Public Administration Australia, *Future Challenges of E-Government. Volume 1*, Canberra.

Moran, Terry 1996, 'Competitive tendering and contracting by public sector agencies', *Canberra Bulletin of Public Administration*, no. 81, October, pp. 18–19.

Moynihan, Donald P. and Ingraham, Patricia W. 2004, 'Integrative leadership in the public sector: a model of performance-information use', *Administration and Society*, vol. 36, no. 4, September, pp. 427–53.

Mulgan, Richard 2002, 'Public accountability of provider agencies: the case of the Australian "Centrelink"', *International Review of Administrative Sciences*, vol. 68, no. 1, March, pp. 45–59.

National Commission of Audit (NCA) 1996, *Report to the Commonwealth Government*, June, Australian Government Publishing Service, Canberra.

Newman, Jocelyn 1997, A new era in customer service, Press release, 26 May.

Newman, Jocelyn 1998, *The challenge of welfare dependency in the 21st century*, Discussion paper, Minister for Family and Community Services.

Newman, Jocelyn 1999, The future of welfare in the twenty-first century, Address by the Minister for Family and Community Services to the National Press Club, Canberra, 29 September 1999.

Newman, Jocelyn 2000a, The government's vision: linking policies, programs and services, Keynote speech to the IPAA Conference, Hobart.

Newman, Jocelyn 2000b, Welfare reform encourages people to reach potential, Media release, 14 December.

Nutt, Paul C. 2004, 'Prompting the transformation of organizations', *Public Performance and Management Review*, vol. 27, no. 4, June.

O'Donnell, M. 2004, HRM in Centrelink: a best practice approach?, Unpublished paper.

O'Faircheallaigh, C., Wanna, J. and Weller, P. 1999, *Public Sector Management in Australia. New Challenges, New Directions*, Second edition, Macmillan Education.

Olsen, Johan 1998, 'Institutional design in democratic contexts', in Nils Brunsson and Johan P. Olsen, *Organizing Organizations*, Fagbokforlaget, Norway, pp. 319–41.

O'Neill, Steve 2003, 'Job Network: the 3rd contract', *E-Brief*, Online only, 11 August 2003, updated 26 September 2003, <http://www.aph.gov.au/library/intguide/ECON/JobNetwork.htm>

Osborne, David and Gaebler, Ted 1992, *Reinventing Government: How the entrepreneurial spirit is transforming the public sector*, Addison-Wesley, Reading, Mass.

Pearce, John A. and Robinson, Richard B. 2000, *Strategic Management with Powerweb: Formulation, implementation, and control*, Seventh edition, McGraw-Hill.

Pfeffer, Jeffery 1998, *The Human Equation: Building profits by putting people first*, Harvard Business School Press, Boston, Mass.

Pfeiffer, E. 1998, 'Future tilt: how and why companies need a culture of continuous renewal', *Straight from the CEO*, Price Waterhouse, London.

Pollitt, Christopher 2004, 'Theoretical overview', in Christopher Pollitt and Colin Talbot (eds), *Unbundled Government: A critical analysis of the global trend to agencies, quangos and contractualisation*, Routledge, London, pp. 319–41.

Pollitt, Christopher and Talbot, Colin (eds) 2004, *Unbundled Government: A critical analysis of the global trend to agencies, quangos and contractualisation*, Routledge, London.

Pollitt, Christopher, Talbot, Colin, Caulfield, Janice and Smullen, Amanda 2004, *Agencies: How governments do things through semi-autonomous organizations*, Palgrave, Basingstoke.

Porter, Michael E. 1996, 'What is strategy?', *Harvard Business Review*, November–December, pp. 61–70.

Radin, Beryl A. and Hawley, Willis D. 1988, *The Politics of Federal Reorganization: Creating the US Department of Education*, Pergamon.

Rainey, Hal 2003, *Understanding and Managing Public Organisations*, Third edition, Jossey-Bass, San Francisco.

Rainey, Hal and Fernandez, Sergio 2004, 'A response to "prompting the transformation of public organizations"', *Public Performance and Management Review*, vol. 27, no. 4.

Reith, Peter 1996, Federal government strategy for reducing size of public service, Press release, 11 April.

Romeijn, M. 2000, Going for gold: managing change in Australian welfare and employment services, Paper for MPA Course, The Hague, December.

Rosalky, David 2002, 'Ministers, secretaries and boards: a perspective from a seat on the Centrelink board', *Canberra Bulletin of Public Administration*, no. 106, February, pp. 9–14.

Rowlands, D. 1999, 'Institutional change in the APS—the case of DSS and Centrelink', *Australian Social Policy*, no.1, pp. 183–201.

Rowlands, D. 2000, 'Purchaser–provider in social policy delivery: how can we evaluate the Centrelink arrangements?', *Australian Social Policy*, no. 1, pp. 69–87.

Rowlands, D. 2002, Centrelink's Relationships, unpublished paper, Canberra.

Rowlands, D. 2003, Agencification in the Australian Public Service: the case of Centrelink, Doctorate of Public Administration Thesis, University of Canberra.

Royal Commission on Australian Government Administration (RCAGA) 1976, *Report*, Australian Government Publishing Service, Canberra.

Ruddock, Philip 1996, 'Second Reading Speech, Commonwealth Service Delivery Agency Bill', *House of Representatives Hansard*, 4 December, pp. 7623–4.

Rush Social Research 1998, *Evaluation of the Strategic Partnership Between the Department of Social Security and Centrelink: A research report*, Presented to Centrelink and Department of Social Security, March.

Schick, Allen 1996, *The spirit of reform: managing the New Zealand state sector in a time of change*, Report prepared for the State Services Commission and the Treasury, Wellington.

Scott, Patricia 2004, Crazy thought or creative thinking—reform in the real world, Presentation to Centrelink's Guiding Coalition, 3 December.

Sedgwick, S. 1996, Challenges for public sector reform, Paper presented to the Conference Challenges & Opportunities: The next phase of public sector reform, 3 September, Canberra.

Senate Community Affairs Legislation Committee (CALC) 1997a, *Child Care Payments Bill 1997 and the Child Care Payments (Consequential Amendments and Transitional Provisions) Bill 1997, Report*, Parliamentary Paper 461, 1997.

Senate Community Affairs Legislation Committee (CALC) 1997b, *Estimates Hansard*, 3 June.

Senate Community Affairs Legislation Committee (CALC) 1999, *Hansard*, 2 February.

Senate Community Affairs Legislation Committee (CALC) 2002, *Estimates Hansard*, 21 November.

Senate Community Affairs Legislation Committee (CALC) 2003, *Estimates Hansard*, 12 February.

Senate Community Affairs Legislation Committee (CALC) 2004, *Estimates Hansard*, 19 February.

Shand, David 1996, The new public management: an international perspective, Paper presented to Public Services Management 2000 Conference, 11 October, University of Glamorgan.

Shaver, Sheila 2001, 'Australian welfare reform: citizenship to social engineering', *Australian Journal of Social Issues*, vol. 36, no. 4, November, pp. 277–93.

Shergold, P. 2004, Plan and deliver: avoiding bureaucratic hold-up, Australian Graduate School of Management/Harvard Club of Australia, 17 November, Canberra.

Smullen, Amanda 2007, *Translating Agency Reform: Rhetoric and culture in comparative perspective*, Published thesis, Erasmus Universiteit Rotterdam, Rotterdam.

Spicer, Barry, Powell, Michael and Emanuel, David 1996, *The Remaking of Television New Zealand 1984–1992*, Auckland University Press, Auckland.

Stace, Doug and Dunphy, Dexter 2001, *Beyond the Boundaries: Leading and re-creating the successful enterprise*, Second edition, McGraw-Hill, Sydney.

Talbot, Colin 2004, 'The agency idea: something old, sometimes new, sometimes borrowed, sometimes untrue', in Christopher Pollitt and Colin Talbot (eds), *Unbundled Government: A critical analysis of the global trend to agencies, quangos and contractualisation*, Routledge, London, pp. 3–21.

Talbot, C. and Johnson, Carole 2007, 'Seasonal cycles in public management: disaggregation and re-aggregation', *Public Money and Management*, vol. 27, pp. 61–8.

Tan, Kwang Cheak 2007, *Service Canada—a new paradigm in government service delivery*, Kennedy School of Government Case Study, Harvard University, Cambridge, Mass.

Tannahill, Lesley 2000, Towards being the premier broker: joining up government and reducing complexity, Paper presented at Second WA Public Leadership Convention, 6–8 August, Joondalup, Western Australia.

Task Force on Management Improvement (TFMI) 1993, *The Australian Public Service Reformed: An evaluation of a decade of management reform*, Australian Government Publishing Service for the Management Advisory Board, Canberra.

Thompson, James R. and Rainey, Hal G. 2004, *Modernizing Human Resource Management in the Federal Government: The IRS model*, IBM Endowment for the Business of Government.

Treadwell, Jane 2001, Centrelink's strategic approach to selective sourcing, Presentation.

Trosa, Sylvie 1994, *Next Steps: Moving on*, Cabinet Office, London.

Tucker, Tony 2008, Corporate governance, Unpublished DPA Dissertation, University of Canberra.

Uhrig, John 2003, *Review of Corporate Governance of Statutory Authorities and Office Holders*, Commonwealth of Australia, Canberra.

Vanstone, Amanda and Abbott, Tony 2001a, Australians Working Together—helping people to move forward—a $1.7 billion fair deal, Joint ministerial media release, 22 May 2001, <http://www.facs.gov.au/internet/minfacs.nsf/vAllMR/australians_working_together.htm>

Vanstone, Amanda and Abbott, Tony 2001b, Australians Working Together—helping people to move forward: a statement, May 2001, <http://www.facs.gov.au/welfarereform/awt/aboutThePackage/governmentStatement/default.shtml>

Vardon, Sue 1997a, Achieving excellence in service delivery—changing service delivery arrangements for the Commonwealth Government, Paper delivered to a conference on service delivery in the public sector, 26 May.

Vardon, Sue 1997b, One stop shopping—perspectives for the Commonwealth Government, Paper delivered to the national conference Service Agencies—Managing the Delivery of Government Services by Agreements, August, Institute of Public Administration Australia, Victorian Division, and Victorian Department of Premier and Cabinet, Melbourne.

Vardon, Sue 1997c, *In the Front Line—The new service delivery agency*, Public Service and Merit Protection Commission, 23 October, <http://www.psmpc.gov.au/media/vardon.htm>

Vardon, Sue 1998a, Global influences on social sciences: how social services will need to react to change and actually change, and the impact of IT, Presentation to Australian Universities International Alumni Convention 1998, 1–4 October, Adelaide.

Vardon, Sue 1998b, Leadership and the executive team, Speech to the ACT Public Sector Quality Network, 21 October.

Vardon, Sue 1998c, Three stages of an evolving model to a one stop shop—challenges at each stage, Paper presented to the IPAA National Conference, Service Delivery to the Community, 26 November.

Vardon, Sue 1998d, 'Creating a responsible service delivery agency: Centrelink Australia', *The Innovation Journal*, vol. 3, no. 3, September–December, <http://www.innovation.cc/volumes-issues/vol3-iss3.htm>

Vardon, Sue 1999a, Electronic delivery of government services—the Centrelink experience, Keynote address to Government of Alberta, Internet Insight Conference, 8 March, Edmonton.

Vardon, Sue 1999b, Creating a customer service culture for a national government, Address given at the International Summit on Public Service Reform, 10 June, Winnipeg, Manitoba, Canada.

Vardon, Sue 1999c, Meeting the challenge, Paper presented 28 September, Brisbane.

Vardon, Sue 1999d, Innovative change management, September.

Vardon, Sue 2000a, '"We're from the government and we're here to help"—Centrelink's story', *Australian Journal of Public Administration*, vol. 59, no. 2, pp. 3–10.

Vardon, Sue 2000b, 'Centrelink: A three-stage evolution', in Gwynneth Singleton (ed.), *The Howard Government: Australian Commonwealth administration 1996–1998*, University of New South Wales Press, Sydney, pp. 96–107.

Vardon, Sue 2000c, The importance of inclusive service delivery and social support for regional development, Paper presented at the Regional Multicultural Conference, Beyond Our Boundaries, April 6, Port Lincoln, South Australia.

Vardon, Sue 2001, Managing change: the Centrelink experience, Speech to MinterEllison Seminar Series, Public Sector in the New Millennium, Service Delivery in the Public Service.

Vardon, Sue 2002a, *Creating Centrelink and the New Journey, Autonomous Service Officers*, 8 March.

Vardon, Sue 2002b, 'Centrelink, changing culture and expectations', in Eileen M. Milner (ed.), *Delivering the Vision*, Routledge, London and New York.

Vardon, Sue 2002c, Managing change, the Centrelink experience: service delivery in the public sector, Speech, 4 November.

Vardon, Sue 2003a, Cultural leadership, Presentation to Australian Public Service Values Seminar, 19 February.

Vardon, Sue 2003b, Creating a customer-focused organisation, Presentation to a Department of Finance and Administration Seminar, This is Your (Work) Life, 6 May.

Vardon, Sue 2003c, Moving service delivery forward: the practical and the tactical: the Centrelink experience Australia, Presentation to the Lac Carling VII Conference, 25–27 May, Quebec.

Vardon, Sue 2004, Internal email to all staff announcing the creation of the Department of Human Services, 22 October, 2.18pm.

Vranjkovic, Ana 2003, 'Taking to the streets', *Malvern Prahran Leader*, 10 September.

WBI Leadership Development Program and the Institute of Public Administration of Canada (IPAC) 2007, *Leadership Matters: Briefs for leaders*, World Bank, Washington, DC.

Wettenhall, Roger 2003, 'These executive agencies!', *Canberra Bulletin of Public Administration*, no. 106, pp. 9–14.

Wettenhall, Roger 2007, 'Non-departmental public bodies under the Howard Governments', *Australian Journal of Public Administration*, vol. 66, no. 1, pp. 62–82.

Wettenhall, Roger and Kimber, Megan 1996, *One-Stop Shopping: Notes on the concept and some Australian initiatives*, Centre for Research in Public Sector Management, University of Canberra.

Whalan, J. 2005, Internal television broadcast and email to all staff, explaining the reasons for change, 31 March, 10.05pm.

Wills, J. A. 1999, Enhancing public sector strategic planning, Unpublished PhD thesis, University of Canberra, Canberra.

Winkworth, Gail 2005, 'Partnering the 800 pound gorilla: Centrelink working locally to create opportunities for participation', *Australian Journal of Public Administration*, vol. 64, no. 3, pp. 24–34.

Woodhead, Ben 2003, 'Centrelink rolls out $100m contract', *Australian Financial Review*, 3 October.

Worthington, Ross 1999, *A Case Study of Strategic Partnering in Australia*, Organisation for Economic Cooperation and Development, Paris.

Yeend, Peter 2000a, 'Welfare review', *E-Brief*, Online only, September 2000, <http://www.aph.gov.au/library/intguide/SP/welfarebrief.htm>

Yeend, Peter 2000b, 'Mutual obligation/Work for the Dole', *E-Brief*, Online only, 27 November 2000, <http://www.aph.gov.au/library/intguide/sp/dole.htm>

Zanetti, C. 1998, 'Managing change: focus on improving service quality and information management', *Australian Journal of Public Administration*, vol. 57, no. 4, December, pp. 3–13.

www.ingramcontent.com/pod-product-compliance
Lightning Source LLC
Chambersburg PA
CBHW061245270326
41928CB00041B/3422